ALZHEIMER'S DAY CARE

ALZHEIMER'S DAY CARE
A Basic Guide

David A. Lindeman
University of California, Davis
Northern California Alzheimer's Disease Center, Berkeley

Nancy H. Corby
University of Southern California School of Medicine, Garden Grove

Rachel Downing
Gerontology Consultant, Baltimore, Maryland

Beverly Sanborn
Alzheimer's Services for Health Care Group
Escondido, California

●**HEMISPHERE PUBLISHING CORPORATION**
A member of the Taylor & Francis Group

New York   Washington   Philadelphia   London

ALZHEIMER'S DAY CARE: A Basic Guide

Copyright © 1991 by Hemisphere Publishing Corporation. All rights reserved.
Printed in the United States of America. Except as permitted under the United States Copyright Act of 1976, no part of this publication may be reproduced or distributed in any form or by any means, or stored in a database or retrieval system, without the prior written permission of the publisher.

1 2 3 4 5 6 7 8 9 0   B R B R   9 8 7 6 5 4 3 2 1 0

This book was set in Century by Hemisphere Publishing Corporation.
The editors were Lys Ann Shore and Deena Williams Newman; the designer was Sharon M. DePass; the production supervisor was Peggy M. Rote; and the typesetter was Shirley J. McNett. Cover design by Sharon M. DePass.
Printing and binding by Braun-Brumfield, Inc.

A CIP catalog record for this book is available from the British Library.

Library of Congress Cataloging-in-Publication Data

Alzheimer's day care: A basic guide / David A Lindeman . . . [et al.].
   p. cm. — (Series in death education, aging, and health care)
  Includes bibliographical references.
  Includes index.
  1. Day care centers for the aged—Administration. 2. Alzheimer's disease—Patients—Care. 3. Dementia—Patients—Care.
I. Lindeman, David A. II. Series.
  [DNLM: 1. Alzheimer's Disease—Rehabilitation. 2. Day Care—organization & administration. WM 29.1 A478]
RC523.A374 1991
362.1′9897′6831—dc20
DNLM/DLC
for Library of Congress   90-5065
                                 CIP

ISBN 0-89116-106-6 (case)
ISBN 1-56032-152-0 (paper)
ISSN 0275-3510

CONTENTS

PREFACE

The purpose of this book is to provide direction to individuals, organizations, and agencies that are considering developing a day care program for patients with Alzheimer's disease (AD) or a related dementia or are at present operating an adult day care program they wish to modify, in one fashion or another, to include persons with dementia. This book was originally developed for the California Department of Aging to assist groups seeking to set up Alzheimer's Day Care Resource Centers (ADCRCs), which are the dementia day care centers supported by state general funds in California. However, it quickly became apparent to us that a reference book of larger scope would be useful to groups planning to provide dementia day care, regardless of the model or setting.

Alzheimer's day care, or dementia day care, is expanding rapidly across the United States. Our goal here is to help readers avoid having to reinvent the wheel by providing them with a foundation of experience and knowledge that others have brought to the field. The experience of directors, staffs, board of directors, family caregivers, and clients of a large number of Alzheimer's day care centers has been combined here to help the widest possible audience. We have focused on the specific knowledge and skills needed to develop or conduct a day care program for persons with dementia, regardless of whether that dementia is the result of Alzheimer's disease, multi-infarct dementia, Parkinson's disease, or any number of other causes.

The book covers the many aspects of developing day care for clients with dementia, including administration, financing, fund raising, public relations, client issues, program activities, program evaluation, supplemental resources, and problems facing participants' families. While some of the material consists of background information that is needed to begin any adult day care program, the emphasis of this book is on material that is required specifically to develop adult day care programs for persons with Alzheimer's disease or a related dementia.

In this book, we assume that readers have general knowledge and skills in a number of important areas not specific to dementia. While we do not expect readers to be experts in all these areas, we emphasize that for an Alzheimer's day care program to be successful, its operators must know or have access to the following information:

- program development
- program administration
- diagnosis, care, maintenance, and prognosis of individuals with Alzheimer's disease or related dementias
- client assessment and care planning
- recruitment, selection, training, and supervision of staff
- record keeping
- budgeting and fiscal management
- grant writing
- working with the elderly and their families
- organizations and resources in gerontology and geriatrics

While this book is not intended as a source for this general type of knowledge, individuals or groups can develop the requisite background and related skills by taking university courses, obtaining professional assistance and consultation, reading books, and networking. In particular, they can turn to specific state programs, such as the California Department of Aging Alzheimer's Day Care Resource Center Program, for further information and guidance. Other resources include State Units on Aging, National Institute on Adult Day Care, state day care associations, the Robert Wood Johnson Foundation Dementia Care and Respite Services Program, and other organizations mentioned in the text.

The organization of the chapters reflects the approximate order in which readers will face the issues involved in setting up an Alzheimer's day care program. Chapters 1 and 2 discuss factors to consider in the decision to begin a day care program for participants with Alzheimer's, and provide a brief history of Alzheimer's day care in the United States. The desire to develop an Alzheimer's day care program needs to be matched with a realistic understanding of the complexity and difficulty of setting up such a program. Furthermore, background on the development of Alzheimer's and adult day care programs nationally, and discussion of the types of models and the variety of programs that have been developed over the last decade, provide a context in which to consider the issues involved in setting up an Alzheimer's day care program.

Chapters 3–7 address administrative and management issues in setting up and running an Alzheimer's day care program. These issues include developing a governing and administrative structure; obtaining, building, or modifying a facility; staffing a program; addressing fiscal issues, such as budgets, fees, and fund raising; and promoting and marketing the program. Chapter 8 addresses the *client pathway*—the steps in the participant's involvement in the program, including definition of the target population, the referral process, client assessment, development of case plans, follow-up, and discharge. Record keeping and documentation for these specific tasks are also discussed.

Chapters 9 and 10 consider the elements of program content and participant issues, particularly in regard to participant and staff activities and scheduling. This discussion includes examples of group activities and individual activities, daily schedules for participants, and daily coordination by the staff. In addition, major problem areas, such as incontinence, wandering, inappropriate behaviors, medical needs, and transportation, are also discussed.

A discussion of staff and volunteer training has been included in chapter 11 to emphasize the importance of special training in finding and retaining staff, and in providing the highest quality services. Volunteers are a critical part of many Alzheimer's day care programs, and strategies for recruiting, training, and retaining these valuable individuals are discussed. This material is followed by chapter 12 on working with the family, which covers the ways in which Alzheimer's care staff can provide assistance to families whose relatives are in day care programs, and the relationships between staff and family caregivers. A basic tenet of this book— and of Alzheimer's day care and adult day care centers in general—is that caregivers are just as much clients as are participants. The provision of respite to caregivers, which allows them a break from constant caregiving, is as much a part of dealing with Alzheimer's as is providing care directly to Alzheimer's patients.

The last two chapters of the text, chapters 13 and 14, have a broader scope. Chapter 13 considers the relationship of Alzheimer's day care centers to the community, and the use of community resources in setting up centers and providing care. It provides information about organizations serving the needs of demented people and their family caregivers, identifies resources for use by day care staff, and considers the importance of relationships with the community. Chapter 14 focuses on program evaluation and research, describing basic strategies for evaluating a program to improve services to participants and their families, and discussing how research can be useful to program staff and policy makers.

The appendix provides four basic types of resources for those interested in setting up an Alzheimer's day care center. The first set of resources is a list of organizations that can provide guidance and expertise in this area, including state agencies responsible for Alzheimer's day care/ respite care, national organizations involved in Alzheimer's care, and Alzheimer's disease and memory disorder diagnostic centers. The second resource is a compilation of specific forms and documents currently being used in a number of Alzheimer's day care centers. These forms can be used as is or modified to meet the needs of any organization or center. The third and fourth resource items are examples of model job descriptions and sample tables of contents for program policies and procedures manuals, respectively.

Throughout this book, we have attempted to present information on day care from various points of view to help readers set up their own programs. Given that a number of successful models of Alzheimer's day care have evolved, we have tried to avoid promoting one particular model over another. There are many exciting examples of medical and social models, integrated and specialized models, private and public models. Regardless of the model employed in developing or improving Alzheimer's day care programs, each center will end up with its own program based on the abilities and interests of its staff, the needs of its clientele and their families, the limitations or advantages of its facility, budget parameters, the number of participants, and program philosophy.

We encourage readers to be creative within the constraints of funding, licensing, regulations, staffing limits, and good participant care, and to develop the best and most imaginative program possible. In the final analysis, all Alzheimer's day care programs reflect the experiences and orientation of their proponents and management. By applying the highest values and using creative strategies to implement a program philosophy, the director, board, and staff of an Alzheimer's day care program can deliver the highest quality and most effective services to demented participants and their families.

ACKNOWLEDGMENTS

The authors are indebted to the California Department of Aging for permission to use *Alzheimer's Day-Care Resource Center Guide* as the basis for this book. The *Guide* was developed by the authors under a contract with the Department of Aging to provide assistance to current and future directors of California Alzheimers' Day Care Resource Centers. Department of Aging staff contributed significant time and support to assist our completion of the project. We especially wish to thank Ellie Huffman and Marita McElvain for their assistance and contributions. Material extracted from the *Guide* for this publication may not be representative of the Department's views nor may any of the recommendations be considered those agreed to by the Department.

A number of individuals have provided valuable contributions to this project. First among them are two individuals who helped develop specific sections of the original *Guide:* Ruth von Behren, Ph.D., and Charlene Young, R.N., B.S.N. We appreciate their hard work and willingness to share their expertise. We would also like to acknowledge the important contributions of the directors, boards, and staff of the Alzheimer's Family Center, Inc., of San Diego and the Berkeley Alzheimer's Family Respite Center. The philosophy and expertise of both of these excellent Alzheimer's day care centers are reflected throughout the pages of this book. This work has also benefited from The Robert Wood Johnson Foundation Dementia Care and Respite Services Program, which is under the direction of Burton Reifler and his associates, Rona Smyth Henry and Kimberly Sherrill. The knowledge and expertise of these individuals, as well as that of the directors, staffs, and boards of the demonstration sites, has been very influential in the preparation of this work.

A number of people provided valuable critiques of this book. Among them are Rachel Billingsley, Barbara A. Blusewicz, Judy Canterbury, LaShawn Chevalier, Dennis Cockrum, Linda Crossman, Michael S. Franch, Barbara Gillogly, Joy Glenner, Betty Hammer, James T. Howard, Lissy Jarvik, Joan Lee, Nancy Mace, Jean Machtweg, Ro Mayer, William Meyer, Paula Nelson, Judy Neubauer, Connee Pence, Renee Pollack, Rosenwald C. Robertson, Rona Smyth Henry, Gary Steinke, Pam Steinke, Catherine Watson, Diane Wong, and Rick Zawadski. We are also grateful for the assistance of Barbara Potter. We thank Ann Trapnell, Ruth Anne Harris, Gail Hayes, and Margaret Hollingsworth for their excellent work and assistance in preparing and editing the manuscript.

Finally, we thank Ron Wilder of Hemisphere Publishing Corporation, who has been very supportive of this effort and provided excellent assistance in getting the book to press.

David A. Lindeman, D.S.W.
Nancy H. Corby, Ph.D.
Rachel Downing, L.C.S.W.
Beverly Sanborn, A.C.S.W.

1

ALZHEIMER'S DAY CARE: AN OVERVIEW

Recent decades have brought a significant increase both in the number of persons with Alzheimer's disease and related dementias, and in requests for help from families who are desperately in need of services to assist them in caring for their family member. As a result, there has been tremendous growth in the number of adult day care programs around the United States that now serve or wish to serve dementia patients. With the rapid spread of programs and the desire on the part of both professionals and communities to start new programs has come the realization that numerous issues and problems are unique to serving this population, particularly within adult day care settings. Before individuals, agencies, and communities begin the long and difficult process of setting up a dementia day care program or modifying an existing adult day care program, they must carefully review all the issues and challenges that need to be faced. This chapter provides an overview of the rationale for day care programs for individuals with Alzheimer's disease or related dementias, a history of the development of Alzheimer's and dementia day care centers in the United States, and a discussion of several of the key philosophical issues concerning dementia day care.

Before proceeding with a discussion of the background of day care programs for victims of Alzheimer's disease, we would first like to define some terms to ensure that readers understand their use throughout the book. The first set of terms involves the interrelationship between Alzheimer's disease and dementia. *Dementia* is a medical syndrome characterized by loss of memory and intellectual functioning. There are different causes of dementia, including *Alzheimer's disease*, multiple small strokes, Parkinson's disease (if the person has an impairment in thinking), and other disorders. Second, it is important to clarify the distinction among *adult day care, dementia day care,* and *Alzheimer's day care. Adult day*

1

care is a generic term that includes all types of day care programs for adults, whether these programs are called health, medical, or social models. *Dementia day care* and *Alzheimer's day care* are community-based, congregate programs with the primary goal of providing healthy and protective day care for people with Alzheimer's disease or other forms of dementia. These programs also furnish assistance to family caregivers and the general community. They frequently provide both health and social services in an adult day care setting for patients with dementia, provide respite and support for caregivers, and offer training opportunities for professionals and caregivers. As will be discussed, any or all adult day care programs, regardless of their focus or services, can serve patients with dementia or Alzheimer's disease. Since day care programs generally serve a range of dementia patients, the term *dementia day care* is used periodically throughout the book, for the sake of consistency as well as to emphasize the broad participant population of these programs. However, *Alzheimer's day care* will be the primary term used to describe programs that serve patients with Alzheimer's disease and other dementias and their families and caregivers. Nearly all of what we say in this book about Alzheimer's day care can be applied to dementia day care in general.

BACKGROUND

Within the last few years federal and state governments have acknowledged the significance of Alzheimer's disease and its physical, psychological, and economic impact on individuals, families, and the general public. In addition, Alzheimer's disease is receiving increased attention from the health and social service community, as well as from the general public, because it is a disease that can have overwhelming social and emotional impact, especially on the patient's family. It is a chronic, progressive, deteriorating neurological disease that afflicts its victims with major declines in cognition, memory, speech, and individual ability for self-care.

It has been estimated that Alzheimer's disease afflicts more than 4 million persons nationally, but recent studies suggest that the number of persons affected by the disease is far higher, particularly in the population over 85 years of age, where the prevalence of Alzheimer's disease may approach 47% (Evans et al., 1989). Alzheimer's victims suffer insidious and unrelenting brain failure, progressing from simple forgetfulness to the need for total care in carrying out the simplest routine activities of daily living. The need for total care may span several years and may eventually result in institutionalization. The monetary cost of caring for chronically demented persons is estimated to be as high as $80 billion annually in the United States alone.

There is a critical shortage in the availability of services to Alzheimer's patients, as well as a lack of appropriate services. Patients with Alzheimer's disease or other dementias are now most often cared for by their families at home or, in the later stages of the disease, in nursing homes. Most Alzheimer's patients, including those who are in the moderate to severe stages of the disease, can remain in a home or community-based setting if families and caregivers are provided with appropriate supportive services. Put another way, given adequate supportive services, most families and caregivers could maintain a demented person in a noninstitutionalized setting for a significant period of time. Evidence suggests that this service arrangement is generally preferable for families because of its greater level of satisfaction and lower financial costs. Evidence also suggests that this service modality is beneficial to society as a whole because it can result in reduced health and social service expenditures as a result of lower utilization of institutional services.

Unfortunately, many moderate to severely impaired dementia patients cannot be adequately served by the existing community-based service system. First, there is a dearth of appropriate, accessible, cost-effective alternative services. Second, the existing home and community-based service system frequently cannot address the special needs of many of these individuals, due to their cognitive, functional, or behavioral characteristics. All too often, families and caregivers of moderate to severely impaired dementia patients are forced to institutionalize their family members for lack of other alternatives.

Over the last decade, many health and social service providers have turned to day care as an appropriate, cost-effective option. Day care or other forms of respite care are important alternatives to having family caregivers exhaust themselves by providing 24-hour-a-day care to family members with dementia, or to the inappropriate institutionalization of dementia patients who could still function at home with the proper supervision and support, as long as the primary caregiver has some relief in providing care. Alzheimer's day care is a community-based, long-term care program, the goals of which are (1) to provide a structured, secure environment in a congregate setting for persons with Alzheimer's disease, and (2) to provide respite from extended caregiving for family caregivers. Alzheimer's day care programs serve patients with various forms of dementia, their families, and their caregivers, regardless of the cause of dementia.

HISTORY OF ALZHEIMER'S DAY CARE

One way to gain a perspective on Alzheimer's day care is to examine the roots from which it has sprung. Alzheimer's day care programs are a natural evolution from the adult day care movement in the United States. Persons with dementia have always been served by adult day care programs and continue to be served by them today. Specialized programs for this population, however, are for the most part a relatively recent development.

Adult day care is a service that began to be provided in the United

States in the early 1970s, when it emerged as part of the movement to shift people out of state hospitals for the mentally ill and to prevent inappropriate nursing home placement. Stimulated by legislative hearings about nursing home care and the enormous growth in nursing home utilization with the advent of Medicaid and Medicare in 1965, consumers and advocates were determined to find alternatives to unnecessary or premature institutionalization. In addition to the growing concern about the quality of nursing home care, various studies found that many persons in nursing homes did not need the level of care provided there, but were there because no other alternatives were available for protective, supervised care. In response to that need, adult day care developed as a grassroots movement throughout the United States. Influenced by the British day hospital program, adult day care programs were started around the United States in the early 1970s by concerned people seeking to find a way to keep functionally impaired persons in the community.

The goals of adult day care programs generally include the provision of health and/or social services in one setting, an attempt to maintain individuals in the community rather than in institutions, and a philosophy that values treating the whole person with emphasis on a therapeutic milieu. The essential elements of adult day care programs are a structured day program in a safe environment where functionally impaired adults can receive the social and health services needed to restore or maintain optimal functioning. Hallmarks of these programs are an individualized, comprehensive assessment and a plan of care, usually involving multidisciplinary staff. Attendance is planned and regular. Although the primary target population is the impaired adult, day programs also serve caregivers. Respite for caregivers is provided while the participants attend day programs, and other direct assistance is provided through support groups, education, training, referrals, and counseling.

While researchers and policy makers have attempted to identify a number of different models for adult day care, over time it has become apparent that there are no clear-cut categories. In fact, what has been developed is a broad spectrum of programs providing a range of social and health services. While some programs emphasize a social orientation, others concentrate on health services. Therapies are directed primarily at maintenance of functional abilities. Distinctions blur between programs that emphasize social day care services and those that emphasize health day care, as programs strive to meet the range of needs of their participants. Categories or models of day care are often developed as a response to licensing and reimbursement requirements. Although some programs receive funds from the Older Americans Act and/or Medicaid, federal and state funding sources that specifically provide for adult day care are uneven, and they are generally inadequate to fund programs at their full operational level. Still, adult day care continues to grow despite the lack of a stable funding base. Attempts have been made in recent years to seek funding support for adult day care programs at the federal level and to expand the level of support from state and local governments.

Although demented clients have always been served by adult day care programs, regardless of whether the programs emphasized social or health services, it was not until the 1980s that specialized programs for dementia day care generally came into being. Persons with minimal cognitive impairments often fit right into day care settings without much adjustment on the part of staff or other participants. And in many cases, adult day care programs can serve a limited number of more cognitively impaired individuals. But as a response to the increasing number of individuals with severe cognitive impairments, who often could not be served in generic day care centers, or who could benefit from more specialized services, a number of programs were established that had a particular expertise in serving demented individuals. Some of the earliest examples of adult day programs specializing in treating persons with dementia were the Harbor Area Adult Day Care Center in Costa Mesa, California, which was established in 1980, and the Alzheimer's Family Center, Inc., in San Diego, which was established in 1982. Other specialized programs started independently throughout the country in the early 1980s.

Specialized dementia day care programs started proliferating in the mid-1980s as a number of states provided funds specifically for Alzheimer's disease services, particularly in the area of day care. One example was the creation of the Alzheimer's Day Care Resource Center (ADCRC) Program in 1984 within the California Department of Aging. Starting with a budget of $300,000 and 8 centers in fiscal year 1984–85, the program has expanded to 36 centers and $2,160,000 for fiscal year 1989–90. These centers may either serve cognitively impaired and noncognitively impaired individuals together or serve demented individuals only. They operate under a variety of licenses, including both social adult day care and adult day health care licenses, and they vary dramatically in size and budgets. California's ADCRCs are day care/respite centers as well as resource centers for families of persons with brain impairments. The most frequently used services in California's ADCRC programs are day care, individual and group family counseling, individual and group patient counseling, and case management.

Many other states have encouraged or funded Alzheimer's or dementia day care programs (see appendix). Furthermore, there are numerous Alzheimer's/dementia day care programs around the country that do not receive any state support. Most of these programs are private, not-for-profit programs. Yet there are an increasing number of public and private for-profit Alzheimer's/dementia day care programs now in existence. Mace and Rabins (1984) conducted a survey to determine the number of day care centers serving dementia patients; they found nearly 450 that served this population, more than 80 of which indicated that 50% or more of their client population was demented. Since that survey was conducted, there have been several initiatives, including those by the Alzheimer's Association, the Robert Wood Johnson Foundation, and the Brookdale Foundation, to expand the number of centers serving dementia patients and their families, and to explore the most appropriate and effective organizational, environmental, staffing, and care systems for service delivery to this population.

The rapid manner in which dementia day care programs have proliferated over the last few years is most clearly shown by the results of the 1990 National Adult Day Care Census Project survey of adult day care programs which was conducted by Zawadski and Von Behren (1990). Funding for the survey was from the American Association of Retired Persons and the Health Care Financing Administration in conjunction with the National Institute on Adult Daycare/National Council on the Aging. This survey of 1118 adult day care centers indicated that the number of adult day care centers in the U.S. serving dementia patients had grown dramatically, with 145 (13%) centers reporting they were established specifically to serve individuals with Alzheimer's disease, 524 (47%) reporting they have special programs for Alzheimer's patients within their center, and another 397 (36%) reporting they serve Alzheimer's disease patients within their adult day care program. Only 52 adult day care centers (5%) indicated they do not serve any Alzheimer's disease patients. This survey also found the median percentage of Alzheimer's disease participants served by all 1118 adult day care centers is 33%, and the percentage of center participants with cognitive impairments is 51% (not mutually exclusive). A particularly compelling point is that 21% of centers, or approximately 235 centers, have at least 50% or more Alzheimer's disease participants, nearly a three-fold increase since the 1984 survey by Mace and Robins. These current figures actually could under-represent the number and percentage of programs serving dementia patients, or exclusively serving dementia patients, given the difficulty in obtaining accurate diagnoses. However, the results of the survey clearly indicate that the number of programs serving this population is certainly very large, and is growing very rapidly.

PHILOSOPHY OF ALZHEIMER'S DAY CARE

Before addressing the planning goals and issues in starting a day care center for patients with Alzheimer's disease, there are several important philosophical constructs that should be understood. These include (1) who the day care client is; (2) day care's role as an alternative to institutionalization; (3) day care's role in the continuum of long-term care; (4) distinctions between integrated and specialized day care; (5) distinctions between health and social models of day care; and (6) day care centers' provision of a range of resources through multifaceted programs. We will address each of these in turn.

Client Dyads: Participant and Caregiver

As in all adult day care programs, programs that serve patients with Alzheimer's disease are providing important services to both family caregivers and patients. The fact that respite for caregivers is often just as important as, and in some cases more important than, the day care services provided for participants is the basis for considering the client of dementia day care programs as *both* the patient and the caregiver. Considering the patient and caregiver as a *client dyad* is a philosophy that is applied throughout this book. It is fundamental to most professionals' approach to serving patients with Alzheimer's disease and related dementias.

Alternative to Institutionalization

As part of benefiting both patient and caregiver, Alzheimer's day care often contributes to preventing premature or inappropriate institutionalization of the patient in a nursing home. Where avoiding institutionalization is possible, and where it is to the benefit of both patient and caregiver, we encourage it. However, we must caution that in the case of Alzheimer's disease and related dementias, there often comes a point where institutionalization is the preferable service alternative for both patient and caregiver. This happens when day care and other home- and community-based services can no longer meet the needs of the patient and/or caregiver. Furthermore, the danger in delaying institutionalization is that the level of care and management of behavioral problems required by persons with advanced dementia may make finding a suitable nursing home much more difficult.

Long-Term Care Continuum

Alzheimer's day care must be considered as part of a continuum of services for patients and caregivers. Alzheimer's disease and related dementias affect individuals differently; symptoms, rates of progression, and impact differ from person to person. Similarly, the impact of the disease on caregivers' ability to manage under the physical, emotional, and financial stress it brings differs dramatically. There are a wide range of services that are appropriate at different times in the course of the disease, to help either the patient or the caregiver. These services include home, community-based, and institutional services. It is becoming more and more apparent that Alzheimer's day care, and other services for dementia patients and their caregivers, has become a significant component of this continuum of care.

Integrated and Specialized Care

Adult day care programs have always served some patients with Alzheimer's disease or related dementias. Adult day care programs are often categorized by whether they have a health or social emphasis. *Adult day health care* refers to an organized day program of therapeutic social and health services that serves elderly persons or other adults with physical *or* cognitive impairment, for the purpose of restoring or maintaining optimal capacity for self-care. These programs provide primarily maintenance services. *Social adult day care* provides nonmedical care and supervision to adults in need of personal services, protection, assistance, guidance, or training essential for sustaining the activities of daily living or for the protection of the individual. Like adult day health care, these programs provide social and related support services in a protective setting less than 24 hours per day, but they differ from adult day health care in that they do not have the same requirements for nursing and rehabilitative services. Regardless of the distinction, the vast majority of adult day care programs can and do serve some dementia patients. Generally, persons in the earlier stages of Alzheimer's disease can be easily integrated into any adult day care program. Difficulties often arise, however, when individuals with more severe cognitive problems or functional limitations try to participate in an adult day care program.

Since many adult day care centers are limited in their ability to serve individuals with moderate or severe cognitive impairments, many programs have been established solely to serve dementia patients, including Alzheimer's patients. Thus, a dementia day care program may be a stand-alone program that exclusively serves persons with Alzheimer's and other dementias, or it may be operated within a broader adult day care setting that serves noncognitively impaired individuals as well. While there are proponents of both forms of dementia day care, there is no evidence to date that specialization or nonspecialization of a center's participant population is any more or less successful. Establishing a dementia-specific versus a non-dementia-specific model is more a function of an agency's history or philosophy, or the range of cognitive and functional impairments of the participants to be served.

Health vs. Social Models

Alzheimer's day care programs operate in both health and social models. There are proponents of the policy that all dementia day care programs should have a nurse or other health professional as director or member of the staff. In contrast, many individuals feel that health care professionals are not necessary as permanent members of a program's staff but should be available on an as-needed basis. While there are pros and cons to each approach (which will be discussed in the text), ultimately it is important to note that both health and social models of dementia day care have been successfully and effectively implemented for patients with Alzheimer's disease.

Multifaceted Programs

Alzheimer's day care programs are often multidimensional, providing not only day care to participants and respite to caregivers, but also information and referral, family assistance, support groups, counseling, financial and legal consultations, and other types of direct services. Most programs are actively involved in training health and social service professionals as well as family caregivers. Many programs also participate actively in health and social service research.

CONCLUSION

The 1980s saw a rapid development in adult day care programs serving Alzheimer's patients and their families in the United States. From a handful of programs to hundreds of programs, Alzheimer's/dementia day care centers have proliferated to meet the demands of the burgeoning population of patients and their caregivers who are in desperate need of respite. Over the last decade a number of major events and initiatives have assisted the development of additional day care programs; these include the availability of public funds, state and foundation initiatives, and a groundswell of community efforts.

As in the case of adult day care in general, growth in Alzheimer's day care programs has occurred despite limited funding and lack of reliable sources of funding. Current and future initiatives may cause traditional funding sources, such as private health insurance, to begin covering Alzheimer's/dementia day care. Successful demonstration projects and proposed legislation may culminate in the inclusion of Alzheimer's/dementia day care as a Medicare benefit. Regardless of the outcome of these initiatives, Alzheimer's day care will continue to grow. Day care is a cost-effective service for both patients and families. Although there are no reliable government figures regarding the number of clients served, costs, or number of specialized programs, as the U.S. population ages and the number of persons with dementia increases, the demand for specialized day programs will inevitably continue to grow.

The development of day programs for specialized populations, such as persons with Alzheimer's disease and related dementias, should continue to be a major theme of health and social services for the elderly for the next several years. Regardless of whether Alzheimer's day care programs are specialized, have a health or social focus, or have any other distinctive features, they will continue to be established, and individuals, agencies, and communities need to understand the issues and challenges to be faced in setting up these programs. For the balance of this book, we will address the fundamental issues involved in planning, implementing, and managing an Alzheimer's day care program. Again, we emphasize that what we say applies to day care for dementia patients in general.

2

PLANNING AN ALZHEIMER'S DAY CARE PROGRAM

Before taking on the challenging task of designing and implementing a day care program for Alzheimer's patients, it is necessary to assess the goals and feasibility of initiating such a major undertaking. The purpose of this chapter is to provide direction and guidance in making the decision to develop an Alzheimer's day care center or to modify an existing adult day care program to serve Alzheimer's patients and their families. Taking time to wrestle with this all-important decision before taking action will prevent program developers from getting in over their heads. It can also assist those who decide to continue with their plans in developing the organizational unity needed to achieve the task despite the ever-present obstacles and problems. This material is designed to assist those who are developing programs from scratch as well as those who have existing day care programs they plan to modify or change in order to serve demented clients.

PROGRAM PLANNING AND GOAL SETTING

Regardless of whether an organization is considering the establishment of an Alzheimer's day care center or the modification of an existing program, good initial planning is the basis for the development of a successful program. As part of the planning process, a day care center or the planning committee for the day care center must first establish a mission statement, goals, and objectives. This process helps conceptualize the fundamental constructs for the organization, and lays the groundwork for future implementation and operational tasks. The framework of a program's mission statement and goals is determined by the chosen model of the center, licensing requirements, funding sources and constraints, or any of a number of idiosyncratic issues related to the specific facility, site, population, and resources. While to some this may seem a rather straightforward process, it often is a complex task requiring a great deal of thought and input from a number of different individuals. It is also a critical step because if the mission statement, goals, and objectives are not specifically laid out, a great deal of effort and time may be put into fruitless planning.

The first step is to develop a clear, concise mission statement. A mission statement is a broad statement that describes the fundamental purpose of the center. This is followed by specific goals and objectives that are expressed as commitments to the program's sponsors, participants, their family members, and staff. After the program is functional, the mission statement can be refined to describe the program better. An example of a mission statement is:

> The mission of this program is to achieve a measurable level of care that is responsive to the needs and values of the participants, the family caregivers, and the community.

The second step is to develop specific and concrete goals. All centers for dementia patients are likely to have somewhat similar goals, particularly in relation to the premises of preventing inappropriate institutionalization, establishing a safe environment, and reducing caregiver stress. The development of specific goals, however, will assist in the conceptualization of a work plan, provide direction to the staff and volunteers, and serve as a useful tool in assessing the program's progress and outcomes. It is imperative that the goals for a center be determined so that the types of services to be provided can be defined. Furthermore, if all parties to the development or modification of a center are involved in setting goals, the organization will have a better conceptual picture of the planned outcome. Most Alzheimer's day care centers develop three or four main goals, such as the following:

1. To provide specific activities to maintain or maximize patients' remaining living skills.
2. To provide respite to caregivers in order to allow them to remain healthy while caring for an Alzheimer's patient.
3. To provide an educational atmosphere where caregivers and professionals can learn and grow.
4. To provide a setting where participants can reestablish and continue to maintain self-esteem in a caring, nurturing environment.

The third step in the planning process is to establish objectives for each goal. Each objective should identify the task, establish who is responsible for completing the task, and set a time frame for completion of the task. Objectives should be very specific and address a single issue. An example of an objective is as follows: The steering committee will determine whether the proposed Alzheimer's day care center will have a social or health focus by June of 1992. Since the focus of the planning process is on the establishment of a new center, a program's initial objectives should be short-term in nature. As will be discussed later in this chapter, objectives should be set by the planning or steering committee. Before objectives can be set, however, those who are developing an Alzheimer's day care program need to conduct a thorough review of the need for a program.

NEEDS ASSESSMENT

Once a mission statement and goals have been prepared, the next step in the planning process is to conduct a thorough assessment of need for the program in the community and to determine the ideal features and characteristics of the proposed program. All too often, there is a general assumption that an Alzheimer's day care center or other form of respite program will be utilized to its fullest capacity. This is not always the case, however. In fact, there are often several different factors that affect the types of services that would be utilized, the amount of money that would be available to pay for those services, and specific utilization problems that may occur because of location, time, or other constraints. In essence, one cannot count on an intuitive belief or anecdotal evidence that the day care center will be appropriate for a given area or utilized to the anticipated capacity.

Several different steps can be undertaken early in the planning process to determine whether there is a need for this service in the community. The first step is to review existing resources and programs within the community and to contact other professional organizations and providers. These include other day care programs, local hospitals, the Department of Social Services, Area Agency on Aging, or the Department of Mental Health. Planners should ask if they have estimates of the number of patients needing Alzheimer's day care.

An even more accurate means for assessing the potential demand for an Alzheimer's day care center is to contact potential users of the program, assuming that they are familiar with the concept of a day care program. A formal market survey of caregivers of Alzheimer's patients provides a much more accurate assessment of the types of services people would utilize, the time in which they would use them, the amount of resources they have to spend on those services, and potential problems, such as transportation, cultural appropriateness, language barriers, and public relations perceptions. If resources permit it, a formal market survey of the potential demand and demographic characteristics of the proposed service area can be very effective. This can be accomplished in a number of ways, including in-kind contributions from organizations such as hospitals and other service agencies; use of university faculty, particularly social work or nursing students; or, when resources permit, hiring of a market research firm.

A number of mechanisms are available to collect information to determine demand for services, including telephone surveys, mail surveys, and focus groups. Each has its benefits as well as its problems. A telephone survey, for example, permits planners to get more detailed information and to identify specific problems that might not be mentioned in a mail survey. On the other hand, it is labor intensive and can be taxing on the caregivers who are responding. Telephone surveys are ineffective if your clients are without phones or if they don't speak English. It is often difficult for caregivers of dementia patients to spend much time on the phone if they are with the patient when the call is received. A mail survey, while it may allow planners to get uniform information from a large number of people for a relatively modest amount of money, usually has a very low response rate. In addition, people for whom English is a second language or for whom literacy is a problem may have more difficulty completing a written survey. Again, the amount of time necessary for caregivers to complete a mail survey may be beyond their ability due to the hardships of caregiving. A marketing firm, particularly one that is willing to provide some community service, can generally offer suggestions as to ways to get the best response for a modest amount of resources. In the absence of resources or funds-in-hand, information might be collected through a survey of providers and potential consumers using Alzheimer's Association mailing lists.

The response from the community needs assessment should provide guidance as to what expectations the center should have in terms of the number of people that will be interested in coming to the center, the staff that will be necessary to run the center, and hidden problems that could potentially have significant costs (e.g., transportation problems). Invariably this assessment will give individuals who are considering setting up a program much better information than can be obtained from professionals who may not have a clear understanding of some of the limitations that are facing caregivers with dementia patients.

Regardless of the technique employed, factual information and data necessary to determine patient, family, and community needs and resources must be gathered as part of the needs assessment process. From a marketing perspective, the information that a planning committee needs includes an environmental analysis, a resource analysis, a demand analysis, a review of current service utilization, an analysis of client resources, an analysis of program features and characteristics, and a financial analysis. To convert these various analyses into concrete terms, a planning committee needs to obtain the following information:

- Local adult day care and respite programs currently in existence (number of clients served, target population, location, fees, operating body, and waiting list).
- Local resources for dementia clients (Alzheimer's Association chap-

ter, respite care, family support groups, caregiver education, centers for diagnosis).

- Total number of elderly and the estimated number of elderly with dementia in the catchment area. Help in obtaining this information may be found through the local Area Agency on Aging, United Way, or other health or social service agencies.
- Data identifying unmet needs of dementia patients and their families. This should help a planning committee ascertain whether or not there is an actual need for such a program. Specific questions that need to be addressed include: Are patients or families going without needed services they would use if they were made available? How many might use them? How much would they be willing to pay? How much do they know about possible reimbursement sources, such as Medicaid, state programs, or private insurance? What other types of respite services do families need? This information may be obtained from Alzheimer's Association chapters, senior citizens' centers, local hospitals, existing service agencies, and market studies.
- Level of community acceptance and support for a program (openness to nonfamilial providers, education or awareness of dementia and respite care, cultural inhibitors, and economic conditions).
- Basic understanding of Alzheimer's disease and related dementias, including diagnosis, management, progression, and intervention.
- State and local licensing requirements and regulations for adult day care in general, and Alzheimer's day care specifically.
- Local fire safety and health department regulations. These regulations can often limit or influence the type of program, the structure of the facility, and programming characteristics.
- The proposed sponsor's financial, staffing, and other resources. Is this something the organization can afford to do at this time? Are additional resources of one sort or another needed? Are they available?
- Other programs serving dementia patients or older clients with whom the planned program might integrate. This would save time and money and might prove more cost-effective than opening a new center.

PLANNING COMMITTEE

The decision to develop an Alzheimer's day care program is rarely the decision of a single individual. There may be one key person who is determined that such a program needs to be developed and who makes things happen, but the long-term success of a program depends on group, organization, and community effort. Therefore, initial steps in deciding whether to begin such a program will be more effective if all interested individuals and those who will be involved, even those who may not initially favor the idea, are included in the planning and decision making.

The first step in decision making is to set up a working group to coordinate program implementation efforts. This should be a *planning committee* or *steering committee*. The group must have a chairperson responsible for setting the agenda, keeping things on schedule, and focusing the group on the task of decision making or on making recommendations to a board or other policy-making body. There is no limit to the size of a planning or steering committee, as long as the group remains manageable. The planning committee will have the following basic objectives:

- To gather information about dementia and adult day care, developing a knowledgeable understanding of the subject.
- To clarify and define the population to be served.
- To decide or recommend whether or not to pursue the proposed program.

The planning committee offers additional benefits in that it provides a vehicle to obtain both official and grass-roots community support. This is vital to prospective programs because it generates community interest and financial support; educates caregivers, providers, and government officials; and provides the basis for future referrals and community volunteers. The composition of the committee is very important as well. By including individuals who will be involved in critical decisions concerning the organization or implementation of the program, other experienced providers of dementia and adult day care services, and most importantly family caregivers, the decision-making process and program start-up will be greatly expedited and improved. Furthermore, individuals with specific skills should be invited to participate. These should include administrators, lawyers, accountants, fund raisers, professionals in the field of aging, and those with skills in marketing and public relations. For an existing organization, of course, participation on the part of board members and staff is critical.

The planning committee will have a number of discrete tasks to complete in order to make the decision as to whether or not to proceed with establishing an Alzheimer's day care center. To accomplish these tasks, it is most productive to develop subcommittees that can address key issues that will determine the feasibility of moving ahead with the establishment of a center. While these subcommittees will differ among programs depending on the resources and needs of the planning committee, there are several key areas that will need to be addressed: reorganization/administration, finance/fund raising, personnel, program structure and content, and facilities/building. A number of other issues may be addressed by each of these subcommittees, or ad hoc subcommittees may be created for special issues, such as transportation or marketing. In an existing organization many of these issues may be addressed by existing board committees, rather than by creating new entities.

The *organization/administration subcommittee* is responsible for helping to determine the best means of setting up the organizational structure and legal entity for managing the center. This may include the time-consuming process of getting the organization incorporated, writing by-laws, obtaining not-for-profit status (if applicable), and developing the framework for the governing body. In an existing agency, this group will also have to address if and how administrative and staff responsibilities and interrelationships will change when new services are offered.

The *finance/fund raising subcommittee* is a critical part of this planning process, as it will determine the general budget for the program and identify potential and existing funding sources. While a great deal of the budget will be dependent upon the nature of the services provided and the staffing required for those services, a general budget can be prepared at the outset of the planning process. This group will also have to address the crucial issue of fund raising and help identify potential resources to support the opening as well as ongoing operations of the center. Resources may include participant fees; federal, state, and local funds; and support from foundations and the private sector. In existing day care centers, this group has an especially challenging task of determining the potential short-term and long-term financial impact of an Alzheimer's program, what extra start-up funds will be needed, and whether the Alzheimer's program will need to be subsidized by the existing program.

The *personnel subcommittee* will work with the *program subcommittee* to determine the staffing arrangements required to operate the center. The principal task of this group will be to develop the job description for the executive director and to develop personnel policies and procedures for the organization (see appendix). The development of job descriptions for other staff and an outline of staff benefits will follow. The program subcommittee will deal with the fundamental content of the program. This group must identify the specific types of program activities that the organization will provide. It also must consider whether the organization will have primarily a social service or health service focus. The group must consider the number of days and the amount of time the organization can operate in its initial stages as well as what the long-term operational goals of the program will be. Program criteria, such as admissions, assessment, and discharge, will be addressed by this subcommittee. Additionally, it will be responsible for considering difficult issues such as transportation, meals, and insurance. Again, in existing day care centers, these subcommittees will have to address intraorganizational issues to ensure the smooth transition and start-up of this new component of the organization.

The *facility/building subcommittee* will be responsible for determining a site for a new center or necessary modifications for an existing site, and what issues need to be addressed related to local fire regulations and building codes.

In a multiservice agency with an established board, the planning committee as a whole might take on these tasks and delegate select portions to existing subcommittees (program, finance, personnel) or form ad hoc task forces to accomplish program set-up and management strategies. It is important to realize that there is no one way to conduct the planning for a new center or for the addition of an Alzheimer's component to an existing program. As in all areas of working with Alzheimer's patients, planning requires flexibility, appropriate use of resources, and thoroughness.

The planning committee needs to set up a timetable for collecting data, scheduling meetings to discuss policy options, and making decisions. This will facilitate the decision-making process and provide valuable structure to committee deliberations. A timetable should include specific tasks, responsible individuals, the date information is due, and recommended decision dates. The timetable for information gathering and decision making must be realistic. Specific priorities must be clearly laid out at the outset. By sticking to a very specific schedule, the planning committee can determine in a timely manner whether or not it is feasible to move ahead on the initiation of an Alzheimer's day care center.

GENERAL FACTORS TO CONSIDER

Those making the decisions about whether or not to develop an Alzheimer's day care program need to consider a number of very important issues. The issues that must be reviewed include facility and location, financial resources, target population, licensing, transportation, insurance, and support from volunteers, the community, and other agencies. We will discuss each of these issues briefly, followed by a rundown of issues particular to existing programs.

Facility and Location

A critical administrative factor is the identification of a site for the program. Buildings that have been used for Alzheimer's/dementia day care programs are single-family residences, church social halls, empty school buildings, stores, clinics, community centers, buildings in industrial parks, as well as units or lounges in hospitals. There is no "best" facility or location—site and program-specific philosophies, resources, and politics play a significant role in determining facility and location. These are some of the key questions to consider. Where will the program be located in relationship to participants, supplemental services, or transportation? Is there an existing building—or can one be obtained—that meets licensing requirements? Are renovation funds available to enable an existing building to meet licensing requirements? Is outdoor space available for participants? Is a parking lot or loading zone available? How easily can the facility be made secure for wanderers? Guaranteeing a suitable facility and location is a crucial step. Some programs have had to turn back funding or delay start-up for months because of difficulty in locating suitable space.

Financial Resources

The costs of running an Alzheimer's day care program generally exceed $100,000 a year, and often are significantly higher depending on the programming and staffing characteristics. The proposed sponsor must have the financial resources to cover start-up costs, including hiring and paying staff salaries and benefits; paying for rent, utilities, and insurance; applying for licensing (and waiting to receive it); and obtaining program and office supplies and equipment. It may be months before revenues are collected to apply to operating costs. It may also be a year or two before the program is actually self-supporting. It is important to note that except in a few states where there is significant state reimbursement, dementia programs are rarely self-supporting from fees alone. For the majority of Alzheimer's/dementia day care programs, financing comes from a number of sources and must be carefully planned for. Organizations should pursue funding from a wide range of sources, including foundations, private corporations, local government, service clubs, hospitals, and volunteer organizations.

Target Population

Defining the target population is a more difficult task than it may appear. Taking time to discuss the characteristics of the population to be served is very important in setting the program philosophy, goals, and policies. It may also determine what funding is available, which type of licensing is best, and a variety of other program decisions. The following list of questions may serve as a guide for thinking and discussion.

- What will be the specific eligibility criteria?
- Will the program serve only clients with Alzehimer's disease and other dementias, or will it also serve cognitively intact patients?
- Will the program serve all levels of the functional/cognitive impairment of Alzheimer's clients—that is, those in the latter stages of the disease (moderate to severe) as well as in the early stages of the disease (mild to moderate)? How will you differentiate between stages?
- Will the program serve clients in only a narrow catchment area or in an extended one? Check with potential funding sources to make sure there are no conflicts.
- Will eligibility restrictions be established for clients? For example, will clients be enrolled who are physically handicapped, who are incontinent, who have no families, who live in board-and-care

homes, who are verbally abusive or physically aggressive, or who wander?

Licensing

Licensing and certification is an issue that varies dramatically from state to state and community to community. In some states, licensing may not even exist, while in other states, licensing requirements will determine the type of facility and program permitted. Planning committees must consider what type of program (dementia-specific or integrated) will be most suitable to develop and which type of licensing will best match the organization's goals and resources.

Transportation

Without transportation, not just a few but *many* clients will be unable to attend the program. Planning committees should consider the question of transportation carefully. Is there an existing transportation system that could be used to serve the day care center? What will be the expected transportation arrangements and costs to serve the day care clients? Will nonambulatory patients—those requiring wheelchairs or assistance devices—participate in the program? Will families be required to provide transportation? If transportation is provided by the center, it will dramatically increase operating costs. However, it may be necessary if the needs assessment shows that most families cannot provide transportation and other resources are unavailable.

Insurance

How will liability insurance for the participants and staff be handled? (Registered nurses, for example, will require malpractice insurance.) Arranging for liability insurance for this type of program may be more costly than expected and may delay the start-up of the program. In turn, delays in start-up can add to the cost of the program. New boards must consider whether there should be insurance to cover board liability—an issue of increasing concern in the past few years.

Volunteer, Agency, and Community Support

A critical factor in program start-up is the availability and interest of individuals and agencies in the community. Is there an individual or core group who are sufficiently interested in starting such a program that they will take responsibility for the development of the program and provide ongoing policy and financial support? This group can include volunteers, board members, or community members. Someone needs to spearhead the project and push it to completion. The process from initial expressions of interest to actual operation of a center may take from 6 to 18 months. Is there major resistance to the project from individuals in the planning organization, another organization, or the community? How can the planning committee/organization involve key community people who will support and cooperate with efforts to develop the program?

Existing Programs

Existing adult day care programs that want to expand to serve demented clients should consider how their program would meet the special needs of these new participants and their families in the following areas:

- Modification of regular day care programming to meet the needs of clients with Alzheimer's disease.
- Modification or relocation of the site/building for control of wandering clients.
- Increased staffing needs in an Alzheimer's day care program.
- Increased publicity and outreach to caregivers of clients with Alzheimer's disease.
- Disaster provision and evacuation plans.

Existing adult day care programs need to assess carefully projected costs and the timetable required for achieving these program changes. They need to ascertain how the provision of Alzheimer's day care services will affect the current program, services to nondemented clients, and outreach and publicity efforts. The start-up of an Alzheimer's day care program by an existing day care center can have a significant impact on time, personnel, and finances.

CONCLUSION

It is important to realize that the planning process is generally an extended one, involving a large number of people and continuing over a very long period of time. While some programs have been fortunate to commence operations in three to six months, substantially more programs have indicated that it took one to two often painful years for them to open, due to construction or personnel budgets that suddenly doubled; delays in licensing, renovation, or fire marshal approval; resistance from the community or other agencies; or just competing priorities. Although the planning process is fraught with potential delays and barriers to getting information and making decisions, a specific timetable can lead to a timely and successful start up. Such a timetable might run as follows: needs assessment, months 1 and 2; site location and licensing, months 2–4; fund development, months 2–6; renovation, months 3–6; personnel development, months 4–6; program content development, months 5–6.

In addition, the planning process must lead to development of a long-range plan for the organization. Besides start-up issues, the planning group must consider the long-term viability of the organization and the challenges it will face. Individuals participating in the planning process must realize that it requires the ability to keep things in perspective, remain flexible, and maintain a very optimistic outlook about the long-term goals of the program.

It should be remembered that at some point the efforts of a working group or planning committee will come to an end, as the decision is made to move ahead. For new centers the selection of a governing board will require the transfer of most of the tasks that have been conducted by the planning committee. A transition from planning body to governing board can generally be made smoothly and successfully, given proper foresight.

Realistic planning and the development of an information base for sound decision making will provide the tools for making an appropriate decision regarding the establishment of an Alzheimer's day care program. While it is hoped that the decision-making process will result in the development and implementation of an Alzheimer's day care program, the process may determine that it will be better for an organization to meet the needs of dementia clients and their families in some other fashion. This might include developing support groups or classes for caregivers, starting an Alzheimer's Association chapter, or joining efforts with another program to develop specialized services.

Whether the process of struggling with this choice leads in the direction of deciding not to begin a program or propels an organization ahead more resolved and enthusiastic than ever, the importance of going through an active, planned, decision-making process cannot be overemphasized. Taking time to gather the information and involve others from the community in a systematic process does not need to slow down the development of the program. Realistic planning and clarification of options will enable those involved with the project to advocate more knowledgeably and achieve the establishment of a more precisely tailored and targeted program to serve the needs of Alzheimer's patients and their families.

3

ADMINISTRATION OF AN ALZHEIMER'S DAY CARE PROGRAM

This chapter will address the primary administrative and organizational requirements of establishing and running an Alzheimer's day care program. While a single chapter cannot convey every requirement or recommendation concerning the administration of an Alzheimer's day care program, the most important of them will be highlighted here. We recommend that readers seek out additional reading material and resources concerning the administration of adult day care in general, several of which are listed in the bibliography. This chapter discusses organizational issues that are appropriate for generic program settings and does not attempt to address specific local or state situations or constraints.

PROGRAM PHILOSOPHY

The administrative and organizational structure of an Alzheimer's day care program is fundamentally determined by the philosophy of the organization and board of directors. Alzheimer's/dementia day care is committed to supporting the human value and dignity of dementia patients regardless of age, sex, race, cultural heritage, and cognitive limitations, and to enhancing the quality and meaning of their lives. Alzheimer's/dementia day care programs must recognize that cognitively impaired individuals can and should contribute to the planning and implementation of their day-to-day activities. In general, these day care programs believe in the therapeutic value of a supportive, caring environment for the cognitively impaired. As previously discussed, the program philosophy is generally articulated in the mission statement and goals of the program. These fundamental points set the stage for the composition and philosophy of the governing body.

A critical component in the development of an Alzheimer's day care program is the governing body of the organization. The governing body may already exist in the form of a board of directors or advisory committee or some subset of a larger organization, which will play a critical role in setting policy and procedures for the new program. If a governing body must be established for the new organization, this has to be one of the top priorities of the planning committee. The level of effort and contributions to the development of the program by the governing body are critical to its success.

In addition to the development of a committed and concerned governing body that has legal authority and responsibility for the operation of the program, there are several other key administrative issues in the establishment and management of an Alzheimer's day care program. These are the appointment of an advisory committee (if deemed necessary), the hiring of an executive director and/or program director, and the establishment of operating policies. A discussion of each of these follows.

THE GOVERNING BODY

For the balance of this chapter, the governing body will be referred to as a board of directors, which is its commonest form. In the initial stages of program development, the board of directors may be responsible for establishing the organization, setting program policy, obtaining initial funding, and designing the program. In general, a board of directors of an Alzheimer's day care program is a formal body, representative of the community structure in which the program is located. The board of directors has legal authority and responsibility for the operation of the program. It determines the purpose of the program, the operating policies, and the lines of authority. The board oversees the program's fiscal affairs and ensures its compliance with all applicable federal, state, and local laws including fire and safety regulations. When the program is a subdivision of a multipurpose organization, the board of directors of the parent organization often serves as the governing authority of the Alzheimer's day care program. In the case of nonprofit agencies, members of the board of directors or any advisory board cannot have any direct or indirect interest in any contract for supplying services to the program.

Board Committees and Functions

Boards of directors generally have an executive committee, standing committees, and ad hoc committees. The executive committee of the board of directors usually consists of the officers (president, vice president, secretary, treasurer, and other appropriate members). While standing committees vary depending on the nature of the organization, some of the more likely committees for an Alzheimer's day care program include: nominating, finance, personnel, program, building/facilities, and public relations or marketing committees. The duties of these specific committees will not be discussed here because they are well discussed in the literature on not-for-profit organizations and adult day care. Ad hoc committees are frequently necessary to deal with specific issues that an individual program may face during start-up or ongoing operations. Ad hoc committees usually function only for a temporary period. Some examples include a special event committee, a transportation committee, or a long-range planning committee. Ad hoc committees may serve to provide an extra amount of effort for specific problems that do not need the attention of the full board or an existing committee.

Board Development and Composition

One of the most difficult challenges to a planning committee in the development of a board of directors is the selection of members. Members must be selected specifically for their qualifications and the types of skills they can bring to the board. The selection and composition of the board are very important and deserve a great deal of planning and attention. There are a range of skills and talent that are necessary to make Alzheimer's/dementia day care programs function effectively. These include administration and management, public relations and marketing, accounting and financial management, legal expertise, knowledge of dementia and the needs of cognitively impaired individuals, familiarity with services and resources, fund-raising experience, and personnel management, among others. It is important that a planning committee carefully assess the qualifications of individuals in terms of their abilities to fulfill these specific requirements. In addition, the board must consider representation of a number of different community groups and populations, including representatives of various social, economic, racial, age, sex, and religious characteristics; representatives of the service provider community; and representatives of caregivers. Wide representation is important in terms of giving a broad perspective to the program philosophy and policies, as well as representing the center to other organizations throughout the community, developing referral patterns, and identifying close contacts with sources of funding and other resources. A difficult issue concerning representation of patients and caregivers is that, unlike many day care programs, Alzheimer's/dementia day care programs cannot have a participant serve on the board. If deemed appropriate, since there can be sensitive issues to be dealt with, such as fee scales and other issues affecting caregivers, caregivers may be allotted one or more positions on the board. However, other mechanisms can be used to ensure caregiver input besides serving on the board of directors. For example, a caregiver representative may attend board meetings, or caregivers may act as an advisory committee to the board.

A number of mechanisms have been developed to select and develop boards. A useful tool that has been applied by a number of Alzheimer's/

dementia day care programs is to use a matrix that identifies the key characteristics wanted on the board on one axis, with the potential applicants for board membership on the other axis. By identifying individuals with multiple skills and attributes, yet without having too much duplication, the planning committee can identify an initial set of prospective candidates for board membership. Once the board members have been selected, they should be given a thorough overview of the program's goals and philosophy and an orientation concerning the nature of Alzheimer's disease, program activities, and the specific roles for which they are responsible in regard to the program. As part of their orientation, new board members should spend time observing an Alzheimer's day care program. Board training and long-term planning are helpful in keeping awareness of the program philosophy and mission at a high level. The size of the board should be dependent upon the needs of the specific organization. Frequently, boards range in size from 5 to 15 members, but they may be much larger in size. In addition, it is helpful to have staggered terms for board members to ensure continuity, so that at least some board members will have a historical perspective of the organization.

ADVISORY BOARDS

Advisory boards are often helpful when it is useful to have a separate group of individuals provide input into the operations of the center. Advisory boards can offer technical assistance in the area of medical supervision, fund raising, publicity, or a number of other areas. The advisory board is a formal body that is appointed by the governing body and is generally composed of professionals from the community, participants' family members, and/or other interested individuals. The function of the advisory committee is to provide professional guidance, strength, stability, and quality to the program. Not all programs have or need an advisory board, but programs generally benefit from an advisory board that is accessible and dedicated to the program's goals. The advisory board should meet at least twice a year to review and make recommendations on program policies that deal with scope and quality of services, quality assurance activities, program evaluation, admission and discharge criteria, and other program and policy issues. Many programs specifically benefit from the establishment of a medical advisory board that can provide clinical oversight and guidance to program staff.

EXECUTIVE DIRECTOR/PROGRAM DIRECTOR

Next to the board of directors, the director of an Alzheimer's day care program plays the key role in setting policy and achieving the goals of the program. The board of directors must hire an executive director and/or program director.

There is an important distinction between an *executive director,* who is generally the overall center administrative director, and the *program director,* who is responsible for the day-to-day program activities. In larger organizations, there is generally an executive director who is responsible for all program policies and procedures, as well as one or more program directors (including the Alzheimer's day care program director) responsible for running specific program operations. In small organizations, the executive director and program director are often one and the same person (see appendix).

The executive director must be given the authority to plan, develop policies and procedures, direct and implement the program, staff the program with appropriately qualified personnel, and manage the budget and day-to-day operation of the center. An organizational chart helps delineate the lines of authority within an Alzheimer's day care program, clearly showing the division of responsibilities between the board of directors and the executive director. By both acting as a liaison between the board of directors and the program and overseeing the day-to-day functions of the program, the executive director is ultimately responsible for the success of the program. This is the most important staff position to fill and requires the utmost consideration on the part of the board of directors and/or planning committee.

Alzheimer's day care centers and other day care programs serving dementia patients generally require a full-time director. In many programs, the program directors are registered nurses, social workers, occupational therapists, or other professionals. They are selected on the basis of their experience in gerontology or administration and management, and of their knowledge of the problems of dementia patients and their families. Program directors frequently spend a significant amount of time actually conducting program activities as well as supervising other staff and volunteers. Program directors must have the ability to interact easily with participants, caregivers, and staff, yet still be attuned to the administrative requirements of the program.

Qualifications and Selection

In the last few years, there have been more and more individuals entering the field of aging and long-term care specifically working with dementia patients. Unlike the early 1980s where Alzheimer's day care was a rare, if not unknown, entity, there are now more programs and persons in this field. It is not hard to find individuals who have some background either in dementia or in adult day care who can be appropriate candidates for positions as executive director and/or program director. There are specific skills, characteristics, and background that should help to determine the person who can best serve as a director. While academic training can be important, there is a difference of opinion as to whether a person with a background in nursing, social work, recreational therapy, music therapy, or gerontology will make the best executive director or program director. Often, the philosophy of the organization may best determine what type of academic credentials a director should have for a specific program.

It is generally more important to look at the skills, experience, and personal characteristics of the individual than at his or her academic credentials. Executive directors and program directors must have a thorough understanding of dementia and its impact on caregivers, but they must also be strong leaders and good decision makers, have budget and accounting skills, be good administrators and supervisors, and have personnel experience. An individual's personal characteristics can be just as important if a person is to function effectively in a program. Individuals who fill these roles must have excellent interpersonal skills, creativity, good common sense, an excellent sense of humor, good verbal and written communication skills, the ability to work with all types of individuals, self-confidence, and above all flexibility. While this may seem an idealistic description, the type of person who has this broad base of characteristics will make the most successful executive director or program director for an Alzheimer's day care program.

Functions of the Executive Director and Program Director

The executive director is responsible for reporting to the board and as such is the liaison between the board and staff, families, caregivers, and community organizations. The executive director has a strong role in helping to shape the board by contributing knowledge and providing input to the development of the board, but he or she is also ultimately responsible to the board. The executive director generally spends time staffing board committees, providing updates to the board, and participating in board meetings.

The majority of the executive director's time is spent in program administration. In this capacity, he or she is responsible for a number of different areas, including program coordination, fiscal coordination, personnel management, public relations, and interorganizational relationships. The amount of time spent on each of these areas depends on the nature of the center and on the resources available through the board, umbrella organizations (if they exist), or other support organizations. The executive director, in the role of administrator, has responsibilities to staff, family caregivers, and, most important, to participants.

The role of the program director (or, in small agencies where staff is limited, the executive/program director) is to play an active role in program activities. One of the most important things a program director can do is demonstrate that he or she can and will undertake any activities required in the day-to-day operations of the center, from interacting with caregivers to toileting participants. Program directors must especially have a hands-on role in all program content decisions; work directly with activity staff, aides, and volunteers; and be cognizant of the needs and concerns of families and caregivers.

Salaries for executive directors and program directors vary considerably depending on the size and scope of the organization, the agency environment in which the center functions, and the scope of work and qualifications of the individual. We strongly recommend that the highest salary possible be given to this individual, within the budgetary framework of the center, because an acceptable salary helps attract and retain high quality individuals. The executive/program director plays a principal role in this organization and as such the position deserves a significant amount of attention on the part of the board and the planning process to ensure that the right person will be hired.

OPERATING POLICIES

Dementia day care programs, like all adult day care programs, must function using a number of different operating policies. The more thorough and comprehensive policies are, the better the program will function. Some of the key policies that the center should be concerned with include the following: board of directors, operations and management, personnel, admission/discharge, program service (including waiting list), fee structure, and confidentiality (including public relations). Each of these will be discussed in turn below. (See also appendix.)

Operating policies of the center set the tone and focus of the program to a large degree. It is important to realize that policies are not written in stone and should be flexible and able to be modified when appropriate. On the other hand, it is important to start out with specific, detailed policies to allow families, participants, and staff to begin with clear guidelines and understanding of how the program operates.

Organizational Policies

A program must have a clear set of organizational policies. These should include: the center's bylaws; listings of the board of directors, the advisory committee, and other related committees and descriptions of their functions; and an organizational chart.

The board of directors, in addition to following the bylaws of the organization, should have its own set of policies regarding its operation and function. These policies should address the responsibilities of each of the committees and the specific responsibilities of the board concerning fiscal, program, personnel, and public relations issues and interorganizational relations.

Operations and Management Policies and Procedures

In developing the administrative structure of the program, the board and executive director and/or program director must consider such issues as days and hours of operation, scheduled and unscheduled closings, participant attendance, participation by volunteers and other professionals, and program format.

Budget Policies and Procedures

The operating policies must describe the budget planning process; budget oversight responsibilities; and bookkeeping, accounting, and auditing procedures. Since many Alzheimer's day care programs are dependent upon participant fees as a primary source of revenue, it is very important to determine the policy for setting fees and the requirements of participants and caregivers in paying fees. Issues such as daily charges, partial day charges, sliding fee scales, scholarship programs, billing procedures, and absences need to be addressed.

Personnel Policies

Developing comprehensive and structured personnel procedures for an Alzheimer's day care program is important to the ongoing functioning of the center. While personnel procedures should follow those of any other health or social service agency, there are several personnel issues specific to Alzheimer's/dementia programs. These include different staff configurations from those used in other day care programs and health and social service agencies, the increased potential for staff burnout, the increased need for staff time off, the need for flexibility in benefits for full and part-time staff, and the use of part-time individuals. All job descriptions should be prepared in written form and reviewed and modified regularly.

Program/Service Policies

The specific program services must be clearly identified for caregivers and participants before their enrollment. Areas that need to be clearly laid out include meals and nutrition, medication management, insurance and liability, caregiver responsibilities, supplemental services, and transportation. Some programs have an admission/enrollment agreement, which participants or their caregivers sign. Alzheimer's day care centers must have very strict admissions, discharge, and waiting list policies to address the needs of cognitively impaired individuals and their families. Admissions procedures may require, in addition to medical examination reports and functional assessments, a visit to the center, a visit to the home, a review of financial and transportation issues, and a thorough review and acceptance of program policies with the caregiver. The special issues that concern discharge can include caregiver knowledge of the center's discharge policy, the specific identification of behaviors and functional determinants of discharge, and specific policies for emergency discharges and readmissions. While some programs do not have waiting lists, many others have constant waiting lists and must determine priorities for how people will be admitted to the program and some means of keeping them informed of their status.

Physical Plant, Quality Assurance, and Disaster Preparedness

A program must also have policies and procedures regarding the physical plant (e.g., safety, maintenance), quality assurance, and disaster preparedness. Specific items related to each of these areas are listed in the model policies and procedures manual in the appendix. One issue that deserves special mention is confidentiality. It is important to maintain the strictest confidentiality of participants' and family records and information, including participant charts, public information, and public relations information. One method to ensure confidentiality is having a consent form available at admission. Confidentiality should be a fundamental concern of the staff and board at all times.

CONCLUSION

A successful Alzheimer's day care program is dependent upon a solid organizational structure, sound program philosophy, excellent personnel, and clear operating procedures. This includes the implementation of a clear and agreed upon program philosophy, the establishment of a broad-based and active board of directors, the appointment of a knowledgeable advisory committee, the hiring of a strong executive director, and the establishment and implementation of sound operating policies. Without this solid administrative structure, an Alzheimer's day care program, much less any other community-based organization, will have a difficult time achieving its aims or adequately serving dementia patients and their families. It is vital that first the planning committee and then the board of directors and executive director put a great deal of time and attention into these areas.

4

FACILITY DEVELOPMENT

The type of facility, physical environment, and atmosphere of a center can have a significant impact on the well-being of both participants and staff. In fact, the quality of a facility can actually affect the long-term success of a day care center. Families often say that the decision to choose a specific Alzheimer's day care facility rests on their perception of its physical environment, or on how comfortable their family members feel with the facility. Thus, it is important in the planning process as well as in the ongoing operations of the center to select and maintain a building and environment that are clean, functional, attractive, and secure, and appealing to participants, families, and staff.

TYPES OF FACILITIES

Alzheimer's day care programs have been established in many types of facilities and locations. Successful programs have been located in single-family homes, church social halls, disused school buildings, stores, clinics, community centers, buildings in industrial parks, converted offices, and units or lounges in hospitals. The environments within Alzheimer's day care programs vary as well, ranging from programs that are very home-like to those that have a more institutional orientation. Facilities are built from the ground up or are modifications of existing structures. The three basic types of facilities/settings that are used for Alzheimer's day care centers are a home-like environment, a traditional health/social day care center, and a modified institutional setting. We will consider each in turn.

A center with a home-like environment provides an excellent atmosphere for Alzheimer's day care, whether it is in a modified single-family home or a facility adapted so that it has a home-like atmosphere. Not only is this environment reassuring to families, it can provide an intimate, comfortable setting for participants. On the other hand, centers in single family homes are generally smaller than those in nonresidential buildings, which may limit the number of clients who can be served; they generally have many small rooms without a large activity area; they can be used only on the ground floor; and they may present problems with zoning and licensing regulations.

A center in a traditional health/social day care facility may be located in a free-standing clinic or building, be incorporated in a large health or social service agency, or be housed in a hospital or nursing home. These facilities are designed specifically for adult day care programming, and generally have the means to address the needs of participants with extensive functional impairments and medication requirements. They often have specialized rooms designated for specific activities, which may include space for group activities, health services and therapies, dining and meal preparations, and individual activity or breakout space.

A modified institutional facility can also provide an excellent setting for adult day care programs that serve Alzheimer's patients. Many programs have been established in a number of unconventional settings, including converted institutional facilities such as elementary schools or modified office buildings or in rooms within larger buildings such as churches or synagogues. These facilities often have extensive open spaces for group activities that permit programs to serve large numbers of individuals. On the other hand, these facilities may be unacceptable to participants and families because they look very institutional, even with modifications in their appearance.

SELECTING AND OBTAINING FACILITIES

The building/facility committee of the planning body or board of directors should base their selection of the site on a number of factors, including program philosophy, programming, participant characteristics, geographic location, facility capacity, and environment/ambience. However, the selection of a facility is often determined by what resources are available, by whether or not a facility or space is donated, or by organizational constraints, rather than by seeking the type of facility and/or location that would be ideal to meet the program philosophy and goals.

The selection of a facility should be one of the first priorities of a planning committee or board of directors, since there can often be significant delays in purchasing or renting, remodeling, and opening a facility. This issue cannot be emphasized enough. Many programs that are otherwise ready to hire staff and enroll participants may be delayed for 6 or even 12 months while a facility is obtained. There are a number of mechanisms available to a board of directors or planning committee to obtain a facility. These include soliciting a donation of a facility or space, renting space, purchasing a facility, or building a facility. Creativity and flexibility are essential in selecting a facility. Purchase/lease/rental costs, remodeling expenses (always more than anticipated), long-term facility expenses, licensing and regulatory restrictions, building and zoning codes, insurance, utilities, transportation and parking, demographic information, the functional aspect of the space, and the potential for expansion must all be considered by the building/facility committee in selecting a site.

DESIGN AND USE OF SPACE

How a facility is designed will affect participant and staff satisfaction, the types of activities and services that can be provided, the safety of participants, and the general orientation of the program. Just as there is no single type of facility that best serves as an Alzheimer's day care center, there is no single type of physical and environmental design that can be best applied to Alzheimer's day care. There are advocates of small, home-like designs as well as advocates of larger designs. Ultimately, the design must address the basic goals and philosophy of the program. Thus, the design of a facility must fit the needs of the participants and staff; accommodate individuals with severe cognitive and functional deficits; provide for maintaining individuals at the their highest cognitive and functional level; ensure safety and security; and present a warm, stimulating, caring environment.

Utilization of space in a facility also is very much a program-specific decision. While there are no minimum space limitations for Alzheimer's/dementia day care programs, many states have specific regulations for adult day care that must be complied with. For example, a state may require that a center provide a minimum of 50 square feet per participant, excluding hallways, offices, rest rooms, and storage areas. Programs should be accessible to handicapped people and meet basic state and local building and zoning codes or ordinances. The ideal facility is one that is located on the ground floor, has plenty of controlled outside room for outdoor programs on nice days and for satisfying participants who wander, and is secured to ensure that participants remain safe.

Access

The building must be easily accessible for the handicapped person with mobility problems. Ramps are easier for the demented person to manage than stairs. Doorways should be wide and may have firmly anchored "grab bars" in place to help guide and steady the individual. The area should be free of obstacles to make it easier for wanderers to pace safely.

Reception

The reception area is critical in that it is generally the first space that participants and families enter, and the space that is used as a transition for participants entering and leaving the center. The reception space must be warm and comfortable, with chairs and enough room for several individuals at once. Ideally, the reception area should also provide a deterrent to patients' attempts to leave the center.

Large Group Activity Room

A center should have at least one large activity room for major program activities. If possible, all obstructions, such as walls or pillars, should be removed to allow free movement and observation. Large rooms that can be made into smaller ones with movable partitions are more flexible than a series of permanently structured small rooms. Using partitions, space can be opened up for large group activities or closed off to create private areas or rest areas; partitions can be arranged to accommodate small group activities or several different activities at once. In examining this option, it is important to take into account the acoustics of the facility. Rooms with high ceilings, even when partitioned, may present noise problems. While wall hangings and drapes may be dangerous, fabric-covered walls and acoustically quiet ceilings can help reduce the noise level.

Special Activity/Breakout Rooms

Most programs have at least one separate room that is reserved for quiet activities or as a place for staff to take a patient who is upset or agitated. Special activity rooms allow staff to provide parallel programming for participants with varying levels of severity of Alzheimer's disease. Smaller, self-contained rooms can also help staff keep an eye on wandering or agitated patients.

Offices

The offices of the director and staff are important for administrative activities, assessment activities, and staff breaks. Ideally, these rooms should provide immediate access to the reception area and/or the large group activity room.

Rest Rooms

Separate facilities should be provided for male and female participants, and each unit must ensure the individual's privacy. There should be 1 toilet for every 10 participants (the National Institute on Adult Daycare recommends 1 rest room to every 6 participants) with 2 or 3 additional urinals in the men's rest room and more than one toilet stall large enough to accommodate one or two staff assistants. If possible, additional toilets and/or rest rooms should be provided so that excessive waits can be eliminated. While many programs function effectively with two rest rooms, staff at many other programs feel they need a minimum of three rest rooms. All cubicles should be equipped with safety grab bars and an emergency call system that can summon help from the main program area (this is more likely to be used by staff). Staff will monitor toileting and rest rooms should be large enough for a participant and two staff members if assistance is necessary. Automatic water faucet shut-offs are helpful in rest rooms. There should be limited use of mirrors as the reflections can scare participants.

During the course of the disease, incontinency of both bowel and bladder often becomes a problem, and frequent toileting is the norm for most participants. When designing or renovating a facility, it may be desirable to provide additional space for bathing or shower facilities, as well as adequate privacy for staff to clean and change incontinent patients. These facilities can often be incorporated into a rest room. It is also desirable to have extra storage space for diapers and clothing changes. Lockable cabinets are helpful, but there should be no locks on the door since participants can inadvertently lock themselves inside. Some facilities install their own washing machine and dryer to clean participants' clothing.

Food Service and Kitchen

A kitchen can be used for therapeutic activities and reinforcing skills of daily living in addition to its use for meal preparation and/or serving. While some people feel that it is better to bring food preparation to the activities tables, others favor doing activities in the kitchen itself. If the area is accessible to participants, the kitchen should have a locking refrigerator, a stove with control handles removed, a sink, and a locked storage area. Most centers have electric ranges so as to avoid open flames. All toxins and cleaning agents should be locked elsewhere. Other safety strategies include activating appliances by a circuit breaker, having a key for the garbage disposal, and having a separate source of hot water for a dishwasher.

Storage

When designing a facility, do not underestimate the need for adequate storage space for program and operational materials, such as participant records, games, puzzles, cleaning supplies, medical supplies, therapy equipment, and files. This space must be provided in addition to activity space. Storage space should be accessible to program staff (not located on another floor), yet secure from and unobtrusive to participants.

Entrance and Exits

Doors and windows must be carefully reviewed to ensure that they are secure and safe. Doors should be quickly accessible to staff, but ideally they should be screened from participants so as not to encourage them in trying to leave the facility. Screening can be a problem when getting fire inspection clearance. Doors may be equipped with buzzers or alarms to alert staff about wandering patients.

Secure Space

Securing a facility through locked doors provides added safety for the Alzheimer's patient and frees staff members for tasks other than guarding the doors. Securing doors during program hours requires the approval of the local fire marshal and may further be prohibited by requirements of the particular license under which the program operates. If doors cannot be locked, a number of excellent alarm or buzzer devices are available that can be installed to alert staff when the door is opened. These include latch keys, key pads, pressure pads, and sensor devices worn by participants. One mechanism that has been used successfully is a door held closed by a magnetized plate which opens automatically when the fire alarm is activated. Some programs use physical devices, such as barriers, screens, and stop signs, to control wanderers. Careful architectural and landscaping design can minimize dangerous wandering as well. For example, if the inside space opens to outside secured space (a locked perimeter fence), interior security measures such as alarms or buzzers may be unnecessary.

Freedom of movement should be encouraged when it is available. Such freedom can reduce agitation. It should be noted that securing a facility does not eliminate the need for staff to maintain constant vigilance. It is very easy for an Alzheimer's patient to slip out an open door when caregivers or visitors arrive and staff are occupied with other activities.

Outdoor Space

There are no specifications for minimum outdoor space for Alzheimer's/dementia day care programs. Some states have minimum requirements of outdoor space for adult day care (such as at least 75 square feet per participant). Outdoor space must be available and accessible to the handicapped individual. Participants using the outdoor space should be protected from traffic, from becoming overheated in the sun, and from hazardous objects. The outdoor area should be surrounded with a visible barrier to prevent wandering, and there should be adequate and sufficient outdoor lighting at all entrances and on the grounds to ensure the safety of participants. Outdoor space generally works best when it is adjacent to the indoor space, is easily accessible to wanderers or restless participants, and is visible to staff working inside. Outdoor patios and walkways are often designed with circular or figure-eight pathways that are structured especially for demented patients who are wanderers. If a facility does not have its own outdoor space, alternatives may include use of a park or similar outdoor space not situated at the facility, if such space is accessible within a short and safe walking distance.

Windows

Large windows with a view of the outdoor area may help decrease participants' agitation while allowing staff to observe the outside space.

Windows and natural light afford any center a warmer feeling. On the other hand, windows that permit participants to look out onto parking lots or streets can have an agitating effect in that participants often think it is time to leave.

Furniture

Furniture must be selected for safety and comfort. Chairs should have high backs and wide-based legs so they do not tip over easily, and arms for ease in entry and exit. They should be covered in plastic or vinyl for easy cleaning and odor control. Some programs have been willing to risk extra cleaning by having upholstered chairs that maintain a home-like atmosphere. A few recliners or cots should be available for persons who need to rest or elevate their legs. Tables should be sturdy, of a solid color, and not shiny. Some centers use portable or collapsible tables to maximize open space for activities. It is desirable to have one or two tables that are adjustable to accommodate wheelchairs. A piano is another great addition. Low coffee tables should be avoided since they can be obstacles to participants' mobility. Furniture should be carefully reviewed to avoid potentially dangerous structures such as pole lamps, sharp corners, or protrusions.

ENVIRONMENTAL ISSUES

Atmosphere

The rooms should be cheerful, clean, and have an attractive appearance. There are different schools of thought regarding interior decorating. Since some Alzheimer's patients become confused easily and/or have diminished hearing and failing eyesight, some individuals argue that bright colors must be used to reduce confusion. Others argue that colors should be muted so as to avoid disturbing or confusing stimuli. Patterned floor and wall coverings, unless the patterns are very subtle, should be avoided because Alzheimer's patients tend to pick at the spots, flowers, or other emblems. Nontoxic plants and home-like fixtures can be very soothing to participants.

Floor

Many Alzheimer's patients have ambulation problems. Keep the flooring one color with no distracting designs, and do not use throw rugs as these are apt to slip and cause falls. There should not be changes in heights or textures between different sections of flooring. If carpeting is used, it should be heavy duty and easy to clean, because it will be frequently soiled with spilled food, juices, and other matter. Programs that have chosen carpet for esthetic and noise control reasons must anticipate the costs of frequent replacement.

Orientation Cues

Clocks, calendars, and name tags should be large and contrasting in color for easier reading. It should be noted that clocks can cause agitation among clock watchers; hence, they should be easily removable. Chalk boards and bulletin boards can be used effectively to post schedules and orientation information. Some programs accentuate rest room doors while screening other doors to help direct participants.

Temperature

The temperature should be kept at a steady level, since Alzheimer's patients may not be able to identify accurately when they are hot or cold. The staff must anticipate and interpret participants' needs and potential problems, help dress participants accordingly, and take into account variations in temperature throughout the day.

Noise

Noise reduction options should be implemented wherever possible, as noise can be very disruptive to program activities. Extraneous noise can come from within a facility or from outdoors. Street noise, for example, can be very distracting to participants.

Light

Bright indirect lighting and nonglare surfaces provide the best type of lighting for day care settings. Natural light, wherever possible, offers a soothing environment.

LICENSING AND CERTIFICATION

As of mid-1990, there are no federal or state licensing or certification requirements specifically for Alzheimer's/dementia day care programs. Planners of Alzheimer's/dementia day care programs must determine the specific rules, regulations, and licensing certification categories that apply. In some states, adult day care licenses are required, while in others they are not necessary. Even in states where licensing is not required, all programs must have a fire and safety check, which is usually under the purview of the local fire marshal. Planners of Alzheimer's/dementia care centers should contact the city, county, or township planning departments to determine what building and use permits might be required in building, remodeling, and operating a center.

Alzheimer's/dementia day care programs need emergency plans for fire and natural disaster. Many programs conduct drills on their own or under the guidelines of government agencies. Programs should consider innovative solutions to these requirements, including using volunteers and neighbors to assist in emergencies. Staff should identify all agencies that need to be notified in the event of an emergency. At a minimum, disaster plans should include 72 hours of nutrition and hydration supplies, first aid supplies, blankets, a radio, and battery-operated lanterns.

CONCLUSION

Selecting and establishing a facility, and determining appropriate interior and exterior design elements, should not be taken lightly. A great deal of preliminary planning should go into determining the type of facility and the configuration and orientation of space. These decisions directly affect the type of programming, type and level of staffing, participant well-being, and caregiver satisfaction with a center. To ensure that you make the right decision concerning the facility, the facility planning committee should review the organization's mission and goals, consider the long-term goals of the program, visit other facilities, contact directors and board members of other facilities, keep fiscal limitations in mind, consider using consultants, and review all possible options before proceeding with the final design and building/modification of the center. Again, there is no single type of facility or single way to use space that is clearly superior to others. The physical design of an Alzheimer's center, like its philosophy and program, is dependent upon the unique characteristics and resources of the center.

5

STAFFING AND VOLUNTEERS

The success of an Alzheimer's day care program, as with all other health and social service agencies, is dependent on the quality, abilities, and management of its staff. Personnel policies, procedures, and approaches to staffing that are utilized in most health and social service agencies apply to Alzheimer's day care centers as well. On the other hand, Alzheimer's day care programs pose some challenging issues in terms of the specific staff configuration and the structure and expectations of staff. Although staff requirements for adult day care centers can be very specific and highly regulated, staff requirements for Alzheimer's day care programs are rarely so carefully defined. This chapter will emphasize the staffing issues that are particularly important in Alzheimer's day care programs.

STAFF STRUCTURE

Staffing must be determined by the type of services provided. If the orientation of the center is toward offering health services, staffing patterns will emphasize individuals with a health or medical background, whereas if the center is more psychosocial in orientation, staffing will include more individuals with a social service background. Regardless of the type of center, the staffing pattern must be adequate to provide the services essential to a full Alzheimer's day care program, and the personnel must be competent to provide those services and meet the individual participant's needs.

We stress that all personnel must be competent to provide the services necessary to meet individual patient needs and must at all times be employed in numbers necessary to meet such needs. When evaluating the appropriate number of staff needed for a particular program, the board and executive/program director should consider the needs of the participants, the services provided by the program, the hours the program operates, the physical layout of the center, and the specific skills of program staff. Although there is no set staff-to-participant ratio required for Alzheimer's/dementia day care programs, such programs generally have staff-to-participant ratios ranging from 1:2 to 1:5. Most commonly, centers operate with a 1:3 ratio of *paid* staff to participants, which is higher than most day care centers serving a population that is not cognitively impaired. The staff-to-participant ratio can often be somewhat lower if the center actively includes volunteers in its programming. Secure perimeters also affect staffing requirements. Ideally, the lower the staff-to-participant ratio, the better.

There is no minimum number of staff required for an Alzheimer's/dementia day care program. However, most centers need at least three to four full-time staff members, including executive/program director, activity coordinator, and program aides, to operate. A substitute list of on-call individuals, particularly for program aides, is helpful in case of illness, vacations, and emergencies. The number of staff needed by a center also depends on the abilities, interests, skills, and cross-training of different staff members and on their ability to substitute for and assist each other as necessary. To ensure a safe environment for participants, it is imperative that at least two staff members be with participants in the primary program activity room at all times. All too often, an individual participant will need special attention or have a problem demanding the full attention of one of the staff members.

In addition to safety and skill factors, there are a number of additional factors that can influence the structure and composition of a day care program's staff. The primary factors are the philosophy, services, and model on which the program is based. A center that provides health services requires more time from a nurse or therapists than one that does not have health services. Other critical factors that influence the structure and composition of staff include a limited budget, constraints imposed by funding sources, number of participants, availability of staff, and participant characteristics. Fiscal issues often determine whether there will be qualified nurses, program assistants, social workers, or support staff available. It is important to note that standards of the National Institute on Adult Daycare (NIAD) may be used to establish particular staffing policies and procedures.

STAFF RECRUITMENT AND QUALIFICATIONS

The executive/program director is responsible for the hiring of new staff. All staff members are hired to fulfill a specific program need, so they must have specific skills. These individuals, however, must first and foremost be people-oriented and capable of working with Alzheimer's patients. They must be caring, compassionate individuals who *want* to work with this population. Working with Alzheimer's patients is very trying and demanding because of the nature of the disease and the unique and changing characteristics of the patients. Working in an Alzheimer's day care program can be frustrating and exhausting. Since patients eventually deteriorate, often do not communicate, and can even be abusive or aggressive, working in an Alzheimer's day care can be very challenging. However, well-selected staff members, many of whom have dedicated years to working with Alzheimer's patients, feel that the rewards of working with these patients and their caregivers can be tremendous. The best staff are able to notice positive changes in even the most demented participant and find great reward in seeing the relief experienced by families.

Staff can be recruited from existing day care settings, nursing homes, and other health and social service agencies. There are more and more individuals who have had experience and training in working with Alzheimer's patients. However, a center should plan to provide extensive training to all new staff members, regardless of their experience. Even those who have long worked with Alzheimer's patients may benefit from a "refresher course."

The staff recruitment, interviewing, and hiring process in Alzheimer's day care is comparable to that conducted in other health and social service agencies. Checking references is extremely important. One mechanism for identifying people who will function well as day care center staff is to have them interact with participants and staff during the interview or recruitment phase. All too often, individuals who may be excellent clinicians, nursing aides in nursing homes, or adult day care staff do not interact or react well in an Alzheimer's day care setting.

While staff qualifications depend on the specific position, there are a number of characteristics that all individuals who work in Alzheimer's day care centers should have, and these characteristics should guide the executive director and the board of directors in selection of staff members. Potential staff members must be able to perform as part of a team, yet be independent and self-starters. They must be versatile, have multiple skills, be people-oriented, be creative, have a great deal of patience, be able to work with people who exhibit unusually difficult behaviors, have high ethical standards, have respect for the dignity and confidentiality of individuals, have a sense of humor, have a high level of energy, and, above all, be flexible. Conversely, there are a number of personal characteristics that should serve as warnings that individuals may not function well in Alzheimer's day care centers. These characteristics include inflexibility, lack of motivation or reliability, prejudice, bias, fear of participants, inability to function with the team, lack of energy, and inability to work independently. Situational or hypothetical questions in the interview can assist the executive director in highlighting these qualities. Hiring someone with inappropriate qualities can be detrimental to staff morale. It may be better to work short-handed than to hire inferior staff.

Regardless of the time, energy, and skill put into the recruitment and selection process, it is often impossible to determine which individuals will work well in an Alzheimer's day care setting and which will not. Often, time and experience alone tell whether an individual will contribute to the program. Those individuals who do thrive and contribute to an Alzheimer's day care program quickly stand out and are valuable employees to retain.

All potential employees should be given a copy of a job description that explains their role in the program. This and a copy of the center's personnel policies should be reviewed with them during the initial interview. They must be allowed ample time to observe the program, meet some of the participants and staff members, and ask questions. It is necessary to stress during the interview process that no staff member can function exclusively within his or her job category. When Alzheimer's day care programs are successful, all staff are not only very good at their own jobs but also pitch in to help others with aspects of the program not in their own field or job description.

A program orientation is critical for both new staff members and volunteers. This orientation should include an overview of Alzheimer's disease, a review of the entire center, and a detailed explanation of their particular position within the center. A comprehensive two-week orientation is usually the *minimum* provided by Alzheimer's/dementia day care programs. An orientation format is provided in more detail in chapter 11.

Employee performance policies vary from organization to organization, but we recommend that evaluations be conducted at the end of a probationary period and annually thereafter. The staff member and supervisor should review and sign the written evaluation together. The signed copies of the evaluation are kept in the employee's personnel file, which is located in a safe, locked area, accessible to authorized personnel only.

PROGRAM STAFF

In addition to the executive director and/or program director, staff usually consists of an activity coordinator, program aides, secretary/receptionist, accountant/administrative aide, and, frequently, a full- or part-time nurse. Alzheimer's/dementia day care programs are often supplemented by a full- or part-time medical director, social worker, or therapist (for recreation, music, or art). In addition to the executive/program director, the activity coordinator is the central figure in the day-to-day functions of the center. The activity coordinator is responsible for structuring and maintaining a full program that runs from the time the center opens until it closes. The activity coordinator generally supervises program aides, volunteers, and adjunct staff, and fills in when the executive/program director is out of the center.

Support staff—that is, program aides or specialists—play a critical role in the functioning of a program and must be well trained and selected. Program aides provide essential help with the specific activities during the day and are often the most difficult individuals to find and recruit. While they will provide a tremendous amount of assistance to professional staff in the day-to-day operation of the program, they should not be expected to replace professional staff. Most Alzheimer's day care centers could not function without a large number of program aides, given the need for high staff-to-participant ratios and the prohibitive cost of hiring professional staff.

Depending on the nature and type of program offered, Alzheimer's/ dementia day care centers often hire additional staff, such as drivers, custodians/housekeepers, public relations specialists, and fund raisers as part- or full-time employees. Flexibility and the ability to function in a number of different roles are important qualities for these adjunct employees as well. Many programs will hire one person to serve as an administrative assistant, secretary, intake worker, and bookkeeper rolled into one. Successful programs find people who can perform a number of different roles and move easily between them. For example, art and music therapists often serve as both activity coordinators and as activity specialists, running the activities they have previously planned. Executive/program directors should be as flexible and creative with staff selection and task assignments as they are with activity programming.

Medical and nursing support is a complex issue deserving a great deal of thought during both the design and operation of a program. Some executive directors and boards feel very strongly that a nurse should be actively involved in program activities and/or administration, and many boards feel that a medical director should be involved as well. Others feel that the program should have a more social service orientation and that health care specialists should be utilized only on an emergency basis. Regardless of the approach taken, this is an important area to review and consider both in terms of staff hiring and program policy.

Most activities in an Alzheimer's day care program can be provided by employees. However, in certain circumstances, it may be more cost-effective and appropriate to bring in supplementary or contractual staff. For example, in the area of activities, a center may use an outside music therapist or art therapist to conduct certain activities if the existing staff are not qualified. Use of outside therapists also gives staff time to complete paperwork and scheduling. Specific activities that may be conducted by supplementary or contractual staff include group activities, health services, nutritional or meal services, custodial duties, fund raising, public relations, staff development, transportation, and social services.

The factors determining which services can be provided in-house are the qualifications of the staff, the size of the program, and, most especially, center resources and funding. In-house staff, however dedicated and creative, will occasionally need relief from the responsibilities of planning activities. There are a number of different options for identifying outside resources that do not necessarily cost the day care program much money. For example, continuing education or adult education programs often will be pleased to provide staff to conduct specific activities for an Alzheimer's day care program. Similarly, Meals on Wheels and Title III nutritional programs often can be utilized to provide meals for a center. Transportation can be provided through joint efforts among a number of different centers or health and social service agencies. It is worthwhile to examine various activities and program components to see if they can be provided through external sources in order to save scarce resources. It is important that all staff coming into contact with participants have sensitivity to and/or training for working with Alzheimer's clients. When selecting outside staff or volunteers to lead activities, executive/program directors and activity coordinators should look for the same qualities they expect in full-time staff. For all of the program staff issues discussed here, it is worthwhile to consult the NIAD standards for additional information.

STAFF ISSUES

Staffing an Alzheimer's day care program involves a number of unique or special issues. These include staff retention, the problem of "burnout," staff meetings, staff relief, the issue of part-time vs. full-time employees, and employee evaluations. We will consider these issues in turn.

Staff Retention and Burnout

Two of the foremost staffing issues facing Alzheimer's/dementia day care centers are staff retention and burnout. Just as the primary caregiver of an Alzheimer's patient needs respite from the demands of assisting the patient, so do day care staff, regardless of their dedication or abilities. Programs have implemented a number of mechanisms to retain staff and help them avoid burnout. First, a critical motivator for many individuals is financial reward. Some programs pay their program specialists or aides slightly more than they would receive in a nursing home or comparable program. Second, many programs reward employees through bonuses or through events that recognize their contributions. Third, the routine and boredom associated with the repetition of a specific assignment can be alleviated by rotating assignments periodically and by allowing staff to choose the activities in which they participate. Similarly, work should be distributed equitably and managed appropriately. Fourth, all staff should be provided with development and training opportunities, including the options of attending conferences, visiting other facilities, and having in-service training. Fifth, executive directors should consider creative solutions to staffing configurations. One solution is hiring a substitute to provide periodic relief for staff so that they can have a break from caregiving (often called a mental health break). Another option is to rotate staff between centers or within a larger center to provide them with new and different job opportunities and environments. Some centers have held annual day-long retreats led by health professionals and counselors. Others encourage staff to interact with participants' families to avoid burnout. It cannot be emphasized enough that much can be done to reward, support, and retain program aides. Program aides need to be acknowledged for work they do well and commended for providing a valuable service to the community. Perquisites such as time off for outside training, a change in job titles (program specialist rather than program aide), and employee recognition events can sometimes do as much as a salary increase to bolster employees' morale.

Staff Meetings

Staff meetings must be scheduled and held on a regular basis. It is imperative that staff have a chance to debrief and decompress regularly. Staff meetings may be scheduled after program hours when possible. Since this is not often possible, provision for regular staff meetings may be made by using volunteers and supplementary staff to work with participants while the meeting takes place. Thus, meetings can be held during the regular program day, and additional staff hours are not required.

Staff Relief and Absence

Given the tremendous and intense pressures on staff and the constant need for one-on-one work with participants, a mechanism must be established to provide relief for staff during the day and coverage for absences. The executive/program director or activity coordinator may provide breaks during the day or coverage for individual staff members during certain activities. Staff should also be asked to identify quickly when they feel that they need a break from the daily work routine. Further, they should be commended, rather than penalized, for recognizing and taking care of their own needs. In addition, regardless of the energy and ability of individuals, staff illnesses will occur. A strategy for covering for individuals during their absences, which are often unplanned, must be put in place.

Part-Time vs. Full-Time Staff

Given limited budgets, many programs are forced to function with a number of part-time workers. This can work very effectively with appropriate planning and anticipation. Executive/program directors can overlap part-time staff to cover heavy periods of participant activity, such as during lunch. The hours worked by part-time staff may be increased during heavy use periods; full-time staff, thus, work fewer overtime hours. Boards and directors must carefully consider trade-offs in selecting between part-time and full-time staff. More full-time staff means more money spent in benefits. On the other hand, more full-time staff means fewer personnel to hire and train and fewer changes for the Alzheimer's day care clients. Boards and directors must carefully consider trade-offs in selecting between part-time and full-time staff.

Staff Evaluation

It is important that programs have a regular evaluation process to provide feedback to staff at all levels. This helps give staff members a sense of their strengths as well as information concerning the areas in which they can improve their skills and knowledge. Regular evaluations help to identify problems before they occur, or before they become serious episodes.

VOLUNTEERS AND STUDENTS

Volunteers are an invaluable component of almost all Alzheimer's day care programs. Like staff, volunteers must have the special ability to work with demented participants. They should never be thought of as free labor or substituted for regular staff members. Instead, they should be given specific, supervised roles within the program. It is essential to provide volunteers with a good orientation to the program and to include them in all in-service training sessions. Volunteers should be utilized according to their specific skills, talents, and interests. Many volunteers will want to work with the participants in music, art, or reminiscence activities, while others may wish to help with office work.

The most effective volunteer programs have a volunteer coordinator or a staff member or volunteer to whom this duty is delegated. Volunteer recruitment, training, and supervision require a great deal of time and energy. It is important that the volunteers enjoy their work, are quickly integrated into the program, are given consistent direction, and are made to feel they belong. Volunteers who are relation-oriented rather than task-oriented and who have good listening and communication skills often interact extremely well with participants.

Volunteers can work as aides, office assistants, or in one-to-one situations with clients. Volunteers work particularly well when a program participant needs to be taken away from a group activity or given some reassurance. Volunteers may also be able to help with planning and carrying out special events or providing assistance in staff development and fund raising. They are a vital link to community resources. Again, the best approach is to encourage volunteers to participate in their area of greatest interest.

Volunteers may be found through a number of sources. Some of the best sources for finding volunteers include families of participants (as long as it is not the primary caregiver), family and friends of staff, social service agencies, schools and universities, civic and professional clubs, churches, and local volunteer centers. To find volunteers, centers can advertise or make announcements on television and radio (called public service announcements, or PSAs) or in newspapers or a center newsletter, distribute flyers to various organizations, give public talks, and spread their request by word of mouth.

In general, there is a greater demand for volunteers than supply. So if a center has good volunteers, they should be treasured. It should always be remembered that they are there to develop their own skills and because they want to help, not because they have to. A successful volunteer program is based on motivating volunteers and providing both informal and formal recognition for their contributions.

Students provide a significant contribution to many Alzheimer's day care programs. They often conduct structured projects in relation to their educational goals, participate through ongoing internships, and volunteer as a community service activity. Students, like volunteers, need to be carefully recruited, trained, and employed according to their skills, abilities, and interests. The development of a student intern program and learning experiences for students requires a great deal of time and energy on the part of the executive/program director and staff, and deserves careful consideration. On the other hand, the time invested in developing an intern program and working closely with students is very rewarding for the student, the staff, and the program participants.

CONCLUSION

More than a center's building, programming, or administration, the staff of an Alzheimer's day care center is the essence of an Alzheimer's program. The staff selected for a center can compensate for a lack of resources, space limitations, or other program constraints, and can make the difference between a superb program and one that is mediocre. Thus, it is critical to hire the best staff possible, to value their contribution, and to provide them with appropriate compensation and support. When considering personnel for an Alzheimer's day care center, it is important to be flexible and creative in finding the best match of individuals for the tasks at hand. Ultimately, selecting the best staff comes down to identifying those individuals who can develop a warm and caring relationship with dementia patients.

6

FINANCIAL MANAGEMENT: BUDGET, FEES, FUNDING, AND FUND RAISING

It is clear that successful Alzheimer's day care programs are dependent upon good financial management and planning. Whether programs are for-profit or not-for-profit, they have to deal with many of the same accounting and fund raising issues. Successful programs have a strong financial team, generally consisting of the director, an accountant, board members, and other individuals who can help in the budget and fund-raising process. Whenever possible, getting staff input can be very productive in improving the fiscal management of a program.

START-UP BUDGET

When considering the development of a new Alzheimer's day care program, it is important to separate the budget into costs that will be incurred during start-up and those that will occur during normal program operations. A start-up budget includes many items that are one-time-only expenses and other items that are much higher initially than in the course of normal operations. A start-up budget generally can be quite large due to specific costs of opening or modifying a center. Since costs and expenses vary from location to location and center to center, we will not present specific amounts here, but will address the general categories of expense. It is important to realize that considerable expenses may be incurred before any fees or revenues are generated by the program.

One of the greatest expenses is likely to be acquiring or modifying the facility. If the program must purchase or renovate a facility, there could be extensive start-up costs involved. At minimum, the start-up budget must include rent or lease expenses for the facility. The start-up costs for personnel can also be an expensive budget item. There is a period of time

TABLE 1   Alzheimer's day care center sample annual budget:
Fiscal year 1990

Income	
Operating revenue	
Private funding	
Program revenues—private pay	$110,000
Private insurance	2,000
Public funding	
State general funds	20,000
Medicaid	30,000
Title III	10,000
Title XX	10,000
County funds	5,000
Total operating revenue	$187,000
Deductions from operating revenue	
Uncompensated care	3,000
Self-pay discounts	28,000
Uncollectable accounts	1,000
Total deductions	$ 32,000
Nonoperating revenue	
Foundation grants	17,000
Private grants	7,500
United Way	10,000
Service organizations	8,000
Corporations	6,000
Fund-raising event	5,000
Individual donations	8,330
Total nonoperating revenue	$ 61,830
Total income	$216,830

Operating Expenses		
Personnel (salary and benefits)		
Executive/Program Director	100%[a]	$ 32,000
Activity Coordinator	100%	23,000
Volunteer Coordinator	50%	11,000
Program Specialist	100%	14,000
Program Specialist	50%	7,000
Program Specialist	50%	7,000
Program Specialist	50%	7,000
Program Specialist Substitute	20%	2,500
Bookkeeper/Secretary	50%	9,500
Total salary		113,000
Benefits (18.5%)		20,905
Social Security, Workmen's Comp., etc.		20,000
Total Personnel		$153,905

(Table continues on next page)

TABLE 1   Alzheimer's day care center sample annual budget: Fiscal year 1990 (*Continued*)

Other operating expenses	
Facility rent/mortgage	$ 7,000
Utilities	
Gas	1,200
Electric	450
Telephone	1,700
Professional insurance	2,000
Board and liability insurance	7,000
Office supplies	950
Program/activity supplies	1,500
Dietary supplies	800
Medical supplies	275
Major equipment	3,000
Minor equipment/rental	500
Equipment maintenance	600
Postage	2,000
Printing and copying	1,000
Data processing	500
Resource library, books, and journals	1,150
Staff training	2,000
Staff travel	1,200
Dietary/meals	7,000
Transportation for program participants	7,500
Promotion/marketing	2,000
Contractual service	3,000
Employee recruitment	400
Repairs/facility maintenance	4,000
Facility/equipment depreciation/amortization	2,000
Housekeeping	700
Audit/financial fees	1,500
Total other operating expenses	$ 62,925
Total expenses	$216,830
Surplus/(deficit)	0

[a]Percentages for personnel denote full- vs. part-time status.

before the program opens during which staff, particularly the director, must be hired. Equipment and furniture, including office and program equipment, must be planned for in the start-up budget. Program, medical, and office supplies, as well as safety equipment, should also be included. Start-up costs related to the opening of the facility may also include other items: legal expenses for the creation of the organizational entity; consultant fees for architectural, fund-raising, and public relations specialists; utilities and installation of a telephone system; and costs for advertising (including fliers, brochures, and business cards).

OPERATING BUDGET

Developing an operating budget for the program, when it is in full operation, takes a great deal of planning. There is no hard and fast rule as to how much money will be needed to operate a program, but a social-model Alzheimer's day care program operating five days a week with 12 to 20 participants can generally require an annual budget of $100,000 to $200,000. (See sample budget in Table 1.)The largest expense items that need to be considered when developing an annual budget are personnel (often up to two-thirds of the budget), lease/rent, insurance, dietary expenses, transportation, equipment, furniture, and renovations. While a center may not use all of these expense categories, a comprehensive list is presented here with some salient examples:

- *Personnel*—salaries, contractual agreements, fringe benefits, workers' compensation, unemployment insurance, and Social Security payments
- *Facility rent/mortgage*—lease/rental, mortgage payments
- *Utilities*—heat/air conditioner, electricity, gas, water
- *Telephone*—monthly fees, long distance
- *Professional insurance*—malpractice insurance for staff such as nurses or social workers
- *Board and liability insurance*—protection for board members and program
- *Office supplies*—paper, pens, pencils
- *Program/activity supplies*—games, puzzles, magazines, songbooks, craft supplies, musical instruments, gardening supplies
- *Dietary/meal supplies*—towels, plates, cups, eating utensils
- *Medical supplies*—first aid kit, blood pressure cuff, stethoscope
- *Major equipment*—office furniture, computer, typewriter, copy machine, file cabinets, tables, chairs, sofas, television, stereo
- *Minor equipment and rental*—office equipment (possibly copy machine or postage machine), cots, kitchen appliances
- *Equipment maintenance*—service contracts and repairs
- *Postage*—stamps or postage machine
- *Printing and copying*—fliers, letterhead, stationery, business cards
- *Data processing*—for data entry of clinical or research records or funding agency reporting
- *Resource library, books, and journals*—reference library for staff and caregivers
- *Staff training*—fees for classes, conferences, in-service training
- *Staff travel*—travel for home visits and community presentations, travel and accommodations for conferences and training
- *Dietary/meals*—food, snacks (may be contract)
- *Transportation for program participants*—transportation fees,

van or minibus purchase or lease, insurance premiums, gas, oil, tires, replacement cost
- *Promotion and marketing*—public relations and outreach materials including brochures, posters, advertising, activity calendars, newsletters
- *Contractual service*—attorney, physician, therapists, social workers, adult education instructors, transportation, meals
- *Employee recruitment*—advertisements and presentations
- *Repairs/facility maintenance*—maintenance and repairs of physical plant
- *Housekeeping*—daily and special cleaning
- *Audit/financial fees*—bank fees, bookkeeping, annual audit

To prepare either a start-up or a general operating budget, an executive/program director must consider both expenses and income, including all sources of income and adjustments to income (i.e., rate adjustments and bad debt). Other factors to be considered in preparing a budget are: the number of days and hours a day the program operates, the number of participants enrolled in the program, the average daily attendance, start-up and seasonal variations in attendance, fixed costs such as staff salary levels, the fee structure, and the financial status of participants. Factors that will specifically affect a budget during the start-up period include whether the program is open a limited number of days and the rate at which the program census builds. Potential operators of Alzheimer's day care programs also need to be aware that there can be delays in receiving funding, so the first year's budget must account for periods of low cash flow. Similarly, when a new program opens, revenues from participant fees and other payment sources may not be received for a long period of time. And even when a program is fully operational, revenues are often received several months after services are provided.

Initial budget planning is based to a large degree on projections of service utilization, income, and expenses. However, after several months of operation, historical data will be available with which to develop future budgets. The minimum goal for developing either an initial budget or an annual program budget should be to calculate the break-even point for the program. This can be accomplished by comparing the total fixed and variable expenses of a program with the total number of annual participant days (i.e., the average daily attendance multiplied by the number of annual program days) multiplied by the daily rate. After a program is operational, net profit or loss figures should be reviewed monthly to assess the financial status of the program.

It is realistic to anticipate that a program may be operational for up to three years before it will become financially stable, again, using multiple sources of revenue. Thus, a large percentage of a program's start-up costs plus operational costs for a year or more should be obtained prior to initiating any building, renovations, or hiring. It cannot be stressed enough that available capital must exceed projected needs by a safe margin because sufficient funds will be needed to maintain the program until adequate revenues are obtained. Many references are available to assist with the proper development of a budget. Obtaining the paid or donated advice and services of an experienced accountant can also be helpful. Programs under the auspices of larger organizations may be able to make use of an established accounting and finance department.

FEES, FEE STRUCTURES, AND BILLING

Fees from participants are an important way to generate program revenue. Services in Alzheimer's day care programs are often provided on a fee-for-service basis, generally ranging from $18 to $45 per day (some programs do not charge fees, while others have fees over $100 per day). Most programs have a sliding fee scale that reflects the participant's ability to pay. Local organizations are often willing to provide scholarships that cover all or part of the daily fee for needy clients to assist them in obtaining appropriate services. This is also true of sponsoring organizations or hospital foundations, if the program is affiliated with this type of organization. On the other hand, some centers choose not to charge a fee, and instead ask for voluntary contributions (particularly agencies receiving Older Americans Act Title III funds).

A fee structure must be established in conjunction with the program philosophy and goals and the commitment of the board of directors to ongoing fund raising and a level of subsidy they consider feasible. Although many programs have a philosophy of wanting to provide services for no charge or as a small a charge as possible, it has become increasingly clear that the viability of programs often depends on having a fee-for-service system. As public and private funding for Alzheimer's/dementia day care specifically, and adult day care in general, becomes more scarce, revenues collected through participant fees will be an increasingly necessary means of covering program expenses. Furthermore, it has often been observed that people value services for which they have paid a fee more highly than services they receive for free. In fact, many older persons will not utilize services unless they can pay something for the service.

It takes a significant amount of planning to develop a fee structure. A fee system can be created in various ways, based on charges per day, per week, or per month, as well as having charges for separate services. The fee may be based upon the total program cost or on the average rate of programs in a geographic area. The fee may be a flat daily or monthly rate, including payment on days of absence, or it may be on a days-attended basis. Some organizations charge supplemental fees for additional services, such as patient assessment, transportation, meals, bathing and grooming, and late pickups. We strongly recommend that fees, if they are charged, be set at a level to cover a program's actual costs. To help establish a fee structure, one could use the following formula:

$$\frac{\text{total estimated operating expenses}}{\text{number of days open per year} \times \text{maximum daily attendees}} = \text{per person daily cost}$$

While centers may not require families to pay the full rate, a fee schedule lets families know the costs of services, allows those who have the resources to pay a higher amount, and indicates to funders the actual costs of running a program. In essence, setting charges at the level of costs shows the true "value" of the program.

When centers try to provide access to services to all interested parties regardless of their ability to pay, they often turn to sliding fee scales where participant fees are based on the individual's financial resources. Sliding fee scales can have a tremendous impact on a center's overall budget if they are established without any external subsidies. However, by combining sliding fee revenues with other sources of funding, a center can enroll a large number of individuals who would not otherwise have access to the service. Sliding fee scales can be created in several ways and should be developed according to the program's philosophy. A sliding fee scale may be based on participant income or on income plus assets. Some programs conduct financial reviews of participants and their families, while others allow families to set their own rates. Many centers state that families are generally very honest and pay as much as they possibly can.

Scholarships may provide another option for allowing people to have access to a program who would not otherwise be able to afford it. The difference between a sliding fee scale and a scholarship is that the scholarship indicates there is a separate fund to be used for subsidizing participants. Scholarships are often attractive to families who would not be comfortable participating in a program through a sliding fee scale or gratis. The awarding of scholarships may be determined through a formal mechanism that is developed by the agency to look at the participant's and family's resources or may be determined informally in conjunction with a request from a family. A scholarship fund, like a sliding fee scale, is dependent upon obtaining significant funding from external sources.

Once a fee structure has been determined, it must also be uniformly and strictly enforced. A billing system or revenue collection mechanism must be implemented to facilitate the thorough collection of fees. Some programs bill families in advance, while others bill retroactively. Billing in advance helps a program's cash flow. Some billing systems permit a discount for multiple visits, while others are very specific about billing for the actual amount of time and services utilized.

A fundamental issue regarding revenues obtained through participant fees is that programs must be very conservative in estimating these revenues. Until a program is financially stable, which can take several years, boards and executive/program directors should not plan on significant income from fees to sustain a program. A program needs to develop a track record of its revenue collection before making specific long-term revenue projections. Revenue projections must also account for actual days of operation, and must consider holidays and snow days. Some programs have established flat monthly rates that include payment for absences, thus making it easier to project revenues. If new programs charge on an average daily attendance (ADA) basis, they should project fees very conservatively, using low ADA estimates and low estimates of an average fee paid. This may result in a need for more fund raising, but if the program exceeds revenue projections, the surplus revenues can be applied to a program reserve. Finally, program fees should include the incremental costs incurred by adding a new participant, such as transportation, assessment, and additional staffing.

SOURCES OF FUNDING

In order to develop, implement, operate, and expand a successful Alzheimer's day care program, most centers will have to obtain additional funds beyond those obtained from participant fees. Depending on a center's location and organizational structure, a number of sources of funding can be used to supplement or subsidize program operations. As previously stated, very few Alzheimer's day care programs have been self-supporting; participant fees rarely cover the full cost of operation. Additional funds for program operations may be obtained through state and local governments, donations, bequests, private foundations, insurance companies, corporations, community organizations, religious organizations, and service clubs. Several issues should be weighed when considering the different sources of funding that may be utilized to operate a program. First, a program should not be dependent on a single source of funding. A program in this situation is vulnerable to political and fiscal changes, and may not be able to respond quickly enough if the funding source is reduced or eliminated. Second, some funds are provided with specific goals in mind or with limits on how they can be spent. "Restricted" funds, while certainly helpful, may limit what a center proposes to do to serve its participants. However, these sources often provide a variety of options for obtaining funds for specialized projects, such as seed money to help with start-up costs, capital projects (including loans), and first-year operating expenses.

Public Funding

Public funds can come from federal, state, or local sources. Depending on the state in which a center is located, Medicaid can be an important source of revenue. Other public sources of funds include Older Americans Act monies (Title III), Title XX of the Social Security Act, state and local general funds, mental health funds, and dedicated Alzheimer's funds from state and federal sources. At this time, the primary government funding source available to cover Alzheimer's/dementia day care services is Medicaid under the auspices of adult day care. Medicaid reimbursement for adult day care is available only in some states. As previously mentioned, there are federal legislative initiatives currently under review to provide coverage for Alzheimer's/dementia day care under Medicare, but any coverage of this sort is still in the future.

Private Funding

Several health care and insurance programs are beginning to provide coverage for Alzheimer's day care. Some health maintenance organizations (HMOs) have begun covering adult day care as a benefit. They realize that adult day care may be a cost-effective alternative to institutionalization or other home-based services for their members. Executive/program directors should check with HMOs in their service area to determine whether Alzheimer's day care might be included in their benefits. In addition, insurance companies may reimburse families or caregivers for some of the therapeutic services provided to specific patients, if they meet the appropriate eligibility criteria.

The private sector provides other options for raising funds for an organization. Businesses and corporations frequently make donations through their corporate entity or through a special foundation. Philanthropic foundations are more and more sensitive to the needs of day care providers and Alzheimer's day care programs specifically. It should be noted that foundations are generally more interested in supporting program start-up or special projects than in supporting general operating expenses. Grants can be obtained from private foundations for training, operations, and research. Community organizations, religious groups, and service clubs often provide support through both financial and staff contributions. The United Way in many communities provides an avenue for support. Some centers charge fees for training or are undertaking research projects as means to expand or supplement funding. Personal donations can be a significant source of revenue for a program. And one should not overlook in-kind donations which can provide substantial benefits to centers. These can range from contributions of space to donations of staff time, program equipment, supplies, and volunteers. In-kind donations should be assigned a monetary value and counted in all budgeting and fund-raising activities.

FUND RAISING AND GRANT WRITING

Fund raising is an essential but often frustrating element in program operations. It requires the development of a comprehensive strategy and must be viewed as an ongoing process. It also requires a significant amount of effort, persistence, and patience on the part of the executive/program director, staff, board, and other interested parties.

Fund raising itself may include grant writing, appeals to corporate and private entities, fund raising events, or a direct mail campaign. A fund raising campaign requires careful planning and a thorough review of all options. It is important that a great deal of time be put into the planning and implementation of a fund-raising strategy because fund-raising activities can take up significant resources, yet have little direct benefit if they are not planned and implemented carefully. For example, the amount of time spent writing a grant proposal to a foundation or a government agency may have the potential for far more financial gain and be far less resource intensive than undertaking a special fund-raising event such as a dinner. On the other hand, fund-raising events can generate publicity and community support for a program. Thus, when a center reviews and selects its fund-raising activities, their potential for increasing community visibility and/or increasing program funds must be considered.

If a center decides to hold a fund-raising event, many different activities can be attempted. Among the successful activities undertaken by Alzheimer's day care centers are the following: a raffle, an auction, a musical event, a dinner, sponsorship of a theater event, sponsorship of a movie about Alzheimer's disease, a walk-a-thon, a sports event or tournament, and a white elephant sale. A fund-raising event should be selected on the basis of the interests of the community, the level of resources available to undertake the event, and the amount of funding needed.

Centers may want to consider assigning a volunteer or hiring a consultant to serve as a grant writer or a fund raiser. Programs should also consider having fund-raising experts or individuals with access to resources on their board of directors. Many community organizations or service groups prefer to work directly with a program and can be counted on to be a primary source of funds. There are a number of excellent references on fund raising and grant writing for nonprofits available to directors and boards.

LONG-TERM FINANCIAL PLANNING AND SELF-SUFFICIENCY

A center's top fiscal priorities should be to achieve a balance between expenses and income—to fiscally break even—and to conduct long-term financial planning to achieve self-sufficiency. Ideally, the budget process and fund-raising efforts should be conducted in tandem, and with constant attention to the program's long-term viability. While the ultimate goal of self-sufficiency may be difficult to achieve, successful programs use multiple options in an attempt to approximate this ideal, including identifying and maximizing all possible sources of income and reducing program expenses.

A number of strategies can be employed in an effort to maximize resources and achieve a sound fiscal base of operations. Executive/program directors can monitor program operations, expenses, and revenues, and insure that excess staff costs and operating expenses are reduced while program utilization is increased to its maximum level. A significant effort should be made to maximize and diversify reimbursement sources and enhance grant-writing and fund-raising efforts. Executive/program directors and boards must anticipate the financial requirements of a program and start identifying future sources of funds as early as possible. It is important to realize that sources of funding that provided start-up money or initial operating funds may not be available to carry a program into future years. Centers should consider maintaining an emergency fund or, like many nonprofit organizations, build up a three- to six-month operating reserve. Some centers try to develop an endowment fund to help the organization over the long term, to be used for daily program operations, or to help clients as needed. In essence, to achieve long-term viability a board of directors and executive/program director must constantly and actively be involved in maximizing existing resources and obtaining additional funds.

CONCLUSION

Sound fiscal management and fund raising are important factors in the start-up and ongoing operation of Alzheimer's day care programs. No matter how good an Alzheimer's day care program is, its viability is frequently dependent upon its ability to raise and manage funds. Fund raising should be considered a constant, year-round part of program operations, with directors and boards always looking for new and innovative sources of funding. Given that programs often have limited resources during both program start-up and ongoing operating periods, it is important that directors and boards develop realistic budgets, monitor income and expenses carefully, develop a long-term fund-raising strategy, and continuously strive for self-sufficiency.

7

PUBLIC RELATIONS AND MARKETING

The success of an Alzheimer's day care program depends as much on its marketing function and its public relations campaign as it does on good management and fiscal accountability. An Alzheimer's day care center must be able to reach out to the public to identify program participants, obtain funding, build strong support from the community, and develop a referral base. In years past, nonprofit organizations have eschewed the concept of marketing, replacing it with community relations and outreach. Public relations has similarly been limited to publicity. In practice, however, marketing and public relations are central to a program's promotion efforts. Marketing and public relations must be viewed as very broad in scope, and should encompass planning, data collection, evaluation, and feedback.

Marketing and public relations are often lumped together. But the two are different in focus and purpose, although they should ideally work in concert. Kotler and Bloom (1984, p. 16) define a marketing orientation as follows:

A marketing orientation holds that the main task of the organization is to determine the needs and wants of target markets, and to satisfy them through the design, communication, pricing, and delivery of appropriate and competitively viable offerings.

Marketing, therefore, is client-centered. As discussed in an earlier chapter, the client in Alzheimer's day care is both the participant and the family. If the day care center has a marketing orientation, it will systematically and regularly determine and redetermine clients' *needs, wants, perceptions, preferences,* and *satisfaction.*

A common error in marketing is to assume that an initial needs assessment is sufficient. Even worse, nonprofit organizations frequently make the fatal assumption that staffs and boards of directors "know" what the client populations want without consulting the client populations first. Even if they have conducted an initial needs assessment, once the day care center has been established, many organizations never again reach out to their publics to find out whether the current service is still satisfying the client population. For the balance of this chapter we will discuss *publics*, in the plural, a term that can be defined as all groups that have an actual or potential interest in or impact on an organization's ability to achieve its objectives.

Many expanded services falter and fail because the all-important marketing process is omitted. Day care boards and staff should institute a rule that whenever a plan to expand services is seriously suggested—such as weekend respite or training programs—a new marketing process should be initiated. The day care staff should once again meet with the relevant publics and find out exactly what those publics want. Then, the new service can be tailored to the specific needs, wants, and preferences of the public. Later, once the expanded service has been established, the day care staff must continue to monitor client perceptions and satisfaction.

Public relations, or promotion, is not the same as marketing. Public relations is often summarized as "getting credit for doing good." Many organizations assume that good works speak for themselves. This approach rarely has an impact on the community. The people of a community do not automatically understand an Alzheimer's day care program and need continual reminders and education to grasp its value and importance.

A public relations program is a systematic and planned campaign to ensure that all the publics who need to know about the day care program are properly informed. A public relations program:

- evaluates public attitudes
- identifies the aspects of the day care program which are in the public interest
- sets up a campaign to earn public understanding and acceptance

Kotler and Bloom (1984) point out three important differences between marketing and public relations:

1. Public relations is primarily a communications tool, whereas marketing also includes needs assessment, service development, fee setting, and distribution (how the days, hours, and location of service are organized).
2. Public relations seeks to influence attitudes, for example, by having staff members give community education talks to raise awareness about Alzheimer's disease and the need for day care. Market-

ing tries to elicit specific behaviors, such as influencing a family's decision to place a patient in day care or encouraging referrals.

3. Public relations does not define the goals of the organization, whereas marketing is intimately involved in defining the center's mission, target groups and organizations, and services. Public relations seeks to change *attitudes*, whereas marketing seeks to change *behaviors*.

Setting up a comprehensive public relations program is the essential underpinning of all fund-raising endeavors. There can be public relations without fund raising, but there cannot be fund raising without public relations. A comprehensive program will follow five steps outlined by Kotler and Bloom (1984)

- Identifying the important publics
- Measuring the attitudes and opinions of the public toward the day care center
- Establishing image and attitude goals for the important publics
- Developing effective communication tools to achieve these goals
- Implementing actions and evaluating results

Just as with finance, programming, and personnel issues, the executive/program director and members of the board must take responsibility for promotion and public relations activities. An individual from an advertising agency, television station, or newspaper can provide valuable support as a board member or member of the center's public relations committee. Individuals who have specific skills in communication, public relations, speaking and writing, and creativity should be encouraged to participate in this critical part of the program. As with fund raising, a substantial and well-thought-out promotion and public relations plan should be developed. The plan should incorporate the short-term and long-term needs of the organization. We emphasize that the experience of existing Alzheimer's day care centers indicates that promotion, while difficult and time-consuming, must be constant and ongoing.

DEALING WITH NEGATIVE DEMAND

Typically, a community needs assessment will show strong interest in Alzheimer's day care. Once the program has been established, boards and staff are astonished to find that family members are not flocking into their center. It can take several months to two years to build up a client base. The dementia day care survey by Mace and Rabins (1984) showed that most day care centers are underutilized—that is, they do not have a wait-ing list and are operating considerably *under* capacity.

The discrepancy between the positive needs assessment and the ac-tual usage of the program is evidence of a marketing situation called *nega-tive demand* or *unsought service.* A negative demand occurs when the consumer may need the service but will go to great lengths to avoid using it. This negative demand is a by-product of the caregiver's *subjective bur-den* (the psychological and emotional feelings) and the caregiver's *objective burden* (the physical tasks).

Subjective burden is probably the greatest deterrent to using Alzhei-mer's day care. The potential user population frequently believes, "Day care is fine for those other people, but my family member is not ready for day care." This kind of denial arises primarily from shame. First, caregiv-ers feel shame about the impaired state of their family member. They do not want to admit to themselves or others just how much impairment has taken place. Placement in day care "announces" to themselves and others that the patient is very impaired. Second, caregivers feel shame about their own feelings of resentment and loss. They fear they are selfish. Third, caregivers feel shame that they cannot "take care of their own." Asking for outside help is always a last resort. Most Alzheimer's day care centers emphasize *respite* as the primary goal of the program. Yet, a refer-ence to respite ("You need the time off" or "You need a break for your-self") arouses these strong feelings of shame. Most caregivers will deny any need for a break or for time off, and they do not like to have the program advertised as a respite (because from the caregiver's point of view, anyone who seeks out respite is selfish and self-serving).

Compounding the subjective burden is the negative attitude toward day care that most Alzheimer's patients express rather vehemently. It is very common for Alzheimer's patients to resist coming to day care during the first days or weeks after enrollment. The resistance, whether passively expressed in delaying getting ready or aggressively stated in accusations, leaves caregivers with highly conflicted feelings. Most caregivers are be-wildered and filled with self-doubt much of the time because the condition of Alzheimer's patients requires that caregivers must take away the pa-tient's right to make choices. Caregivers will say, "How can I bring him to day care? He does not want to come. I don't feel right about making him do something he does not want to do."

Taking a patient to day care may also compound a caregiver's objec-tive burden. Alzheimer's day care is an out-of-home respite program. Out-of-home respite requires more physical effort from caregivers than does in-home respite. Many caregivers spend anxious hours anticipating the negative reaction they will encounter when they try to get their patient ready for the day care program. The act of getting the patient dressed, groomed, fed, and in the car is oftentimes more exhausting than it is re-lieving to family members.

Marketing Strategy for Negative Demand

A carefully designed marketing program can help to counteract negative demand. Such a program should include the following elements.

1. Conduct a survey or focus group of nonusers, dropouts, and families who inquire about but do not attend the center. Find out how they perceive the center, and what objections they have to it. Ask how the service can be altered to meet their needs.
2. Conduct a survey of users of day care. Ask the same questions that were asked of nonusers and dropouts, but *add* questions about client satisfaction and participant satisfaction.
3. Emphasize the *therapeutic benefits to the patient* in all literature and all interactions with families. *Deemphasize respite.* This strategy reframes the experience for the family—placing day care in the context of the patient's best interests—and reduces caregivers' guilt and shame.
4. Prepare families for the expected negative reaction of patients, and explain how this reaction is part of the disease process. First, describe the length of time it takes a patient to become adjusted to the program (at least two to three weeks). Next, present the benefits of the program for the patient (increased socialization, heightened stimulation, reduced excess disability). Finally, show how the benefits outweigh the negatives.
5. Assign a staff person to follow up regularly with new clients' family members or family members of potential clients. Staff should provide reassurance and handle objections expressed by caregivers.
6. Set up services for families, such as support groups and family training programs. These programs not only help families, but they also provide the staff with an ongoing feedback mechanism.
7. Assign a staff member to be available for feedback from families. Keep an open-door policy for families.
8. Conduct surveys periodically to assess caregivers' satisfaction and caregivers' perception of the program.
9. Conduct surveys with the referring publics to learn about their needs, wants, perceptions, preferences, and satisfaction with the program. These referring publics may include physicians, social service agencies, hospital discharge planners, and senior centers.

Public Relations Strategy for Negative Demand

Many promotional and public relations strategies can be employed in getting information out to both potential participants and current and future supporters of an Alzheimer's day care program. These include the following:

1. Develop public talks and audio-visual materials that emphasize the therapeutic benefits of day care for both Alzheimer's patients and families.
2. Hold public talks for those who have contact with elderly people (churches, senior centers) and emphasize the important role friends and professionals play in encouraging caregivers to seek appropriate services for their patient.
3. Plan events that are open to the public and will expose the community to the therapeutic benefits of the program (a "Renaissance Faire" conducted by the day care participants, a participant kite-flying contest held on the premises).
4. Cultivate the local media, and submit press releases on a regular basis that highlight the therapeutic benefits of the program—particularly articles that show the potential for participants to have fun and to be creative.
5. Set up a speakers' bureau, and seek out opportunities to tell the center's story. Speaking engagements with local community organizations provide an excellent opportunity to promote a program as well as to let the community know of program needs. These are especially beneficial when community organizations are trying to determine their philanthropic goals. Speaking engagements offer a secondary benefit, since many people still do not understand what Alzheimer's disease is or the toll the disease exacts on caregivers. By actively seeking opportunities to impart information to various groups, one can help demystify the disease and enlighten the public about what constitutes "care," as well as educate a potential user of services or someone who knows a family struggling alone and who are not aware of available services.
6. Have a "high profile" in the community. Key staff and board members of the center should belong to important community groups. Take a leadership role in the community on senior citizens' issues. Define the Alzheimer's day care service broadly, as an important component of the long-term care continuum. Interact as an important player in all community consortiums.
7. Help the community to set up important consortiums and linkages; be at the center of the network of senior service providers.
8. Encourage visitors to the center, including persons from around the state and nation, and from overseas. This not only provides excellent publicity but provides a morale boost for staff as well.
9. Staff can open the program to agencies and organizations for tours, or offer the site for meetings or organizational activities

during the hours the program is not operating. People are more likely to make referrals to a place they are familiar with.

10. Cultivate all publics that are referral sources. The most reliable and regularly used promotional strategy is networking with referral sources. Through face-to-face contact with agency staff or invitations for referral sources to visit the center, you can help them become more comfortable and encouraging to inquiring families seeking day care. Keeping contact with referral sources by providing updates on their clients is an effective way to maintain a good exchange of knowledge. Desired referrals—for example, low income or minority clients—can be targeted by contacting agencies already connected to specific populations.

ROLES OF STAFF, BOARD, AND THIRD PARTIES

Selling the Program

The marketing and public relations components overlap on the issue of staff and board members' goals and activities in regard to determining demand and promoting the program. An individual from an advertising agency, television or radio station, or newspaper can provide invaluable assistance as a member of the board of directors. The executive/program director should plan events and experiences for board members to ensure that all board members have an intimate and positive knowledge about the program. *Do not take the knowledge of board members for granted.* It is very common for the board—and sometimes even for the staff—to have only a vague awareness of the program's mission, purpose, goals, and effectiveness. It is also desirable to hold training programs for all staff to ensure continuity in the presentation of the program to the public. Staff should know how to interact positively with family members, with visitors and volunteers, and within their own community networks. Staff must realize that they are part of the public relations process and that they are always representing the center to the public.

Third Party Opinions and Accountability

A second group that should be a target of promotional and public relations efforts are those individuals who are responsible for making referrals and supporting the organization. First, identify all publics that have an impact on the success of the Alzheimer's day care program. The list should include: physicians, Alzheimer's Association, local support groups, senior centers, government regulatory bodies, government funding agencies, philanthropic organizations, local opinion leaders, universities and medical centers, diagnostic centers, other health and social service providers, other day care programs, home health agencies, city and county government officials, and other long-term care providers. Next, set up a program to determine for each of the publics their needs, wants, preferences, perceptions and satisfaction with the day care program. Then design a public relations program that will provide these important third parties with information about the mission, purpose, and successes of the Alzheimer's day care program. This strategy can include:

- Designing and distributing quality brochures targeted to specific publics, such as families, providers, and referral agencies
- Regular mailing of press releases to the media
- Mailing of a newsletter to the center's publics
- Invitations to important events, sent to the various publics
- Responding to or initiating speaking engagements
- Taking advantage of public service announcements (PSAs)
- Holding promotional events
- Making slide and video presentations

The media can be very instrumental in the success of a public relations program. It is important to note that the executive/program director and staff of the center must ensure confidentiality and conduct all media activities ethically and appropriately. Finally, the center's *public relations strategy* should include a plan for staff and board members to become active participants in community groups that interface with its publics.

It is important to address potential public relations problems, whether they be participant problems in the day care setting, caregiver problems at home or with the day care program, or administrative issues related to the public perception of the program. Problems must be tackled immediately by the executive/program director and the board so that the center can go on about its business. One unresolved problem can create a negative impact that takes long public relations work to end. Prevention of negative situations is a much better way to approach this issue.

CONCLUSION

The public perception of the organization is critical to an Alzheimer's day care center's ability to maintain referrals, financial support, and viability. This perception cannot be left to chance. It must be constantly nurtured by a sophisticated, planned marketing orientation and public relations program.

Alzheimer's day care programs operate in an atmosphere of negative demand. This situation requires a sensitive understanding of caregivers' subjective and objective burdens and a shaping of the program to lessen these burdens. The public perception of the organization is very important in terms of referrals, support, and viability. While it may appear obvious, it is important that the center provide the most positive image possible to the community overall. There are still individuals who have a misunderstanding of dementias and need to be educated and informed about Alzheimer's disease and related dementias. Furthermore, there are misconceptions as to what an Alzheimer's day care center is about. It must be clearly articulated by authorities, such as Alzheimer's Association doctors, that centers provide very important services to both participants and caregivers.

As previously mentioned, one must present the issue of respite very carefully. The concept of respite care is not widely understood by society as a whole, nor by many of the individuals who may want to have access or should have access to the program. It is very important that board members, staff, and volunteers constantly present the best image of the center and its positive impact on participants, and avoid emphasizing respite care. The emphasis should be on the fact that the center offers a secure, safe, and structured program for participants with less emphasis on relief and support for caregivers. Thus, a marketing strategy that emphasizes therapeutic benefits rather than respite will also encourage utilization of the program and ultimately lead to greater program success.

8

THE PARTICIPANT PATHWAY

The purpose of this chapter is to clarify the process of individualized care for participants in an Alzheimer's day care setting. This process begins with the identification of the target population and continues through referral, intake and assessment, setting of care goals, and reassessment, concluding with discharge of the participant from the program.

Alzheimer's day care is a group program with care based on individualized assessment and care plans. Thoughtful service provision structures will enhance the quality of the program. Centers should take time to plan the participant pathway carefully. This will maximize smooth functioning of the program. The following steps constitute the *participant pathway* in an Alzheimer's day care setting.

1. Definition of the target population, determination of participant eligibility, and criteria for exclusion from the program.
2. The referral process.
3. Intake and assessment of the participant.
4. Development of a care plan.
5. Participant orientation to the program.
6. Reassessment.
7. Discharge from the day care program.

This chapter will discuss each of these steps in turn, as well as the record-keeping and forms necessary for each step.

DEFINITION OF THE TARGET POPULATION AND CRITERIA FOR PARTICIPANT ELIGIBILITY AND EXCLUSION

It may, at first, seem obvious who will be the target population for an Alzheimer's/dementia day care program. Participants will certainly include individuals with Alzheimer's disease or other forms of dementia. But in actual practice clarifying the definition of the target population and participant eligibility raises many issues and questions, such as how the center will be certain of the diagnosis of Alzheimer's disease or other dementia, and what the rules are for inclusion in and exclusion from the program.

Participant Diagnosis

The day care program has a responsibility to be as certain as possible that the person attending actually has dementia and that medically treatable and reversible causes of confusion, if present, have been diagnosed and are being treated. Deciding on a clear policy and holding to it are very important. This will make it easier to manage crisis calls. For example, the spouse of a confused older person may want to bring him or her into your program—but the individual's dementia has not been medically diagnosed. The policy of prior medical evaluation can be explained at that time. It needs to be clear to the family that the day care center is not a diagnostic center for the evaluation of dementia.

Most Alzheimer's day care programs require diagnosis by a medical doctor or evaluation by a geriatric evaluation service, ideally through a multidisciplinary team assessment program. Often day care programs have a requirement that new participants must have been seen by a physician within the past six months or that they are receiving ongoing treatment from a primary care physician. Ideally a diagnosis based on the National Institute of Neurological and Communicative Disease and Strokes/ Alzheimer's Disease and Related Disorders Association (NINCDS-ADRDA) (McKhann et al., 1984) criteria will have been made. This includes a medical history, neurological examination, laboratory evaluations (blood tests, urinalysis, CT scan, etc.), and psycho/social assessment. In reality, many centers must accept the best diagnosis available, which might not come from a specialist. Whenever possible, a comprehensive diagnosis by exclusion should be required.

In most cases, a mental status exam has already been done for participants who have been evaluated for dementia. However, these exams fail to evaluate people's ability to participate successfully in programs, their social abilities, or their degree of interest in day care programs. Hence, it is important to evaluate potential participants' reactions to the group and the setting, in addition to their formal mental status scores.

Participant Eligibility Criteria

After the diagnosis of dementia has been established, several factors remain to be considered in determining the participant's eligibility for the day care program.

Level of participation   Some programs require participants (with the help of their caregiver) to attend the program on a regular basis. This is often defined as three times a week or having more days of attendance than absence. Minimum attendance criteria are used in a number of programs, because regular attendance generally helps participants to adjust to the center. Infrequent attendance may produce crises and severe problems of adjustment.

Participant functional abilities   Some programs do not or cannot serve participants with certain impairments, including those who are wheelchair-bound (cannot move in or out of the wheelchair without assistance), who cannot feed themselves, or who are incontinent. Many specialized programs specifically target individuals who can control incontinence through frequent toileting, and who can perform other activities of daily living with modest assistance.

Participant behaviors   Although some programs do not serve participants with severe behavioral problems or a dominant psychiatric problem, the benefits of Alzheimer's/dementia day care programs are that they are often able to handle difficult behavioral issues, such as wandering. Some behaviors, however, often cannot be handled at day care programs. These problem behaviors may include the following: a history of violent behavior toward themselves or others (suicidal or assaultive), psychotic or severe anger or agitation, hitting of other patients or staff, wandering that cannot be contained in the facility and by the staff, the consistent need for one-on-one supervision and assistance to participate in the program, screaming/ yelling as the primary mode of communication, or inability to adjust to the day care setting.

Family/caregiver and living situation   Some programs require that participants with dementia have stable support systems. They may require the participant to live at home or with a caregiver (not in a board and care or nursing home, although some programs do accept this) or that the center have access to a primary caregiver when the participant is under stress.

Other considerations   Some programs may also set limits on eligibility for participants who need certain types of nursing care and/or need to be given medications. Common criteria for automatic exclusion from day care participation include communicable diseases requiring isolation and active alcoholic or drug-addicted behaviors.

Criteria providing for *temporary* exclusion from an Alzheimer's day care program may include (1) participants who are ill (colds, flu, or fever) and are requested not to attend the program during their illness; (2) those with a sudden change in physical or psychological functioning who are required to have a medical/psychiatric evaluation before continuing in the program; and (3) participants whose functioning temporarily changes so that they no longer meet the criteria for program participation. Individuals who are temporarily excluded from the program should be reevaluated regarding the appropriateness of their continuing in the program once their status changes.

Clear written policies of patient eligibility for the Alzheimer's day care program are essential to all aspects of program development, ranging from publicity to staffing of the program. In deciding on these policies the center needs to consider several factors, including program goals and objectives, the space and physical environment, the staff's abilities, the number of participants, and the staff-patient ratio. The basic goal of Alzheimer's day care is to provide appropriate care for persons suffering from Alzheimer's disease. Establishing reasonable eligibility policies for the program ensures that this can be accomplished.

THE REFERRAL PROCESS

After the eligibility criteria have been set and this information has been publicized in the community, the day care program will begin to receive referrals. We emphasize that referral and outreach are important and frequently difficult. Referrals will be from the family, caregivers, or health care providers. The referral will usually begin with a telephone call. Policies and procedures need to be set for the following questions, in order for the center to handle these calls:

- Which staff will handle these calls? It could be the receptionist, executive/program director, social worker, or intake worker.
- What form will be filled out? How much information will be taken over the telephone? Will the telephone contact be used to screen appropriate/inappropriate clients, or will this be done in an in-person interview?
- Will materials about the program be sent to the caller? Can intake forms be sent to the caller, filled out in advance, and brought to the first interview?
- What records or documentation will be required for telephone referrals?

INTAKE AND ASSESSMENT
OF THE PARTICIPANT

Most centers conduct intake and/or assessment interviews in person to make a final determination of the participant's appropriateness for the day care program. One must consider whether the intake and assessment for the family and/or demented person will be conducted at the center, during a home visit, or both. Some day care programs have instituted trial periods when participant eligibility is reviewed. For example, a caregiver might state that the relative wanders. During the trial period, day care staff members evaluate the frequency of this behavior and ascertain whether changes can be made in programming or supervision to accommodate the wandering pattern of this particular participant. If changes can be made and the participant safely accommodated, the strict eligibility criteria are modified. Many Alzheimer's day care programs consider a home visit/assessment integral to their program, in that it provides extensive background information on the potential participant, as well as insights into life-style, likes, dislikes, and home environment. It is important to note that NIAD standards for assessment of admission to adult day care require a home visit.

Intake Interview

During the intake interview, data collected on the participant include, at a minimum, the following:

- A basic participant profile consisting of physical health status, current medications, allergies, sensory deficits, living situation, family/caregiver situation, functional status (ability to handle activities of daily living), and level of cognitive impairment. Interests, hobbies, and former occupation are also very helpful for activity planning.
- Emergency information, including name, address, and telephone number of the participant's medical doctor, relatives, and/or caretaker, and hospital, and instructions on how emergencies are to be handled.

During the intake interview the Alzheimer's day care program is explained. If it is agreed that the individual will participate (even on a trial basis), the following agreements are made. First, an agreement to participate is signed, and days and hours of participation are agreed to. Fees for the services are agreed to, and a release for medical information from other providers and an emergency care authorization are signed. Finally, transportation arrangements are clarified.

The center should have a patient's bill of rights, a procedure for handling complaints or grievances, and/or a public relations release form, which would also be explained and signed at this time. This is also the time for clarifying services or assistance to the caretaker. If the Alzheimer's day care program is part of a research project, there may be additional forms to be signed or data to be collected.

The intake interview is a very important step in the process of bringing participants into the program. Clear communication with the participant and the family member/caregiver about the program goals and mutual responsibilities of the family and of the center will prevent future problems. As will be discussed later, this is also a critical time to discuss participant discharge issues.

Assessment Interview

In order to plan appropriate services for participants and to meet the individual needs of participants, the following areas of need must be assessed.

Cognitive impairment. Some form of mental status exam should be conducted at entry to the program. There are many standardized mental status exams that can be used, including the Folstein Mini-Mental Status Exam and the Blessed-Roth Dementia Rating Scale. A mental status exam score may be obtained from an individual's diagnostic evaluation results.

Communication style and/or limitations. Knowledge of the participant's communication skills and style is important for the staff. Which does the participant understand better, pictures or words? Does the participant have nonverbal cues to indicate toileting and other needs? Does the participant use certain objects or words to represent an idea or thought, such as *keys* to represent going home? Assessment of communication style or problems is usually done by interviewing the family member or caregiver.

Sensory impairments. Difficulty with hearing or vision will affect the participant's communication and participation in the program. Clarifying the participant's sensory capacities can be done when interviewing the family member. In some cases a referral will be needed for a professional assessment.

Social skills and coping style. Getting a historical and current picture of the participant's social skills and coping style is also valuable to individualized care and program development. For example, in terms of social skills, is the participant usually sociable, talkative, or quiet? Does the participant prefer male or female companionship? In terms of coping style, how does the participant handle frustration, new situations, and misunderstandings? Is it better to leave the participant alone or to stay beside him or her?

Previous and current interests. What types of activities does the participant like or dislike? Did the participant once have hobbies or recreation interests? Does the participant prefer to observe others doing activities or to participate in them?

Family, work, or social history, and current situation. Some day care programs diagram a "family tree" with the names of relatives listed. That way, when the participant refers to a staff person or volunteer as "Mary," then the staff is aware that Mary is the name of the participant's daughter. Knowledge of the participant's occupation may help the staff make sense out of the participant's references. For example, a demented patient who was a lawyer may continually refer to a courthouse.

Functional status. This is defined as the ability to handle activities of daily living, such as dressing or toileting. Assessment of functional status is needed to know how much staff assistance will be required during the program day for each participant. This can be assessed by asking the family member and/or observing the participant.

Multidisciplinary Assessment of Alzheimer's Participants

Obtaining a comprehensive profile of a participant's current abilities and limitations is essential to the development of an individualized care plan and to a smooth transition of the patient into the Alzheimer's day care program. If a recent assessment has been done as part of a diagnostic work-up, these records should be requested and reviewed by day care staff. If there has not been a recent assessment, the program should consider other options. Since different programs have different staff and resources available to them, centers may consider the following options to obtain a comprehensive evaluation: a full assessment in-house by day care staff and consultants; a mini-assessment by day care staff with a referral to other professionals to complete the assessment; or referral of individuals to a local evaluation clinic (hospital-based or university-based) for a full assessment.

When programs conduct their own multidisciplinary assessment of the participant, it may include the following components: nursing (including review of medical records), social work, physical therapy, occupational therapy, and recreational therapy. This comprehensive assessment is generally determined by the level of program resources or access to professionals in the community. For patients with special needs or concerns, additional assessments may include audiology/speech therapy, pharmacist review of medications, dental assessment, and psychological and/or psychiatric evaluation.

DEVELOPMENT OF A CARE PLAN

After the participant has agreed to attend the Alzheimer's day care program and the intake/assessment has been conducted, a care plan must be developed. This plan will include program goals for the participant, and guidelines for staff regarding the participant's needs. Examples of participant goals might include: (1) group participation plan, including activities most beneficial to this patient, most difficult for this patient, and groups the patient should or should not participate in; and (2) individual participation plan, including individual treatment or services needed by the participant. The latter may include nursing services, counseling, occupational therapy, and/or physical therapy. Guidelines for staff regarding special needs of the participant might include identifying whether assistance is needed with dressing, feeding, or toileting, and identifying special communication needs, such as that the participant understands pictures better than words.

PARTICIPANT ORIENTATION TO THE DAY CARE PROGRAM

Many programs have found it extremely beneficial to have potential participants come to the day care program before agreeing to an ongoing enrollment. That way, staff can see how they respond to staff, other participants, and the environment. Other programs use the initial visit as a trial period, after which the family and the staff decide whether the person is appropriate for the program. Most participants take a period of time to adjust and settle in at an Alzheimer's day care program. This orientation can be done through a short visit or over the course of one or two days before the participant enrolls in the program.

REASSESSMENT

Policies and procedures for reassessment need to be established before the day care program begins. In some cases, these will be determined by the funding source. Many programs conduct reassessments every six months, or every year, or at times of cognitive or functional change in patients. In general, reassessment can be done on an as-needed basis when the participant's functioning is observed to change; at regular intervals, such as every six months or every year (because changes in dementia generally occur very slowly, participants do not need frequent reassessments); or when the participant is discharged from the program. Reassessment at discharge is important for both clinical and administrative reasons—to track the cognitive and functional levels of participants at this stage, as well as to provide information for other care providers and facilities.

DISCHARGE

Usually participants have to be discharged from the Alzheimer's day care program at some point. Often this is a result of physical and cognitive deterioration of the participant due to the dementia. Other times it occurs as a result of behavioral or functional changes. Generally, when a discharge is required, the reason is that the patient's needs for care have changed to such an extent that the Alzheimer's day care program can no longer care for him or her appropriately or safely. Quite often the participant can no longer be taken care of at home either. In fact, many discharges occur because family members are no longer able to cope at home, even though the participant can still function in the day care program. Discharge usually occurs when a participant has deteriorated to where he or she requires full-time attention or assistance. This includes participants who can no longer ambulate or feed themselves, participants who have become incontinent and are not manageable by a toileting schedule, participants who are aggressive or exhibit menacing behavior, or participants whose wandering cannot be managed by the staff. If a participant has excessive absences or attends infrequently, discharge may be appropriate as well. Discharge must be based on the needs of both the participant and the family.

Caregivers need to know and fully understand the criteria for program participation and what problems *cannot* be handled by the program, so that they may more easily understand if the need for discharge arises. Development of realistic expectations cannot be emphasized enough, because no matter how appropriate discharge is, it may be very traumatic for the family caregiver and other members of the family. The issues and conditions related to discharge should be openly discussed as early as the intake interview. Clearly, discharge and subsequent referral are as important as intake into the program. The decision to discharge must be carefully considered and not pursued too quickly. When the decision has been made, staff should assist families in the transition to long-term care placement or other appropriate options. While staff can make the transition a smooth one, the program staff must balance providing assistance with letting families assume responsibility.

PARTICIPANT RECORD KEEPING AND FORMS

Records are an important part of the participant pathway in order to verify what has been done to and for the participant and to show that required procedures have been completed and necessary certifications obtained. For administration, evaluation, and reporting purposes, it is also important to be able to track the number of participants served, their characteristics, and program activities. Many administrators tend to develop very complicated and technical record-keeping systems. We recommend that Alzheimer's day care records be kept as simple as possible, and geared toward the needs of staff as well as provision of documentation to local, state, or federal reviewing agencies.

Generally, participant clinical/program records, staff records, administrative and licensure/certification records, and program policies must be kept. Examples of each type of document or form are provided in the appendix.

Participant Clinical Records

Participant clinical records generally include intake information, assessment data, a care plan, an agreement of participation, medical records, progress notes, service utilization, medication information, and discharge data.

Most programs have at a minimum the forms listed in Table 3. (See appendix for examples of these documents.)

TABLE 3   Participant clinical forms for Alzheimer's day care

Initial intake and assessment forms
   Referral form
   Home visit evaluation
   Intake
   Emergency information sheet
   Agreement of participation
   Patient's rights form
   Release of medical information form
   Participant profile (medications, ADL, social situation, etc.)
   *Activities of daily living evaluation
   *Nursing evaluation
   *Social work evaluation
   *Recreation therapy (or interest list)
Discharge or termination forms
   Discharge summary
Ongoing treatment records
   Attendance
   Transportation
   Medication
   Treatment plans
   Problem list
   Charting behavior
   Charting activities
   Charting episodes
   Charting family meetings
Special-purpose and other forms
   Attendance summary
   Fees and billing
   Authorization to bill
   Correspondence
   Permission for field trips and outings
   Accident report
   Consent to photograph
   Grievance procedures

Note: Asterisk indicates optional forms. ADL = activities of
daily living.

Staff Records

Staff records contain personnel information and include the staff
member's name, address, telephone number, and Social Security number,
and the name, address, and telephone number of the person to be called in
an emergency. They should also contain information about a staff person's
educational background and previous experience, any licenses that are
required for the position, a copy of a current driver's license and proof of
insurance (for drivers), a birth certificate or green card documenting na-
tionality or immigration status, and date of employment. The staff record

should also include a detailed copy of the person's job description signed by the employee, and signed performance evaluations.

Administrative and Licensure/Certification Records

Administrative records, and records of licensure and certification, should include fire clearance from the state fire marshal; a disaster plan that designates administrative authority, employee assignments, plan of evacuation, and areas of relocation; attendance records for both participants and employees; records of hours served by volunteers; salary records for staff members and applicable taxes withheld to meet state and federal requirements; monthly billing reports; inventories of supplies and equipment; current income and expense statements; and monthly/annual statistical reports.

Program Policies

Policies that delineate responsibility and define administrative plans are generally required of all Alzheimer's/dementia day care programs. They must be developed by the executive/program director with approval of the governing board. These policies are to be kept current and available for review by the staff and representatives of appropriate licensing/certification agencies. Program policies must be kept in a written form. They include a disaster plan, personnel policies, a policy on management of medications, emergency medical plans, transportation safety and vehicle records, reporting of cases of abuse, and reporting of any unusual occurrences.

CONCLUSION

The Alzheimer's day care center must set policies and procedures for each of the steps of the participant pathway, including eligibility and exclusion criteria, referral, intake and assessment, care plans, participant orientation, reassessment, and discharge. Guidelines must be clear, specific, and in writing to enable staff to direct participants and their families through the day care process. Having the right documents and forms and a comprehensive and detailed record-keeping system will ensure that this system works efficiently and effectively. Throughout the participant pathway the needs and experiences of participants must be considered at all times. However, it is also important to be realistic about the capacities of the program and the capabilities of the center's staff. A carefully planned, detailed, and well-tested participant pathway offers the best mechanism possible for delivering individualized care in an Alzheimer's day care center.

9

ALZHEIMER'S DAY CARE PROGRAM CONTENT

The purpose of this chapter is to provide an overview of activity program concepts that are basic to any well-run Alzheimer's day care program, regardless of program model or philosophy. Alzheimer's day care is not babysitting. It is a therapeutic endeavor with powerful potential to restore a demented participant's feelings of usefulness, sociability, and capacity to celebrate life.

At the heart of this endeavor is the *activity program*. Activities are the core of Alzheimer's day care. It can be said that the quality of a day care center—its ambience, therapeutic benefits, and staff satisfaction—reflect the success of its activity program. Activities serve a two-fold purpose: (1) to encourage each participant to function at the highest level possible, thereby building self-esteem and shedding any excess of disability; and (2) to serve as a primary tool in managing problem behaviors.

This chapter will discuss activities with an emphasis on generic concepts revolving around philosophy, goals, and objectives of program content; program implementation issues, including staffing patterns, group size, and set-up procedure; scheduling and coordination for the program day and for group and individual activities; and special issues concerning programming. The chapter offers guidelines rather than instruction on specific activities. Sources of instructional material for specific activities may be found in the bibliography.

PHILOSOPHY OF ALZHEIMER'S DAY CARE PROGRAMMING

Every Alzheimer's day care program faces two dilemmas that must be addressed, resolved, and evaluated. The first results from the nature of the impairment itself: Alzheimer's day care programs deal with an extremely confused population having shortened attention spans, poor alertness, poor concentration, loss of recent memory (including orientation to person, time, or place), and high levels of verbal, visual, and motor coordination impairment combined with, in some cases, a tendency toward combative behaviors. This group of people has virtually no ability to start an activity—and if one is begun, they cannot continue or complete it. The first dilemma, in short, is whether an activity program can work.

The second dilemma is a philosophical one: Do people with impaired judgment and reasoning still possess the right to self-determination (autonomy)? Do they have a right to choose among offered activities, decide that they want to leave the premises, or even decide whether they want to come to day care in the first place? Stating the dilemma in another way, is it philosophically possible for a day care staff to take away some of the choice-making rights but still allow self-determination in other, selected areas?

The answer to both dilemmas—will activities be successful, and is selective choice making compatible with individual rights—is, of course, yes. But boards of directors and staffs of Alzheimer's day care centers rarely state the dilemmas openly. An examination of the philosophical underpinnings of successful programs, however, invariably shows evidence of grappling with these issues. To best address these issues, we recommend that an Alzheimer's day care center specifically articulate a program philosophy, followed by a resolution expressed in the form of goals and objectives.

Applying the Program Philosophy

The program philosophy and mission statement that a center develops should address and attempt to resolve the two dilemmas presented above by striving both to achieve respect for the individual and to define success for the participant.

Respect for the individual may be expressed through the following goals:

1. Tailoring the program to individual needs and preferences through a process of assessment and development of care plans.

   Example: Each program makes a determination about participant levels of functioning. Activity programs are designed to appeal to each level. If one activity appeals only to high or moderately functioning individuals, a parallel program for the lower level people is added to the activity hour.

2. Developing a concept of delegated autonomy for each person. A participant will retain the ability to make choices, but will delegate to a surrogate (the day care staff) those aspects of self-

determination that are necessitated by the mental or physical incapacity.

Example: The choice to leave the premises cannot reasonably be made by the confused participant whose safety would be jeopardized by such a decision. This choice is therefore delegated to day care staff. Participants may leave only when supervised. In contrast, the decision to join a particular activity while on the premises is self-determined by the participant. Making the decision about coming to day care is a more difficult philosophical issue. Generally, family members are the decision makers because most participants are initially reluctant or negative about coming. Some day care centers get around this self-determination issue by considering the first week or two of adjustment as a trial period. The best way to address this philosophical issue is to have each participant experience the program before making a decision about attending.

3. Protecting the participant from experiencing unpleasant environmental factors.

Example: When one participant has a delusion about another ("you are my wife") and continually bothers and annoys that person, staff will separate the participants without offending either person. Often it is enough simply to stop the behavior. Occasionally, providing separate activities for these participants is enough. Sometimes, the two individuals will be assigned different days for attendance at the center.

4. Selecting activities that reflect participant preferences.

Example: Intake tools should be used to solicit information about individual preferences. In addition, the activity coordinators and staff continually evaluate participant response and enthusiasm about each activity. Parallel activities are always provided for people who like to keep busy but do not enjoy a particular program.

5. Selecting adult-level activities, even though the skill level may be more commonly seen in childhood.

Example: Coloring, cutting, and pasting are craft activities that can be enjoyed by the whole range of participant functional levels. These crafts must be placed in an adult context, however, in order not to seem "babyish." Coloring, cutting, and pasting can be craft skills used to make decorations on a weekly basis or for a specific festival time. Sophisticated "coloring books" can be used, which are actually learning aids in biology, art history, and other college classes. A "Lifelong Learning" Series is interesting to participants, and can be followed by coloring these unusual pictures.

6. Presenting parallel programs with other choice options. Parallel programs are a key component of the participant's right to self-determination.

Example: Activity coordinators plan an activity program for the whole group. At the same time, parallel activities are also planned with appropriate staff assignments. The parallel activities are designed with specific nonparticipants in mind and are set up with goals and objectives just like the main activity schedule.

7. Selecting activities that reflect the participant's daily living skills.

Example: Grooming, health (beauty care, manicures), helping another person, setting the table, cleaning, and preparing meals are all activities that reflect and reinforce the skills of daily living that participants possess.

Defining success for the participant may be expressed through the following goals:

1. Selecting activities that are meaningful to the participants.

Example: Reality orientation can be retitled "Current Events." The current events can be presented in a format that is like a business meeting. Instead of merely reading the newspaper, staff can discuss several current issues. Even though the verbal impairments of participants may limit their ability to join a discussion, each participant can feel that they are participating if the question addressed to them has a "yes, no, I don't know" response. Discussion of an intriguing issue can begin with a description of the issue followed by staff asking each participant: "Did you ever experience . . .?" Thus, current events can also be used to stimulate reminiscing. Both of these rely primarily on active group participation rather than on passive listening. As a rule of thumb, active group participation is more meaningful to participants.

2. Presenting activities in a simple one-step-at-a-time format so that participants can follow each step (a prototype model is shown to participants first to orient them to the purpose of the craft or activity).

Example: Many complex tasks can be handled by people at a wide range of functional levels if each step is presented on a one-step-at-a-time basis. Cooking, simple origami, and even such complicated activities as square dancing are possible with this format. In fact, a successful activity is usually labor-intensive and has several steps that will keep the participant occupied over a long period of time. Another advantage to multiple steps is that staff have an opportunity to move on to another step at about the time most participants have lost attention with or concentration for the existing step.

3. Engaging and reengaging the participants in the activity.

Example: Sometimes participants say no when invited to join an activity. *No* may actually indicate that the participant does not know how to begin and does not know the sequence of steps needed to continue with an activity. Staff must invite each participant individually, and reassure each person in the special way that works with that individual. Gentle coaxing and reassurance plus enthusiasm about the activity will usually persuade most people. Staff must be aware and vigilant about the attention span and concentration level of each person. Staff circulate around the group, reengaging each individual when necessary. Staff must also be skilled in a repertoire of strategies to get and maintain attention and alertness. Some participants will need to be shown how to do an action. Others will need staff-hand-on-participant-hand to begin the activity. Some participants need help with some steps but can accomplish other steps alone. This individualized approach is essential if the participant's attention span is to be expanded from the average of about 1–2 minutes to the desired 30–45 minutes.

4. Matching activities to skill levels.

Example: Very few activities appeal to individuals at every skill level. Many times it is necessary to have parallel programs designed for each functional level. Sometimes the entire group can be involved by modifying aspects of the activity (see Table 4).

5. Having activities build on participant strengths.

TABLE 4 Matching activities to skill levels

Activity	Modifications
Ball toss	High level participants stand in the middle of the circle and toss the ball to moderate and lower level people.
Cooking	High level participants read the recipe and measure. Moderate level participants stir. Low level participants pound nuts in a bag and squeeze oranges with a portable juicer.
Square dancing	The addition of many volunteers can assist one to two low level people at a time in very simplified instructions. Moderates need a 1:3 staff/volunteer ratio. High level people can follow the instructions.
Lifelong learning	High level participants help with the lesson. Moderates help by passing out materials. All groups color the learning materials. Staff and volunteers assist the low level people with hand-on-hand coloring activity.
Weekly participant meeting	High level people participate in discussion and raise questions. Moderates make simple statements. Low level participants respond to staff-directed questions with yes or no answers.
Sing-alongs	All participants can be involved since no one needs to know the lyrics. High level participants can lead the singing.
Ballroom dancing	This activity works best if many volunteers are available to encourage dancing among all participants. All levels can interact together.
Indoor bowling	All levels can participate with staff assisting the lower levels. High levels can help staff maintain the scoreboard.

Example: An assessment of each person's strengths will show a range of abilities in the areas of activities of daily living; sociability; music, dancing, and singing talents; specialized interests and expertise; ability to help others; ability to make others feel welcome; and many more. A former clockmaker may bring in his collection of clocks to share with staff and other participants. Other hand-crafted items and/or mementos from important times in a participant's life can be brought to the center and displayed. All these strengths can be incorporated into the program. The strengths will be used to enhance the self-esteem of each individual as well as to enrich the program day. There are also symptoms of dementia that can be transformed into strengths. Perseveration—the tendency to perform an action over and over and over—can be used in some crafts such as coloring or sanding. The need to be in motion can be transformed into a vigorous walk with the group.

Addressing Behavior Problems

When each individual is accepted as he or she is, with a sensitive understanding of strengths and limitations, it is possible to set up an environment that helps each individual function at the highest possible level. This basic philosophy, which respects the individual and provides for the success of participants, is also the primary method for managing problem behaviors. This technique for managing problem behaviors is based on the philosophical position that advocates having the environment adapted to the individual—not the other way around.

The activity program becomes the vehicle for moving participants in and out of appropriate environments where their behaviors are manageable. Some Alzheimer's patients are prone to periods of agitation, or can become agitated through boredom or inactivity. Activities channel this energy into positive experiences. When groups of Alzheimer's patients mill around with nothing to do, the group as a whole becomes more agitated. Activities that engage the whole group—sing-alongs, bowling, ball toss—can immediately lower the tension and allow staff to regain control.

Setting up parallel programs for nonparticipating groups is important as much for behavior management as for development of participant self-esteem. In Alzheimer's day care settings, some form of activity should be scheduled for each hour of the day—even if the "activity" is quiet time, massage, or listening to music.

Behavior management strategies are usually viewed as a by-product of a well-run activity program. Rarely are these strategies expressed in goal and objective statements by boards of directors or staff planners. But every goal and objective statement has an implicit component that states: When these activities are working and participants are interested and active, their behavior will also be positive and manageable. More specific points and illustrations of dealing with behavior problems and other participant management issues will be addressed in chapter 10.

Translating Philosophy into Goals and Objectives

Program goals and objectives are an important mechanism for translating the program philosophy or mission statement into concrete actions. The primary goal of the activity program is to provide therapeutic activities that match the ability and needs of the participant population and restore or maintain maximum participant functioning and sense of well-being. The program should enable the participant to participate "successfully" despite limitations. An Alzheimer's day care program should address the following objectives:

- To provide experiences and activities that promote maximum functioning and do not make participants more dependent than they need to be; that prevent or delay deterioration; and that maintain participants' functional and cognitive levels (acknowledging that dementia of the Alzheimer's type cannot currently be reversed)

- To provide activities that achieve specific goals of individual treatment in the following areas: cognitive, physical exercise, self-care, socialization, and psychological well-being
- To provide activities that allow participants to set their own style and pace of participation—initiating, participating, and observing
- To plan and schedule activities in a manner that makes the most effective use of staff, space, and other program resources
- To provide activities that participants enjoy and feel satisfied/ proud about
- To recognize the value of activities in managing problem behaviors and to ensure that an environment is adapted to the special behavioral needs of each participant

IMPLEMENTING THE ACTIVITY PROGRAM

There are four elements in an activity program: the participant group, the staff and volunteer, the environment, and the activity schedule. All four elements must be addressed, planned for, and subjected to ongoing evaluation. This section will present the key issues that staff should consider in implementing an appropriate activities program.

Know the Participant Group

To plan for the needs of individual participants, staff can use several techniques. An individual assessment of each participant should be conducted; it should include assessments of cognitive functioning, degree of language capacity/disorder, physical disability, and impairments in activities of daily living skills. (The assessment process itself is addressed at length in chapter 8.) Staff should interview both the participant and family, using direct observation to assess preferences and interests. Staff members should observe an individual's social preferences, as well as the effect of each individual on the other members of the group.

To plan for the needs of participants as a group, staff should observe and evaluate group preferences with each activity and also note the change that occurs when particular members are present or absent. Staff can also observe and evaluate the differences when there are groups of 5, 10, 15, 20, or larger numbers. How do these numbers change the strategies for enticing individuals to join activities? How do numbers affect the need for several small group activities as opposed to one large and one small group activity? Does the size of the group affect the length of time for an activity—1-hour segments vs. 30-minute segments? Does it change the use of space or increase the potential for overstimulation?

Know the Staff and Volunteers

The executive/program director of a center must recognize the special strengths and talents of staff and volunteers so as to determine what kinds of programs work best for each staff/volunteer mix. Staff and volunteers need to be people with personal characteristics of patience, flexibility, caring, and a sense of humor. Administrative staff also need to reflect these qualities.

Different staff/volunteer combinations require different styles of supervision. Developing and encouraging staff cooperation and communication enables the staff to meet the full range of patient needs better. In addition, the executive/program director will set the tone of the program by communicating a respect for staff and volunteers as well as for the participant groups.

In hiring staff, it is important to consider what types of prior experience and what kind of training can compensate for lack of direct knowledge of or experience with Alzheimer's patients. In many cases, staff and volunteers have specific skills or related experience that can adequately prepare them for working with Alzheimer's patients. In other cases, staff and volunteers have abilities and interests they have not previously applied to Alzheimer's patients. These skills, if employed, allow program innovation and expansion.

Staff/participant ratios are an important factor in planning an activity program. What works best with the participant group? Alzheimer's/ dementia day care programs generally have staff-to-participant ratios between 1:1 and 1:5 (the average appears to be one staff person to three participants). The best case is having ratios that provide the most individualized attention. In any activity, it is advisable to have at least two staff members with the group—one to lead the group and the other to provide support or assistance to individuals.

Staff must also consider the best way to use volunteers. Volunteers can provide valuable assistance during program activities. They may even lead certain activities with the approval of program staff. In all instances, however, responsibility for the program remains with the program staff.

Know the Physical Environment

All elements of the physical environment can affect the planning and the success of an activities program. Key aspects of the environment include rooms, noise, lighting, chairs, space, outdoors, movement, safety, and memory aids. We will discuss each of these briefly.

Rooms What are the size and number of rooms? What activities work best in these spaces? Two or three small rooms will work well for groups focused on different activities, such as crafts, reality orientation, or group therapy. To achieve this effect, a large room can be divided into different activity areas with screens or movable room dividers, and a different staff member can lead each activity. Kitchen space large enough to

allow a small group permits participants to assist with cooking and preparation of special meals and snacks. The kitchen can also be used for occupational therapy on a group or individual basis.

Noise   How can extraneous auditory stimuli—such as noise generated
by participants, outside noise, background noise, traffic sounds, and distracting conversation—be minimized? Large groups generate considerable
noise. Experiment with group size and noise levels in each space. Sometimes a space requires a "rule of 10" or similar number as a maximum
allowable group size. Outside noise, particularly traffic noise, is especially
distracting to the functioning of the program, and may be addressed by
using specific "noise free" rooms.

Lighting   Lighting will need to be brighter than usual to compensate
for changes in visual perception. Avoid glare since that will interfere with
participants' ability to see.

Chairs   Chairs need to be very sturdy because participants' physical
impairments cause them to lean on chairs in ways that stress the joints.
Participants often need to have their chairs pushed up to tables once they
are sitting down—another stress on joints. Chairs need plastic fittings that
allow for this kind of movement; otherwise, the day care center will be
filled with chair carcasses and kindling wood. Chairs should have arms to
enable participants to sit and stand easily. Plastic molded chairs or large,
vinyl-covered chairs have often been used effectively. Recliners are also
helpful when participants want to rest.

Space   Program space should be bright and cheerful and have a
homey atmosphere. It should be easy to survey the environment visually,
keep track of participants, and spot potential problems. Thus, the space
needs to be safe and secure, yet feel good. Every Alzheimer's day care
program needs to determine how best to handle wandering. Some programs assign a staff or volunteer "door guard"; others use alarms or wind
chimes to alert staff that a door has been opened; still others provide an
activity to distract the participants who wander to the door.

Outdoors   What opportunities exist for outdoor walks? Can activities
be moved to outdoor patios? In many mild climates or during the summer
months, the outdoor areas can serve as another room. Sometimes people
with dementia are calmed by getting outdoors for a while.

Movement   When activity groups are moved from room to room, participants have a chance to stretch and to take a break from concentrating
on activities. This might also increase their attention span for the next
activity. This renewed alertness can also be induced if participants can
"step outside" for a moment between activities.

Safety   Review the arrangement of rugs, lamps, appliances, extension cords, and equipment to ensure safety for visually impaired and
coordination-impaired persons. It is also important to notice how participants are seated—are their feet outstretched waiting for someone to trip?
Are there canes, walkers, sweaters, or purses in the main pathways?

Memory Aids Surround the environment with memory aids, such as clocks, calendars, an activity board with a daily schedule, a reality orientation board, names over coat hooks, pictures on cabinets that identify the content, the word *bathroom* with a picture of a toilet to identify the room, and name tags for staff and participants.

Know the Activity

An activity program should be developed as a whole unit, for each day, each week, and each month. This approach will allow programmers to view the plan as a whole and will encourage variety in program activities.

The activity program *for the day* for large group and individual or parallel activities should include a balance of large motor, fine motor, sensory, and cognitive stimulation; sitting activities interspersed with movement activities; a prototype day that is regularly followed; scheduling of more cognitive tasks in the morning; and special activities to reduce the "sundowner effect," which occurs each afternoon as participants become more agitated.

The activity program *for the week* should include themes that can be repeated throughout the week, a balance of large group activities to achieve variety throughout the week, and selection of activities that appeal to the participant population of each scheduled day.

The activity program *for the month* should include a balance of events, parties, and festivals to reinforce participant awareness of time and place, and observance of local traditions and holidays.

GUIDELINES IN SETTING UP ACTIVITIES

The success of specific activities and programming as a whole is often dependent upon the proper preparation for each activity. This includes attending to individual activity steps, having appropriate materials, selecting the right type and mix of activities, providing proper assistance and direction, and monitoring individual levels of ability and stress. The actual activities will go more smoothly if the following guidelines are observed:

Prepare a prototype of each craft or comparable activity. Practice the steps before presenting it to the group.

Have all materials ready and available.

Remove all materials from preceding activities.

Plan program activities that require new learning, and pace the presentation of this material, taking into account the individual capacities of the participants.

Include a mix of familiar and new activities when programming. The emphasis, however, should be on activities that use the participant's existing skills and strengths.

Plan program activities with a realistic understanding of how the different stages of cognitive impairment will affect the individual's ability to participate.

Use the special interests and backgrounds of the participants as the basis for specific small group activities, such as preparing ethnic foods.

Avoid childish games or children's activities.

Divide complex tasks with a series of steps into individual steps (sit here, hold this, put this in the box), and give instructions in a paced, sequential way rather than all at once.

Be prepared to repeat instructions many times.

Repeat the same program activities to provide needed structure and comfort. Providing the same program activities at the same time daily may achieve the same objective.

Avoid stimulus overload for the patient. Stimulus overload may evoke nonverbal behavioral problems or reactions.

Structure activities so that participants move from a high level of physical activity to a quiet or slow paced activity and back again.

Try to be flexible and to respond to the needs of the group and its individuals, rather than forcing a specific activity.

Gathering Basic Program Supplies

In preparing supplies for the program, staff should consider the activities to be conducted and obtain supplies to help accomplish these goals. Program directors and staff have indicated that the following items, among others, will provide the means to conduct basic, yet stimulating, activities:

- Chalk board, white board, dry marker, eraser board (chalk, dry markers)
- Paper, felt-tip marker pens, pencils, scissors (blunt-tipped or safety scissors)
- Craft supplies, such as construction paper, crepe paper, tissue paper, glitter, masking tape, cellophane tape, nontoxic glue and crayons, an assortment of ribbons, old greeting cards, and a supply of milk cartons, egg cartons, and old jewelry and buttons
- Art supplies, including watercolor paper, watercolors, brushes, stencils, sophisticated adult coloring books
- Indoor bowling supplies, beach balls, small soft balls
- Plastic or cushioned horseshoes or ring toss
- Games
- Puzzles
- Calendars, reality orientation board, clocks
- Storage carts

Additional supplies and resources, particularly those available only through an expanded budget or donations, include the following:

- Stereo or tape player
- Song sheets
- Gardening tools and supplies
- Indoor plants or outdoor planters
- Specialized games and equipment for physically handicapped participants
- Piano
- Slide projector and screen
- Overhead projector
- Large screen television and videocassette player
- Expenses for field trips
- Microphone
- Pinball machines

ORGANIZING AND SCHEDULING THE PROGRAM DAY FOR PARTICIPANTS

Programs vary dramatically in terms of the number of hours, the time of day, and the number of days that they operate. The program hours and the number of days a program operates will affect the daily activity plan. These factors will also affect the type of participants that can be served. For example, a program that is open from 9:00 a.m. to 3:00 p.m. will have the participants at the highest cognitive levels, because participants will leave before the agitation from sundowner effects becomes pronounced. In contrast, a program that is open from 8:00 a.m. to 5:00 p.m. will have to include programming for late afternoon sundowner reactions, as well as provide for one meal and two snack periods. Programs that open at 7:00 or 7:30 a.m. will have participants who are drowsy and want to nap. Programs that operate in the evening will have a participant population that is likely functioning at a lower level and one that will require small group (as opposed to large group) activities. Late afternoon and evening programs also should have comfortable chairs or places for participants to nap.

Every Alzheimer's day care program must consider common issues in planning and organizing the program day. The day activities need to include time for transition—on arrival, between activities during the day, and at departure. A generic program day would typically include the following divisions of organization and scheduling: transportation, arrival, morning orientation, activities, lunch, and departure. We will briefly discuss each of these.

Transportation

Whatever arrangements are made for transporting participants to the program—families providing transportation, a van from the program, or volunteers—the time of arrival and departure and the special needs of participants using the transportation must be coordinated with program staff. Although a clearly designated time for arrival makes programming easier, it is often extremely difficult for families to arrive at a specified hour. The morning program should reflect flexibility and be set up to absorb the arrival of participants at different times. For example, the van at one day care center, which transports 25% of the participants, has an arrival time that ranges from 9:30 a.m. to 10:45 a.m. Staff have adapted the program by putting the large group in a room that is out of view of the front door. When the late arrivals appear, the large group is not disrupted. Meanwhile, one staff member is assigned to assist the late arrivals, who are settled into the program in another room. It is a good idea to assign the transportation issues and coordination to one staff member so that the other staff are free to focus on the program.

Arrival of Participants: Greeting and Orientation

When participants arrive, staff/volunteers need to be available to greet them and to assist them in taking off and hanging up their coats and hats, and pinning on name tags. Participants need to be reoriented to the program, and reminded of time and place, in a tone of respect, welcome, and encouragement. This is also a time when family members can update staff about issues and concerns for the day.

During this time of day, the more functional members may help with greeting and assisting other participants to get settled. These higher functioning people can also assist with program preparations, such as putting supplies on the table for crafts or bringing juice and coffee from the kitchen to the dining room.

Morning Orientation Meeting

Most Alzheimer's day care programs begin with an orientation meeting. The plan for the day is reviewed and written on the chalk board. Staff and participants are reintroduced, and information about each other is shared. Discussion about the season, weather, the date, and everyday events may help orient participants. The information is repeated in different ways throughout the meeting. This morning group is a good time to assess the "pulse" of the group and to note any changes in participant behaviors that may have an impact on the program for the remainder of the day. For example, a discussion of the season might begin: "What season is this, anyway? It certainly is dark and rainy for summer. Believe it or not, it is summer. Do you remember a summer with rain?"

Scheduling of Various Program Activities

It is important to set a basic schedule that is usually followed every day. Groups are usually scheduled for 30–60 minutes, with time between group activities to assist participants with toileting and other self-care tasks.

Lunch

Most centers serve a hot noon meal. Lunch time is an ideal time for relaxation, personal interactions, and, most important of all, treatment. It is very important to promote a home-like or family atmosphere, rather than one that feels institutional. The use of round tables, placemats or vinyl tablecloths, and standard place settings can enhance the dining atmosphere and encourage interaction. A designated space for meals should be established that can be set up prior to lunch time and have minimal distractions. A planned seating schedule will avoid problems such as having a lower functioning "food stealer" sitting next to a participant who will be upset or embarrassed by this activity, as well as permit staff to sit next to participants who need special assistance or monitoring. Meals should be served in courses with attention to participants who eat at different speeds. Soft background music provides an excellent atmosphere for meal time.

Participant involvement in meal preparation is up to the discretion of the program staff. While this may be very useful to some participants by reinforcing daily skills, it may be too difficult for other participants or provide too great a burden for staff. The same holds true for having participants help with set up and clean up.

All staff and volunteers need to be trained in assisting during this time. It is important that staff and volunteers know when to tactfully intervene and provide assistance and when to allow certain behaviors to continue. All meals must be supervised since choking and aspiration can be a problem. The importance of a supportive and normal social environment around meal times cannot be emphasized enough, and it is staff who are the most instrumental in setting this tone.

End of the Day/Departure

Smaller group activities need to be introduced as group size diminishes. Some large group activities can continue as group size dwindles. Some staff must be assigned to run activities while other staff assist participants with jackets and give reports to families. If a van is used by the center, staff should plan to have a "break" in activities while the van is loaded. Even higher functioning persons are often concerned at that time about how they will get home and will need to be reminded that their family member will be there soon. Ask higher functioning participants to assist lower functioning ones to the van. This will distract them while making them feel helpful.

An example of a prototype day, with activities balanced between large and small motor, cognitive, and sensory activities, is given in Table 5.

SCHEDULING/COORDINATING STAFF FOR THE PROGRAM DAY

The task of coordinating and scheduling staff to handle a variety of program tasks and responsibilities usually requires setting up standard pro-

TABLE 5   Prototype daily activity schedule

Time	Activity
9:00 a.m.	Arrival. Participants are greeted and reacquainted with each other.
9:30 a.m.	Coffee time and introduction to the activities of the day.
10:00 a.m.	Current events or reality orientation.
10:30 a.m.	Exercises.
11:00 a.m.	Outdoor walk.
11:15 a.m.	Craft activity.
12:00 p.m.	Lunch, stretch, move the body, wash hands, and toileting.
12:45 p.m.	Clean-up.
1:00 p.m.	Quiet time, soft music, massage, toileting, napping.
2:00 p.m.	Exercise or another walk.
2:30 p.m.	Small group activity: bingo, cards, etc.
3:15 p.m.	Snack and juice or coffee.
3:45 p.m.	Physical exercise game, such as bowling, shuffleboard, ball toss, parachute ball (holding a parachute and tossing the ball in the center).
4:15 p.m.	Quiet activities and sitting-down options, such as cards.
5:00 p.m.	Saying good-bye, wrap-up.

cedures and forms both for managing everyday activities and for dealing with emergencies. The areas in which specific schedules need to be made include transportation and program activities.

Transportation

Setting up a transportation schedule is critical to the smooth functioning of the program. This transportation schedule should include a list of participants attending on each day, their source of transportation, geographic area from which each participant is coming, whether the participant needs a reminder call on the day of the program, expected arrival time, whom to call or notify if the participant doesn't arrive or if the person is not picked up on time, special instructions for the driver, and whom to contact for back-up transportation. While most centers use written records for scheduling and transportation, some centers are now automating their transportation scheduling using a computer. Responsibility for this aspect of program coordination should be clearly defined, and that person should be freed from other aspects of program responsibilities. Transportation issues are addressed in greater detail later in this chapter.

Program Activities

Setting up a written schedule of program activities with space to indicate which staff and volunteers are responsible for which activities will result in a more smoothly run program (see appendix). Often the schedule will be determined during a preprogram staff meeting designed to review staff/patient needs. Schedules may be developed for the following tasks:

- Staff responsibilities for lunch pick-up, lunch duty, crisis counseling, emergency coordination, coordination with outside consultants, and clean-up after craft/program activities.
- Staff responsibilities for individualized participant assistance with toileting and individual treatment. Some programs have a notebook or discreetly posted special-need sheet to help keep track of this. Other programs assign staff or volunteers to participants for the day.
- Staff responsibilities for preparation of program activities, greeting/orienting, participation in clean-up after program day, and follow-up with families about participants.
- Staff responsibilities for assisting or coordinating with administration activities.

GROUP ACTIVITIES FOR COGNITIVELY IMPAIRED PARTICIPANTS

Even though individual interventions may occur throughout the program day, Alzheimer's day care is basically a group program. The group experience needs to focus on activities that minimize the cognitive deficits of the participants and support the current strengths and skills of the participants. In order to accomplish this, it is important to select activities that do not require "new learning" but can be done using previous knowledge and over-learned social skills.

The need to focus a program on these types of activities has been reported by Mace and Rabins (1984) in their survey of 346 centers serving demented participants. These centers listed the following activities, in rank order, as most successful with demented participants:

Sing-alongs
Physical exercise, including dancing
Walks
Reminiscence groups
Visits from children
Active games
Outings
Listening to music
Reality orientation
Visits from pets

Anecdotal reports indicate that music and dancing are very successful activities for participants. This section will describe five basic types of activities in Alzheimer's day care programs, including physical activities, social activities, cognitive/intellectual activities, functional activities, and miscellaneous activities. Again, this book does not address the specific details of each activity; the bibliography lists references on activities for Alzheimer's/dementia patients.

Physical Activities

Several goals may be achieved by physical activities at an Alzheimer's day care program, including (1) increasing or maintaining physical fitness and preventing excess physical disabilities; (2) increasing clients' participation despite cognitive limitations through activities requiring little or no instruction or new learning for joining in; and (3) bringing on a natural fatigue that may enable participants to sleep better and wander less at home (or even at the day care program).

Center staff should plan for including the physically disabled in the activity (for example, as observers), modifying the activity or using special equipment so that those physically limited may still participate (participation while remaining seated), or providing alternate activities for those who are physically handicapped.

Physical activities in an Alzheimer's day care program may include taking walks, dancing, shopping trips, throwing a beach ball, indoor bowling, physical exercise, swimming outings (include walking), gardening, and shuffleboard.

Social Activities

The goals that can be achieved by social activities include (1) emotional satisfaction from social relationships and social experiences; (2) participation, if it does not require new learning and reinforces familiar skills and life experiences; (3) an increased sense of self-esteem from relationships; and (4) lowering of anxiety and agitation through familiar, emotionally rewarding, and successful experiences.

In a basic way, all group activities in an Alzheimer's day care program are social activities. This list of activities focuses on the "social" aspect of the experience and emphasizes social skills as the primary skill of attention: reminiscence, sing-alongs, intergenerational activities, visits from children, visits from pets, meal or snack time, meal preparation, parties, holiday celebrations, listening to music, and watching movies.

Cognitive/Intellectual Activities

The goals that can be achieved by cognitive activities include (1) preserving and maintaining cognitive functioning; (2) enhancing self-esteem and well-being of participants; (3) providing sensory stimulation; and (4) minimizing excess cognitive disabilities that may actually be caused by depression or other reversible conditions coinciding with dementia.

The activity must be matched to the level of the participant's ability. Staff must be able to conduct cognitive activities with participants who have sensory impairments (especially vision and hearing) that limit their ability to participate, and to conduct activities with participants who are aware of losing cognitive abilities. It is very important to be attuned to the abilities of participants so that they will not fail or feel inadequate. Some examples of cognitive activities are reality orientation, sensory awareness, quiet games, reminiscence, naming familiar items, remotivation, current events discussion, and jigsaw puzzles.

Functional Activities

Functional activities consist of activities of daily living, including dressing, eating, grooming, toileting, cooking, cleaning, and other self-care or household maintenance tasks. There are several goals to be achieved through functional activities at an Alzheimer's day care program, including (1) increasing or maintaining the participant's self-care ability; (2) minimizing or preventing excess disability in self-care and activities of daily living; (3) providing participants with increased self-esteem from continued participation and management of self-care and activities of daily living; and (4) increasing positive emotions by participating in activities of daily living.

Problems with providing functional activities in an Alzheimer's day care setting are that some participants may need one-on-one assistance with handling, learning, or conducting these activities, and it may be difficult for staff to distinguish between functional impairment and excess disabilities in these areas. Examples of functional activities include grooming, meal preparation, cleaning, cooking, eating, dressing, and toileting.

Miscellaneous Activities

Art and Music Therapy   The goals to be achieved through art and music therapy are similar even though the activities are different and may require different skills for active participation by Alzheimer's patients. The goals are to stabilize or increase social functioning, increase a participant's sense of well-being or self-esteem through participation in activities that do not require linear thinking, decrease anxiety or depression, provide sensory stimulation, and increase positive feelings by having a good time. Art and music therapists should be considered for permanent positions with, or as consultants for, the day care program.

Art and music activities include drawing, music therapy, dance therapy, crafts, painting, art therapy, and sing-alongs.

Religious Services and Religious Activities   Religious services and religious activities in Alzheimer's day care programming may achieve several goals, including recognizing and providing the opportunity for participants to meet their spiritual needs, and providing comfort and a sense of belonging through participation in religious activities and in familiar rituals.

Problems with religious activities include determining how to meet the varying needs of individuals from different faiths and different religious orientations, planning parallel programs for those who do not wish to participate in religious activities, and being attuned to the feelings, attitudes, and policies of staff or the sponsoring agency about inclusion of religious activities in the program.

Religious activities may encompass religious services, reading of prayers, singing hymns or religious music, and celebrating religious holidays.

Work or Community Service Activities   The goals achieved by providing work or community-service activities in a day care program include giving participants the opportunity to engage in meaningful and contributing activities, and increasing participant self-esteem and emotional satisfaction through participation in work or service activities. These activities might include folding flyers, winding yarn for others to knit or crochet, painting blocks as children's gifts, stuffing envelopes, or packaging simple items.

INDIVIDUAL ACTIVITIES FOR COGNITIVELY IMPAIRED PARTICIPANTS

Even though most activities in an Alzheimer's day care program will be conducted in groups, some activities may be provided on a one-to-one basis. The goals to be achieved by individualized activities include (1) providing special assistance to participants; (2) providing individualized approaches to learning or participating in the activity; and (3) separating individuals from the group who need special assistance so the group may proceed more smoothly (this may be a "time out" or individual instruction in conducting an activity).

Providing individualized activities may be difficult because of insufficient staff, lack of staff training, or other constraints on staff time and energy. These obstacles may be overcome with good planning and thorough training of paid staff and volunteers. Individual program activities may include some or all of the following: personal care (grooming, changing clothes); nursing care (medication, change of dressings, vital signs); assistance with activities of daily living (eating, dressing, etc.); walks or exercise; naps or time out; reality orientation, sensory awareness, naming; and drawing or quiet games.

SPECIAL ISSUES IN ALZHEIMER'S PROGRAMMING

The purpose of this final section is to summarize the specialized aspects of program development that relate specifically to serving a population primarily composed of Alzheimer's patients. For program staff who know how to plan, implement, and evaluate an adult day care program, this section will address the issues specific to serving Alzheimer's patients.

Staffing

Even though the basic guideline for participant-to-staff ratio in adult day care is 8:1, with dementia participants the ratio will often be 5:1, 3:1, or even as low as 1:1. In some cases, attendance of a new participant or an evaluation of a potential participant might temporarily require a 1:1 ratio. It should be noted, however, that many programs use continuing need for 1:1 staff assistance as the basis for discharge from the program. Although the ratio of participants to staff will vary based on participant needs, type of activity scheduled, and space/building design, nearly all directors of Alzheimer's/dementia day care centers indicate it is imperative to have a low patient-to-staff ratio.

Staff Training

Before being hired or starting work with Alzheimer's patients, staff should be trained in the following areas (for a more detailed review of training see chapter 11):

- Knowledge of various types of dementia: diagnosis, stages, and symptoms.
- Management of persons with dementia.
- General center guidelines.
- Handling specific problems: wandering, incontinence, catastrophic reactions, and crisis situations.
- Ability to deal with special medical situations such as falls or choking. (Staff should be trained in CPR.)
- Communication needs and skills of Alzheimer's patients.
- Being able to assist the caregiver of the Alzheimer's patient, including understanding the effects on the caregiver, common concerns of caregivers, and handling problems with caregivers. Most centers find that caregiver concerns and problems are best handled by a few staff members—the executive/program director or social worker.
- Developing or modifying program activities for Alzheimer's patients.
- Identifying signs of illness or problems that participants cannot articulate.

Space Needs

Alzheimer's patients may need more space per participant than non-dementia participants. This may include either creating room for participants to pace or having a room for participants to withdraw, rest, or have "time out." Many programs feel it is imperative to have large activity space artificially divided into several areas, or one or more rooms specifically set aside for individuals or problem periods. Even in geographic regions that do not have good weather throughout the year, an outdoor space is generally considered a very important adjunct to programming.

Nutrition

A minimum of one midday meal should be provided, meeting one-third of an adult's daily nutritional requirement as established by the food and nutrition board of the National Research Council. Most programs have a mid-morning and mid-afternoon snack. If participants arrive at 7:00 a.m. or earlier, the program may provide breakfast for them, unless it can be definitely ascertained that they had a nutritious meal before arrival. Also special modified diets should be available if required, such as diabetic, low fat, or low sodium diets. "Finger foods" work particularly well, as do foods that can be prepared in separate, small servings.

Many programs contract with another source to provide meals for their participants. If the day care program is hospital-based, meals and all necessary supplies as well as dietary counseling and education can be contracted for and provided by the hospital's dietary department. Some programs contract for meal preparation and delivery from nearby skilled nursing facilities or residential care facilities, while others have developed reciprocal agreements with the nutrition site of Volunteers of America or another organization, thereby providing space for their program and receiving meals for the participants. Still other centers contract with a Meals on Wheels program to supply their lunches or become designated Title III congregate meal sites. Programs report that their contract cost can range from $.50 to $4.00 a meal. (Adult day care centers providing their own meals are now eligible for USDA subsidies.)

Regardless of their source, meals should be attractive, nourishing, and easy to eat for an elderly person who may have dental or swallowing problems and/or diminished taste. The meals may be served in a homelike setting at a table set with plates, cups, napkins, and tableware. Meals and snacks should be served at conventional times. Breakfast may be served between 7:30 and 8:30 a.m. Mid-morning snack and/or a juice break may take place at approximately 9:30–10:30 a.m. Lunch may be served between 12:00 and 1:00 p.m. Mid-afternoon snack and juice time is approximately 3:00–4:00 p.m. All programs should stress to their participants' families the necessity of reporting missed attendance early enough to reduce the waste and expense of meals that cannot be utilized.

Transportation

Transportation is often a difficult and/or expensive problem for day care programs to resolve. In most cases, however, transportation is an essential service for the program to offer. Many centers, as well as families, prefer to have the participant's family provide transportation to and from the program. This not only eliminates the cost of transportation and insurance, but also provides staff with an opportunity to communicate with families regarding the participant. Having families drive participants to the center can be the most comfortable and secure form of transportation. The benefits of having families drive—such as reduced anxiety, shorter transit time, and easier transition to the program—can be offset by the physical and time demands on the family, possible unreliability of the family, and the burden that may be placed on a family. Another alternative to consider is carpooling by family caregivers. Again, this comes with potential problems as well as advantages. Alternative arrangements need to be available for families where the caregiver works or does not drive.

Some areas have public transportation accessible to the caregiver and participant through buses and subways, although the level of dementia of most participants precludes use of these forms of transportation without the strict supervision of a caregiver. Taxi programs such as Dial-A-Ride or Share-a-Ride are often effective but are usually prohibitively expensive. Many drivers need special instructions regarding Alzheimer's patients and have been known to let patients off at the curb rather than seeing them to the door. Another method of providing transportation is through volunteers. The director may keep a list of persons willing to transport participants if an emergency arises. In some cases, families may even be able to pay drivers to get their family member to and from the program.

An alternative to which many centers turn is purchasing a van or coordinating van services with another agency. If a center offers transportation with its own van or minibus, the executive/program director and staff must determine the geographic range that can be served both efficiently and cost effectively. Many centers set a limit on the distance their vehicle will travel, such as offering the service only within a seven-mile radius. Charges range from nothing up to $7 each way depending upon actual costs, subsidy, and regulatory limits. Fees can be paid separately or incorporated into the total program fee. Policies must be developed regarding transportation safety and vehicle maintenance. Consideration must be made for safety devices to protect participants during transportation as well as accommodating participants with physical limitations. States generally have specific requirements for drivers. One strategy used to deal with the staffing pressures resulting from provision of a van service is to hire an individual as a driver/program aide or driver/housekeeper, so that the employee will have other duties as well.

An alternative to having the center purchase its own van is to coordinate with or use an existing van system. This can reduce costs and resources needed for coordination, and allow the staff to concentrate on program activities. If the agency has a contract for van service, the contract should require drivers to meet with center staff for orientation to the needs and behaviors of Alzheimer's victims. The relationship of staff with the van drivers is particularly important because of the difficulties involved in picking up and transporting cognitively impaired individuals. Staff must work closely with drivers. There are numerous problems that must be considered, including that of drivers having to go to a participant's door and leave the van unattended. Drivers must be able to cope with problem behaviors in transit; staff must ensure that participants are taken directly to the center door or their home door so that they do not wander away; and families must deal with billing and scheduling.

Regardless of whether a program runs its own van or contracts out, there is one crucial consideration in having demented participants on a van. Most Alzheimer's/dementia day care programs report that another person in addition to the driver is needed to help if a participant decides to get out of his or her seat and move around the vehicle. This takes another staff member away from direct participant care and can be very costly for the program. Many programs have a transportation aide as a paid staff member or a volunteer.

Regardless of the method used, transportation creates a number of problems, including a drain on staff resources, added expense, the need for increased interorganizational coordination, and increased liability risks (including insurance costs for staff and volunteers). However, transportation is a critical part of a successful Alzheimer's day care program.

CONCLUSION

Specialized program development for Alzheimer's day care provides "successes" for both participants and staff. When program staff members find the right mix of activities for their participants, both the participants and staff will experience increased self-esteem and a sense of accomplishment. Staff will become more comfortable with serving more impaired participants and serving a higher percentage of Alzheimer's patients. Thus, activities and their successful implementation are at the core of an Alzheimer's day care center's operation. They require a significant and ongoing level of attention to ensure that the program is successful for participants, family caregivers, and staff.

10

MANAGING PROBLEM BEHAVIORS AND MEDICAL ISSUES

Managing problem behaviors is perhaps the greatest challenge facing caregivers of Alzheimer's patients. Virtually all Alzheimer's patients have these difficult behaviors, although in varying degrees, because the brain deterioration robs patients of the ability to initiate action or to make adaptations to their environment. Managing problem behaviors is a *process* rather than a formula—there are no easy, universal solutions. Mastery of the process, however, can ensure that most problem behaviors will either disappear or will become less disruptive.

Problem behavior is usually defined on a subjective basis—that is, a problem is whatever seems like an unmanageable behavior to a specific caregiver. But problem behavior can be defined objectively. It is useful to make such an operational definition because the definition will clarify the boundaries of the problem-solving process. One definition of problem behavior is that it exists when a dementia patient exhibits a behavior that causes disruption either to self or others and requires intervention by another person. Thus, a patient who wanders has a problem behavior in an unsecured environment because someone has to watch and/or retrieve the patient. If the environment is secured, wandering is not a problem behavior. The solution to the problem behavior lies in the adaptation of the environment to the patient—not the other way around.

Since Alzheimer's day care is a group program, problem behaviors occur in a group context. Changing problem behaviors, therefore, requires that the whole staff have an understanding and commitment to the problem-solving process. It is wise to hold weekly staff meetings in which the difficult behaviors are introduced and the entire staff participates in the solution process.

The problem-solving process begins with an analysis of the problem behavior.

1. Describe the problem in behavioral terms. Be very specific. The description should be clear enough for an outside observer to understand exactly what's happening.
2. Determine who in the environment has the problem: participant, caregiver, staff, day care group, or more than one of these.
3. Consider the extent of the problem. Since day care is a group model of care, a problem exhibited by one participant will ripple throughout the group as a whole. In analyzing the problem, day care staff must explore the question of how the problem affects the group: Does the behavior affect a small group of participants, or the group as a whole? In what way is the group affected? Do they become distracted? More irritable or agitated?
4. Determine whether the behavior is a sudden onset, a recent problem, or a typical pattern.

When the analysis is finished, staff are ready to move to the next phase of the problem-solving process. The process will be most influenced by whether the problem is a sudden onset or a typical pattern. The following discussion will set up a problem-solving process for each type of problem behavior.

SUDDEN ONSET BEHAVIORS

Managing sudden onset behaviors involves three steps. First, determine the antecedents to the problem—that is, what are the conditions that occurred before the appearance of a problem. Second, design a strategy that will adapt the environment to fit the behavior so that the consequences of the problem are reduced or disappear (the behavior does not necessarily disappear). Third, evaluate the plan. We will discuss each of these steps in turn.

Determining the Antecedents

The Participant's Physical/Emotional Health   In any sudden onset situation, it is imperative that the physical health of the patient be checked. Physical distress caused by medications, acute illness, dehydration, constipation, fatigue, or other physical discomfort are often expressed as behavior problems.

Example: Jim has both expressive and receptive aphasia. Staff have to interpret body language cues to understand his wants and needs. Usually, his messages are clear; today, Jim is pacing with much greater agitation. He angrily refuses his lunch, and he takes a swing at another day care participant. Staff have noted that his forehead is cold and clammy, his hands are cold, and he is sweating profusely. The nurse examines Jim and determines that he is extremely constipated. She calls the doctor and receives an order for milk of magnesia and Fleet's enema. After Jim has had a bowel movement, his behavior returns to the normal patterns.

Changes in the Environment   Pay attention to the size of the group, changes in the staff, excessive stimulation, or addition of new participants or new volunteers.

Example: Marie is very charming and appears to be higher functioning than her Mini-Mental scores indicate. She has severe expressive aphasia but masks the deficit with strong interpersonal skills and the ability to make people join her in playful interactions. Within the last week, staff have noticed that Marie is morose, refuses to join group activity, and has had two combative outbursts with other participants. The staff met as a group and asked the question: Has anything changed in the environment? The discussion revealed that staff members were feeling somewhat overwhelmed themselves because the center had admitted four new participants in one week. All of the new people were very demanding, and there was little time to pursue relationships with the longer time participants. Staff members were feeling more tense, and they were not responding to Marie with the relaxed playfulness she had previously enjoyed.

Tensions at Home   Alzheimer's patients have an "emotional memory." They may not remember the content of a scene but they do remember the tension, anxiety, and anger. These feelings can set the tone of the participant's mood and create a resistance to day care that can last the entire day.

Example: Al arrived at the day care center tense and resistant. His wife, Alice, looked harried and exhausted. The center director met with Alice and asked her to describe, step by step, what it was like to get Al ready for day care. Alice wept as she confessed that she looked forward all week to her two days off. The thought that she might have to give up this respite was unbearable. The center director pointed out that this feeling may have made Alice more anxious when she was getting Al ready. The anxiety was conveyed to Al, who then became frightened, confused, and resistive. The more he resisted, the more anxious Alice became, setting up a vicious cycle that ended with Al's statement: "I'm not going anywhere!"

Communication Problems   Most Alzheimer's patients have communication impairments that severely limit meaningful verbal interactions.
Staff must rely on nonverbal cues—a skill that requires considerable trial
and error, particularly with new participants. When a participant feels he
or she is not understood, behavior problems, such as angry agitation, resistance to activities, and combativeness, may occur.

> Example: Usually, Charles was a very easy-going, cooperative
> participant. He suffered from severe expressive and receptive
> aphasia—talking in a kind of "word salad"—but staff had learned
> his patterns and his nonverbal cues and were able to communi-
> cate with him. A new staff person complained of his combative
> behaviors and resistance to help. She tried to use eye contact and
> a reassuring manner, but to no avail. The center director ob-
> served her interaction and discerned the difficulty. The new staff
> person did not realize that even though Charles had severe apha-
> sia, he was highly verbal and needed acknowledgment for the
> verbalizations. Charles' response to a suggestion such as "Let's go
> to the bathroom" might be "We need to put 10% down before the
> rates rise." The new staff person continued to insist on moving
> toward the bathroom. Charles would escalate his statements
> ("The pipes will fall out, and he does not understand"). These
> nonsequiturs had some meaning to Charles and needed to be ac-
> knowledged first with statements such as, "Charles, I understand
> that we need to put the 10% down, and we do not want the pipes
> to fall out." While echoing his statements, the staff person could
> gently guide him into the bathroom. Echoing the statements had
> a calming effect and acted as a necessary bond of contact be-
> tween staff and Charles.

Designing a Strategy

When the problem behavior is caused by a participant's *physical condition,* the physical condition must be treated. In the case of Jim, his constipation caused the outbursts. When the constipation was resolved, his
former disposition returned. In this case, it is also important to be alert to
Jim's vulnerability to constipation and to discuss with his wife the proper
diet, need for fluids, and need to monitor Jim's bowel movement schedule.

When the behavior is caused by a *change in the environment,* experiments with altering or adapting the environment must be attempted. In
the case of Marie, staff realized that Marie was actually the most visible
but not the only participant who was having difficulties with the admission of the four new participants. In fact, the entire day care community
was feeling some stress. At the staff meeting, the staff designed strategies
for integrating the new people, for working out new teamwork styles, and

for finding creative ways to give one-on-one attention to Marie and others who needed this kind of validation.

When the behavior is caused by *tensions at home,* the social worker or center director will need to counsel the family members and introduce them to the problem-solving process. Families require information about the disease, support for their feelings, and help with experiments to handle behavior problems. When Alice understood how her own anxiety affected Al, she was able to change her style of interaction and reduce his tension.

When the behavior is caused by *communication problems,* depending upon the problem, either the staff should discuss the issue at a group meeting or the social worker or center director should counsel the staff. It is important for staff (1) to understand the nature of the communication deficit (expressive and/or receptive aphasia, anomia, paraphasia, agnosia); (2) to receive feedback about their communication styles; and (3) to be given suggestions and guidance when experimenting with new communication styles. In the situation with Charles, the staff person had mastered some of the communication skills but did not understand how to interact with such a severe expressive/receptive aphasia.

Evaluating the Plan

Evaluation of the strategies is usually incorporated into the regular staff meeting. Staff should participate at every level: analysis, design, evaluation. If a plan has not worked, the problem-solving process should be initiated again. If a behavior is persistently disruptive, escalating in intensity, or threatens the group, the family and physician should be brought into the process. In some cases, medication may reduce or eliminate the problem. In other cases, the staff and family may need to evaluate whether the participant can continue in the day care program.

PROBLEM BEHAVIOR THAT OCCURS TYPICALLY OR REGULARLY

Describing the Pattern of Behavior

Do not look at the behavior as though it is a separate or discrete occurrence. Instead, look at the total pattern and its relationship to the way the participant interacts with his or her environment.

Example: Eloise wandered and paced during three-fourths of her waking day. She sat down only to snooze for a few minutes in a chair, then she was up and about. She was not angry, nor unduly agitated, unless someone attempted to disrupt her pacing. She would not sit down long enough to finish a meal, and she often disrobed in front of other people.

Each of the behaviors could be viewed as a problem, but each behavior was a manifestation of a highly mobile individual whose organic brain changes were manifest in a need to be in almost constant motion. There was no way to change her behavior (medications were ineffective). Staff realized that they first had to understand the smallest nuance of her actions.

Staff members individually and in group discussion compiled a description of her patterns. It was observed, for example, that Eloise followed a very consistent route. She became combative if anyone attempted to change the course of this preset route. But she was cheerful if someone accompanied her on her pacing journey.

Designing Adaptations in the Environment

By experimenting, staff learned that Eloise did not resist help with dressing (when she disrobed) or assistance with toileting if this assistance took place on her route. For example, she would go to the bathroom if she was already pointed in that direction. She became combative, however, when she was pointed the other way.

Eloise ate her meals standing up. Staff provided her with small bites of finger food, and placed her meal at three locations in the center—all on her route.

In the afternoon, Eloise was able to participate in large, focused motor skills activities such as ball toss. Occasionally, she would dance, and she enjoyed music, even though she would pace after a few minutes.

Evaluating the Plan

The evaluation of the plan must include satisfaction for the participant, satisfaction for the entire day care group, and ability of the staff to carry out the plan. In the case of Eloise, the plan worked very well. She enjoyed her day care program, her family received much-needed respite, and staff members were able to manage Eloise's needs without extra effort or stress.

COMMONLY OCCURRING BEHAVIORAL PROBLEMS

The problem-solving process should be applied to any strategy session for behavior management (a checklist is presented in Table 6). For some of the more commonly occurring problems, the need to analyze and to design a strategy is not as demanding or complex because the range of participant reactions is usually predictable. Some suggestions follow for dealing with these more commonly occurring problem behaviors.

TABLE 6　Behavior management checklist

 I. Analyze the problem:
　　A. Describe the problem behaviorally.
 II. Who has the problem:
　　A. Participant _____
　　B. Caregiver _____
　　C. Staff _____
　　D. Day care participants _____
　　E. All of the above _____
 III. Is this behavior:
　　A. Sudden onset _____
　　　　1. What are the antecedents to the problem?
　　　　　　a. Physical or emotional health _____　Describe.
　　　　　　b. Change in environment _____　Describe.
　　　　　　c. Tensions at home _____　Describe.
　　　　　　d. Communication problems _____　Describe.
　　　　2. Design a strategy to adapt the environment to the behavior.
　　B. Long-term typical behavior _____
　　　　1. What is the pattern? Describe in detail using time, place, and person.
　　　　2. Design an adaptation of the environment to accommodate to this behavior.
 IV. Evaluate the plans: Give method, time, and date.

The New Participant's First Days

The first day at a day care center is a frightening and disorienting experience for nearly all Alzheimer's patients. Typically, the participant believes that he or she has really been placed in a residential facility—the day care center is a nursing home in disguise. Anxious behaviors and repetitive questions mask this fear. The new person can be very disruptive to the group, raise staff tension, and reduce staff effectiveness. It is a good idea to plan for each new admittance in advance. Tell the staff what to expect about the person. Remind the staff that the first two weeks are a trial period—a time for close observation.

Assign a staff person to give one-on-one attention to the new person. Sometimes the program director takes on this role. Introduce the new person to every member of the group (participants and staff). Point out similar interests and backgrounds that the participant has in common with other group members ("You are both retired teachers").

Reassure the new person that this is a day program. Everyone—staff included—goes home at night. Say, "Your family will be here to get you soon." However, avoid giving a definite time when the family member will return. "Two hours" can sound like forever to someone who is disoriented to time and place. Use events rather than time to describe when the family will return ("Your wife will pick you up after lunch" or "Your husband will be here after bingo").

Allow the new person to have time alone and to observe rather than participate in activities. Find opportunities to integrate the new person into the group that feels comfortable for him or her ("Come join Esther and Bill for lunch on the patio; I think you will enjoy them—they are both golfers").

Prepare the family members for the adjustment period. Let the family know that it takes about two weeks to a month for the adjustment to be complete. Tell them that many participants believe that the day care center is a nursing home in disguise, so that they will need to remind their patient that this is only a day program. Find a euphemism for the day care center that makes sense to the participant (club, health spa). Tell the family not to overprepare the participant. Suggest that it might be best to get the patient dressed and into the car, and to say, "Here we are at the club," when the day care center is in sight. Too much preparation increases anxiety and resistance.

The Catastrophic Reaction

What It Is   A *catastrophic reaction* is an Alzheimer's patient's negative response to being overwhelmed by stimuli. Behaviorally, it looks like: hitting or threatening to hit; becoming stubborn; saying "no, no, no" to any request; blushing, weeping, looking ashamed; shouting; resisting any assistance or resisting directions; exhibiting sudden agitation or wandering.

When It Occurs   Alzheimer's patients have a difficult time processing stimuli and become confused very easily. The reaction may occur any time a person feels overwhelmed or confused. The following are examples:

- When the participant is asked to make a decision he or she does not have the conceptual skill to make ("Do you want to play bingo in the dining room, or would you rather play cards in the living room?").
- When there is too much noise in the environment (background music, loud laughter, and people coming in and out talking in loud voices).
- When the participant feels rushed. For example, a staff member asks the participant to put his clothes back on after going to the bathroom. The participant is resistant because he is confused, but the staff person continues to say, "Let me put your clothes on." As the participant becomes more resistant, the staff person becomes more intense with the request. This provokes the participant to even greater resistance and possible combativeness.
- When the participant feels that he or she is not understood. For example, a participant who has aphasia tugs at his clothes when he wants to go to the bathroom. If no one responds and helps him, he will wet himself. The shame of the wetting can provoke weeping or angry behaviors in which the emotional memory for the event remains for several hours.

- When someone has a negative reaction to the participant or shouts "Don't do that!" or "No, no, no," or belittles the participant ("I just showed you how to do that. Can't you remember anything?").
- When other participants become angry with the participant, bump into the participant, or belittle him or her. For example, a low functioning participant sits down in the chair that is regularly "claimed" by one of the higher functioning participants. The "owner" of the chair shouts, "Get out of my chair! How dare you!"

How to Prevent the Reaction   Several precautions can be taken to prevent catastrophic reactions. Make eye contact and get the participant's attention before initiating any interaction. Do not come up from behind or shout across the room. Make sure that the environment is free of clutter, excess noise, or confusing stimuli. When one activity is completed, remove materials before launching into another activity.

Speak in slow, reassuring tones, and give the participant plenty of time to process the request. Give tactile and visual prompts and cues in addition to making verbal requests and suggestions. Keep all verbalizations simple, in one- or two-step directions. Ask questions that have a yes or no answer, and do not ask a participant to make complicated decisions. Use the phrase "Let's go to the bathroom now" rather than "Do you want to go to the bathroom now?"

Know the participant group. Prevent potential conflicts among the participants by anticipating problems and using strategies that distract participants from potential conflict.

Rely *primarily* on nonverbal cues or body language to understand and communicate with participants. Respect all nonverbal communication. Take time to pay attention to *any message* from a participant, and be respectful of the attempt to communicate. Avoid *all* negatives. Staff members should avoid saying "no," "stop it," "don't touch that," "come back here," "don't go in there," and similar phrases.

Know yourself. Staff members may be tense and anxious. Alzheimer's patients are extremely sensitive to feelings, and staff tensions can generate tensions among the participant group or individuals. If a staff person or group is feeling anxious, tense, or angry, the staff must plan for a way to reduce tension, such as leaving the group temporarily or trading activities with another staff member.

What to Do if Staff Have Caused a Catastrophic Reaction   Catastrophic reactions can happen quickly and can be very subtle. Many times, staff do not recognize that the resistance they are experiencing is actually nothing more than a catastrophic reaction. It is, therefore, important to learn to identify a catastrophic reaction in each participant. Some will become stubborn; some will become ashamed; others will hit, shout, or become aggressive. Some will talk about wanting to go home, or they may become agitated or begin to wander. Most participants have a characteristic style of response. This style should be identified at staff meetings and case conferences so that all staff and personnel share the observation.

When a catastrophic reaction is recognized, staff should immediately stop the interaction and back off. In some situations, staff can leave the room for a few moments. The staff member should come back later and resume an interaction with the participant. *Act as though nothing has happened before.* Do *not* remind the participant about the past resistance or feelings.

If the interaction is necessary for participant safety (in the middle of toileting, getting dressed), gesture to another staff person to come and take over. The new staff person becomes a *change of face.* The new staff person should enter the scene, make eye contact, and talk to the participant *as though nothing has happened.* The new staff person can use additional distracting strategies ("Hi! We are waiting for you. Here, let me help you finish dressing. We are having a party and everyone is waiting for you.").

In all interactions, as the participant becomes more agitated, staff should use lower, softer voice tone and use a rhythmical style of speech. The speech itself should be soothing. Tone is more important than words.

What to Do if Other Participants Have Caused the Catastrophic Reaction   Make a judgment about which of the participants in an altercation is most distractible. Move between two disputant participants to break their visual awareness of each other. Attempt to distract the *most distractible* of the two. As soon as possible, move the most distractible participant away from the other disputant. Use soothing tones to calm the participant. *Immediately,* another staff person should come over to the other disputant and use calming tones to soothe him or her.

If a participant becomes more combative, abusive, or verbally assaultive, gently move the participant to a quieter location away from the others. Occasionally, the participant cannot be moved easily. In that case, calmly encourage the entire group to move to another area ("Let's all go outside and play ball now").

Anticipate which participants "rub people the wrong way," and set up activities and distractions for the disturbing person that will prevent unwanted intrusion on other people's space.

Behaviors that Disrupt the Group

We assume here that the problem-solving process is applied to all the behaviors listed below. Is the behavior a sudden change or a typical pattern? Describe the behavior in detail. What are the antecedents to its appearance? What changes can be made to lessen the behavior or to adapt the environment so that the behavior is no longer a problem? The discussion will highlight several features that should be given attention in any problem-solving analysis.

The Shouter   What time of day do the episodes occur? What makes the shouting stop? Are there spaces in the day care setting where the shouting can continue but it will not bother anyone (outside)? Is the shouter getting enough attention? How distractible is the shouter? Are there any activities or any roles that will make the shouter feel useful or needed?

The Criticizer   What happens if someone takes the criticism seriously? Is there a role or activity that will make the criticizer feel special? Is the criticism masking low self-esteem and feeling of shame at having lost memory and independence? Can the criticizer be separated from other participants who will feel wounded by the criticism? Are there specific activities that seem to intensify or provoke the criticizing behavior?

The Person Who Bothers Others with Touchy-Feely   Can staff pay more attention to the touchy-feely person and provide more tactile stimulation? Can staff be more vigilant and watch out for an inappropriate touchy-feely encounter with another participant (or staff) and ward it off with distraction before it arises? Are there other stimuli that will be satisfying (folding towels, stacking and unstacking wooden objects, wiping tables, putting hands in warm sudsy water, holding a stuffed animal)?

The Person Nobody Likes   What are the behaviors that are disagreeable to the other participants? Does everyone dislike this person, or are there some neutral persons who don't mind him or her? Can staff place the person next to a more neutral person in each activity? Will staff acceptance of the person persuade any others to accept him or her? Are there any roles or activities that will lessen the disagreeable behaviors?

The Distracter Who Interrupts Activities   When do these distractions occur, and what appears to trigger them? Can the distracter be distracted? What parallel activities can be found to entice the distracter away from the group?

The Person Who Takes Someone Else's Things   Are there times in the day when this behavior is more pronounced? Can the environment be set up so that there are enticing boxes of "things" to rummage through so that other people's things will be left alone? Are there ways to retrieve the other people's possessions without causing a catastrophic reaction? Are there "things" brought by other people that can be placed in hiding or in a less obvious location? Does the person need more attention or a different kind of activity?

The Person Who Eats Someone Else's Food   Is there a way to arrange the tables so that the person is not sitting with highly functioning people who will notice and strongly object to the behavior? Can supervision be available at all times when food is placed on the table?

The Person Who Refuses to Participate   Is there a role, activity, or way to make the day care experience meaningful to the person? Can the activity be brought to the individual rather than having him or her come to the activity (perhaps by surrounding the person with a craft project as though he or she had agreed to join in)? Are there companions at the day care center who will make an activity more enticing or palatable ("Come join Al and Dick to play cards. They need you.")? Does the person feel comfortable just watching, and is there a way to help him or her feel included while watching ("What did you think of that catch, Lee?")?

The Person Who Is Angry and Agitated Does the person feel "heard" and understood? Is the anger masking depression, confusion, despair, or shame? Is there a way to help the person ventilate feelings? Is there a physical activity that will siphon off some of the angry energy and distract the person? Is there a way to raise the person's self-esteem? Are there roles he or she can perform and feel good about? What provokes the anger and what calms it?

Wandering Behaviors

Wandering is a common occurrence in day care settings. But wandering may not be the problem. Instead, it may be a symptom of a catastrophic reaction, or it may indicate that the participant needs to go to the bathroom or is in physical discomfort. Wandering may also occur when the participant feels lost or useless or anticipates being picked up to go home. When wandering is a symptom of another problem, it is important to tend to the real problem (take the participant to the bathroom; find activities that will enhance self-esteem and will distract the participant from lonely feelings).

Wandering itself may be the problem behavior, especially when the participant continually tries to leave the premises, bolts and runs away, or is in a state of heightened agitation. The process for behavior problem solving can be applied to wandering. Several suggestions for coping with wandering problems follow.

- Make sure that every wandering participant wears an identifying bracelet and a name tag with an address of the day care center. A current photo should be part of the client's record.
- Camouflage exits through the use of large screens or visual cues or discourage families and staff from using the most obvious exits. (Any camouflage attempts must meet fire marshal's approval.)
- Remove items that may suggest the desire to go out, such as coats, hat, or purse.
- Try to identify preliminary signs of wandering or agitation at the earliest possible time.
- Distract the participant with highly focused activities, such as folding laundry, sing-alongs, ball toss, or parachute ball.
- Monitor the group closely during arrival and departure and during emergencies.
- Assign a staff person to watch all potential wanderers at all times. This assignment can be rotated among all the staff.

- Use door fasteners and signals that will delay exits (if the fire marshal approves) and will signal when someone opens the door. While buzzers and other sound devices may be distracting, they will provide an important backup to visual monitoring.

If the participant is highly agitated, try to engage him or her in activities that reduce anxiety and drain off energy, such as ball toss, taking a walk with staff, or dancing. Make sure the participant drinks enough liquid and does not become dehydrated. Reduce noise and confusion. Check that there are no problems with medications. Set up indoor and outdoor spaces that are secure and allow for safe wandering. Finally, toileting may be appropriate.

Once a participant wanders out a door, he or she is potentially in danger. When staff attempt to bring the participant back onto the premises, participants often have catastrophic reactions. Staff need to remain calm in voice tone and body posture and need to avoid physically restraining the wanderer. Ask the participant if staff can join him or her for the walk. Ask as though this is a pleasant activity. When the time feels right, suggest, "Why don't we go inside now? I'm getting thirsty, aren't you?" or "I'm cold—let's go inside." If this does not work, another staff person can take over and can try a similar strategy (this is called "change of face"). Walkie-talkies with a two-mile range may be useful to keep a staff member who is with a client outside the building in contact with the center.

A participant may continue to resist coming back to the center. The staff member needs to stay with the participant even if it means walking a few paces behind. Before leaving the premises, alert another staff member that you are accompanying the participant. Sometimes another staff member can get in a car, drive to the participant, walk up to him or her as a "new face," and convince him or her to return to the center.

Unfortunately, nearly all Alzheimer's day care centers need to address the problem of a participant wandering off. No matter how rigorous a center's security system is, participants tend to find ways to get out through a door temporarily left open or through other unexpected means. Centers must have an established procedure for instances when a participant wanders off. When it is noticed that a participant is missing, the staff person should alert another staff member and proceed to look for the missing person around the entire program area. If staffing permits, another staff member can drive around the immediate area. Specific staff members should be assigned different locations to be searched, while a coordinator remains available to all staff. If possible, volunteers and other available individuals should be asked to help with the search. If the person cannot be located within a few minutes, police should be notified. Caution: do not spend too much time looking before notifying the police. Participants have been known to move amazingly quickly in open space. Copies of photographs of the participant and a written description should be prepared for searchers. In addition, do not hesitate to contact the family and ask for suggestions as to where the participant could be heading. The well-being of the wanderer must be the highest priority for center staff.

Hallucinations/Delusions and Paranoia

Hallucinations, delusions, and paranoia are all beliefs that have no basis in fact. *Hallucinations* involve unreal sensory experiences; *delusions* are beliefs that persist even though they are contrary to fact. *Paranoia* is a type of delusion because it is a blaming belief that cannot be assuaged by facts.

The problem-solving process should be applied to these behaviors to determine if the belief is a symptom of another problem that must be attended to first. In handling delusions, hallucinations, and paranoia, it is very important for staff to maintain a calm, reassuring manner. Do not try to argue with the participant. There is no way to talk him or her out of the belief. Arguing will often provoke catastrophic reactions. The participant will also think staff members are in collusion with the tormenters. Instead of arguing, determine the underlying feeling that prompts the false belief. Fear caused by confusion, loneliness, depression, and feelings of abandonment can cause these beliefs.

Find a way to offer support without making the participant think that you don't believe him or her.

> Example: Olive says, "I must go downstairs to see mother now." Staff respond, "Your family knows where you are, and your lunch is waiting. Let's eat lunch first." Or when John is frightened about the man with the knife who is behind the door, a staff member responds, "Here, take my hand, and we will walk out together. The man won't hurt you if we are together."

A participant may simply need to be reassured that everything is all right, that the staff has everything under control. Sometimes participants will respond to factual material.

> Example: Art, age 94, becomes agitated every afternoon. He "knows" that his family needs him and he must get into the car and go to them. He is convinced that they live only a short distance away. He persists with this belief despite the use of distraction strategies. Each afternoon, staff members show him his chart. They point out that they have the name, address, and telephone number of his son. "Yes, yes, that is my son all right." Staff members then say, "Art, if anything is wrong with someone in your family, your son Sandy will call us immediately. You know he will do that for you." Art responds, "Yes, I'm sure he will." In this example, Art still maintains the delusion, but the strategy

reassures him that things are probably all right at home. He is then able to participate in activities.

Incontinence

Incontinence may be an intermittent occurrence or a regular problem. There are also varying levels of incontinence ranging from "needs reminders" to "needs supervision" to "needs assistance" to "must wear diaper at all times."

Even for the participant who wears diapers at all times, a toilet schedule can be an effective strategy to reduce incontinence. Setting up the toilet schedule requires understanding the toileting patterns of each participant. A simple charting of times for urination and defecation can be maintained for a three-day period. That observation period should be sufficient to set up a toileting routine for any of the levels.

An assessment of the incontinence problem should cover two main areas. First, it should include an exploration of physical problems. Does the participant have any chronic illnesses, such as diabetes or Parkinson's disease, that can make it difficult for the participant to go to the bathroom? Does the participant have a urinary tract infection or a physical problem that leads to loss of bladder control? Is the participant taking a medication that can cause incontinence? Is the participant dehydrated?

Second, the assessment should explore memory or coordination problems. Has the participant forgotten the physical sensations that indicate a full bladder? Is the participant unable to communicate the need to go to the bathroom? Has the participant forgotten what to do while in the bathroom? Can the participant sit down on the toilet without assistance? Is clothing too complicated to get up and down or on and off? Is the participant unable to find the bathroom?

To lessen the incontinence problem, there are several steps that may be helpful.

- Select furniture and floor coverings that are washable and impervious to urine.
- Locate bathrooms close to activity and meal sites and be sure they are well marked.
- Select clothing that is easy to get on and off.
- Keep a change of clothes on hand for each participant.
- Learn the participant's pattern of urination and defecation, and give proper cues and prompts at bathroom time.
- Maintain a toileting schedule or checklist for staff.
- Assign staff to specific participants, ensuring that toileting is equally shared by all staff.
- Properly train staff in toileting techniques and incontinence, including using verbal and physical prompts and hands-on assistance.

- Alert the family to possible medical problems, and ensure that the participant sees a physician.
- Make sure the family knows about incontinent undergarments and how to use them.
- Make sure assistance is given to individuals needing toileting before they leave at the end of the day.
- Discuss effects of medications with the participant's physician.
- Make sure the participant drinks adequate amounts of liquids—five to eight glasses daily.
- Make sure the participant urinates when taken to the toilet. Turn on a faucet and let water run for a while if the participant cannot relax his or her sphincter.
- If the participant has an accident, be sure to wash skin thoroughly, provide a change of clothes, and clean the floor or furniture immediately. Cleaning incontinent patients should be done quickly, but with dignity and reassurance.

Sundowner Reactions

When day care programs extend beyond 3:00 p.m., the *sundowner reaction* among participants is very common. This reaction intensifies during the winter months when the days become dark early, and it can begin as early as immediately after lunch in some participants. The reaction is characterized by agitation and preoccupation with going home. Sometimes, over half the participants are peering out the windows, waiting for their family member or their ride to appear.

To cope with sundowner reaction, it is best to set up a group activity that requires focused attention. A strong group feeling and absorbing activity will allay most sundowner behaviors. Plan a bowling tournament, a sing-along, a dance, or a parachute ball.

This is also a good time to have a parallel activity with one or two small groups. Card games, word games, or repetitive activities such as rolling balls of yarn can be effective in reducing late afternoon agitation.

MEDICAL ISSUES

It is important to remember that persons with Alzheimer's disease have the same probability of having other illnesses or needing additional medical treatment or medications as other older persons. Programs must have the proper staff, as well as have policies and procedures in place, to cope with all ongoing medical issues and emergencies. Each of these issues will be addressed below.

Staffing Issues

As indicated in chapter 5, having the proper health care personnel for a program can be very problematic given funding constraints and/or a program philosophy that emphasizes a social day care model. While a nurse can handle most program health care issues, many programs do not have a nurse available on a full-time basis. Programs should have appropriate health care professionals, including nurses, internists, neurologists, and psychiatrists on staff or available as consultants to deal with day-to-day health care issues, medical emergencies, and medication management.

Medical Conditions

Programs must set up policies concerning patients who are ill with colds, the flu, and other infectious diseases, and be attuned to rapid changes in patient health status or behavior. Most programs require patients with communicable illnesses to stay home since they may not be able to maintain proper hygiene or avoid infecting other participants, much less be able to participate actively in group activities. Rapid changes in a health condition warrant review by a health care professional at the earliest possible time to identify any underlying illness or potential problem that would limit a participant's functioning in the program.

As persons with Alzheimer's disease progress through their disease, they will lose the ability to communicate about how they feel. Caregivers and staff must become aware of the changes in behavior that could indicate a change in the health of the participant. For example, increasing agitation might indicate pain. Reluctance to be taken to the bathroom or changes in the pattern of incontinence could indicate a urinary tract infection. Lethargy or increased confusion could indicate a chest infection, including pneumonia. When behavior changes occur, it is important to consider these possibilities to avoid overlooking a problem that could be taken care of easily.

Many dementia patients have increasing difficulty swallowing. They also may forget how to chew properly. These participants can still attend a day care center successfully with some planning and extra attention at meal time. Chopping food or adding supplements, such as Ensure, can help maintain the participant's nutrition intake.

It can be useful to monitor participant's weight and blood pressure. A certified nurse's aide will have had training in these procedures if a licensed nurse is not available. The local public health nurse or a home health agency may be able to donate an hour or two twice a month to assist the staff in these activities. While patients with Alzheimer's often seem healthier than the general aged population, they are still subject to the usual effects of age, including hypertension. Treating elevated blood pressure can prevent additional complications, such as a stroke.

If the center has a nurse, that person may also provide invaluable help to families by teaching them how to set up the home environment to deal with bathing, incontinence, or even bed-making problems. If there is no nurse on staff, a home health agency may be able to arrange a home visit by a nurse and an occupational therapist to teach the family how to give the care needed at home.

Medical Emergencies

A center must have procedures in place to address a medical emergency. Regardless of the attention and expertise of center staff, participants will fall, have seizures, or have some other form of medical emergency. All staff must know their specific duties in the case of an emergency. A communication system must be in place to contact the nearest emergency medical care team or police, and emergency telephone numbers should be located at all telephones. This emergency medical plan should be written down, presented in the initial staff and volunteer training, and reviewed at least once a year with all staff. Each participant should have as part of their chart a medical record, list of medications, and emergency contacts.

All staff should be trained in first aid and how to perform cardiopulmonary resuscitation (CPR). Staff should know how to recognize and deal with an obstructed airway since that is one of the most common emergencies they will need to address. Training can be obtained through the Red Cross First Aid or CPR classes or through the American Heart Association. Many local hospitals and medical clinics also provide training classes that are open to the public. Some centers have found it useful to have a staff member take the instructor's course so that they can provide their own training in-house.

Medication Management

What types of medications are given and how they are administered or supervised will be determined by the program philosophy and by licensing guidelines. While some programs have established policies prohibiting the administration of medications, most programs deal with the medication needs of participants. Medication policies, procedures, and guidelines should address who will be responsible for administering medications, who is in charge of medications, where they will be stored to protect them from accidental ingestion by another participant, who is responsible for communicating with the family and physician regarding changes needed, and how medications left at the center after discharge or outdated medications will be destroyed. If a nurse is not at the center each day, a staff member or on-call health care professional who can supervise over-the-counter and prescription medications needs to be designated.

For specific information on medications for Alzheimer's patients, particularly those used for managing behavior, we recommend obtaining additional information from pharmacological references and experts in the field. One medication issue that should be discussed with families is whether participants have any difficulties swallowing pills. Many people who can swallow anything else without problems have difficulty swallowing pills. They may need to have a pill crushed and mixed in applesauce or jelly. Inexpensive pill crushers can be purchased at most pharmacies. It is a good idea to contact the pharmacist to make certain that the pill can be crushed and mixed. Some medications are designed to dissolve in the intestines and should not be crushed. Many medications have liquid forms, or the pharmacist can make up a suspension that can be given in place of a pill.

CONCLUSION

Successful management of problem behaviors and medical issues requires good team interaction, well-developed problem-solving skills, a strong imagination, patience, maturity, and experience. Even the most successful day care teams can find their repertoire of solutions for problem behaviors running dry for a particular participant. Sometimes, nothing works. If that happens, family and physician must be brought into the process. There are participants who cannot be managed in a day care setting. Fortunately, these participants are the exception. Most participants will thrive in a setting that uses behavior management strategies that respect the individual and make adaptations to the special needs of Alzheimer's patients.

11

TRAINING

An effective training program is an important part of a successful Alzheimer's day care center. In order to manage people suffering from Alzheimer's disease, staff must use a range of skills that are not commonly found among new recruits to staff positions. Staff must learn how to communicate with the aphasias, how to adapt to the apraxias and agnosias, and how to use their own personality as an effective tool in managing problem behaviors. Staff must adapt the environment so that it is safe for a very old population, and they should be able to differentiate between normal and abnormal aging. Since day care is a group effort, it is very important that staff receive ongoing training in team building and group problem solving.

Training should be divided into three components: orientation to the program, specialized in-service training on topics related to understanding dementia, and team building/problem solving. Each component uses a different format, but all share a common set of goals and objectives.

GOALS AND OBJECTIVES OF THE TRAINING PROGRAM

There are at least three basic goals of a training program for Alzheimer's day care staff:

- To create a training model that emphasizes the worth and value of day care participants, staff, and family members.
- To develop and reinforce teamwork and group problem-solving skills.
- To teach staff how to enhance the highest functioning of each par-

ticipant by using planned activities, behavior management strategies, and other appropriate interventions.

To achieve these goals, the training program has several objectives. First, it should give staff a working knowledge of Alzheimer's disease and dementia through a specified number of didactic and hands-on experiences. Second, it should contain didactic sessions intended to develop staff alertness to changes of aging (such as incontinence, osteoporosis, or heart/hearing/vision deficits) so that staff can set up and follow through health and safety plans. Third, it should feature group discussions to reinforce a teamwork/problem-solving style in developing behavior management care plans for each participant. Fourth, training should build staff ability to take on responsibility for carrying out a routine that adheres to a structure but has the flexibility to respond to changes in participants, group dynamics, or emergencies. Fifth, it should continually improve staff skills in engaging participants in activities. Sixth, training should help staff develop a professional but warm, caring attitude in working with families. Finally, a good training program should improve staff knowledge and, ultimately, staff morale.

ORIENTATION TRAINING FOR NEW STAFF

Working with a dementia population is a highly unusual experience for most people. Until they have had direct experience with Alzheimer's patients, it is hard for them to imagine the energy, resourcefulness, humor, and teamwork that will be needed in every member of the staff. For this reason, the orientation sessions that work best use a combination of didactic material and hands-on experience with close supervision. In designing the orientation session, it is important to include a simplified taste of every element of the program that a new person needs to know before beginning to work on the floor with participants. A suggested format for the didactic session that provides a broad, thematic overview is presented in Table 7.

At the end of the didactic session, trainees should be assigned to a seasoned staff member for an orientation to the participants and the program. It is often useful to provide the seasoned staffer with a checklist to make sure that every important detail is covered. A checklist should include the following statements, along with the date and names of new person and trainer (each statement should be checked off as it is covered in the orientation):

New staff member has been introduced to every participant.
New staff member has seen demonstration of behavior management strategies for the following participants: _____.
New staff member knows where activity supplies are stored.
New staff member knows where Depends, wipes, etc., are stored.

TABLE 7 Overview of Alzheimer's disease, day care, and the program

---

I. Introduction
   A. What is day care and Alzheimer's day care?
   B. Brief history of this program
   C. Who is who in the milieu—especially, who is your supervisor?
II. Philosophy of the program
   A. The difference between "babysitting" and a therapeutic program
   B. The mission and purpose of the program
   C. The right of self-determination and how and when parts of that "right" are delegated to staff
III. What is dementia?
   A. Global brain dysfunction, or an acquired cognitive impairment
   B. Difference between *dementia, delirium, depression,* and *amnesia*
IV. What is Alzheimer's disease?
   A. Statistics about Alzheimer's disease
      • 3%of elderly between ages 65–74
      • 18.7% of elderly between ages 75–84
      • 47.2% of elderly ages 85 and over
   B. Alzheimer's disease is about 60% of the dementias
      Multi-infarct dementia is about 20%
      There are about 70 other types
   C. Review of recent literature
      • No known cause
      • No known cure
      • Progressive and terminal
      • Use a graphic to show the changes in the neurons—the formation of plaques and tangles
V. Impact of changes in the brain (brain graphic that shows the global impact on the selective parts of the brain)
   A. Hippocampus—impact on recent memory
      • Recent memory orients people to time, place, person
      • Memories range from a few seconds to about 15 minutes—use names of participants and give examples
   B. Changes in vision
      • Give trainees a plastic bag and have them look through it to illustrate the vision change
      • Have trainees block off their peripheral vision by circling their own eyes with rounded hands
      • Trainer stands beside a trainee who is looking straight ahead. Trainer says: "You can see me with peripheral vision, but the dementia participant cannot. This means that you must communicate ONLY when you are in front of the participant and have direct eye contact."
      • Trainer stands at a distance from one of the trainees and says: "Now, I will call you by name. See how you look at me and notice me. But the participants will NOT respond this way. Therefore, do NOT try to get their attention in this way. Shouting or yelling across the room will also cause agitation in the group."
      • Reinforce this important point by then walking over to the trainee and again demonstrating eye-to-eye contact
   C. Changes in language
      • Aphasias: *expressive aphasias* and *receptive aphasias*—explain what they are and that a participant might have one or both. Use examples of actual participants in program.

(Table continues on following page)

TABLE 7   Overview of Alzheimer's disease, day care, and the program (*Continued*)

- Ask the group how this deficit will affect their interaction with the participants
  —use of body language
  —use of more than one stimulus to communicate (e.g., visual, auditory)
  —use of calm, reassuring tone
  —use of one-step directions
- Demonstrate, using role play, how to assist specific participants with sitting in a chair, putting on a jacket, using the toilet

D. Point to the other areas of the brain that are affected and give an example of how this condition impacts program
- Visuospatial—example is not being able to find the bathroom or not recognizing three dimensions
- Sensory-motor—example is not being able to follow visual instructions in the exercise program, so staff must help some participants move their body parts until participant's memory and skill are triggered
- Judgment, alertness, personality, concentration, attention span—example is repeating the importance of eye contact; expressing the goal of expanding the attention span to 30- or 45-minute segments and demonstrating how to engage a participant in an activity and then to reengage him or her

VI. Day Care Program Day
A. Philosophy
B. Organization of the program day
C. Staff schedules
D. Group activities
E. Individual activities
F. Meals
G. Transportation
H. Program and participant record keeping and forms

VII. The Catastrophic Reaction
A. What is it? The definition: When a participant becomes overwhelmed by stimuli or something in the environment, he or she responds in a characteristic way that looks like:
- Hitting
- Yelling, shouting
- Blushing, weeping
- Stubborn refusal, saying "no, no"
B. What are the causes? Use examples in the day care environment and include:
- Tension or angry tone of voice
- Saying "no" to participants or shouting at them
- Asking questions they cannot answer
- Too much ambient noise
- Rushing the participant
C. What do you do if it happens?
- Use a calm, reassuring tone
- Use a minimum of words
- Back off—come back later
- Use a "change of face"—let another staff person come in and take over
- Move the group to a larger space—take the group for a walk, begin a sing-along, or start an activity that is calming

TABLE 7 Overview of Alzheimer's disease, day care, and the program (*Continued*)

VIII. Other Commonly Occurring Behavioral Problems
    A. New participant's first days
    B. Behaviors that disrupt the group
       • The shouter
       • The criticizer
       • The person who bothers others with touchy-feely
       • The person nobody likes
       • The distracter who interrupts activities
       • The person who takes someone else's things
       • The person who eats someone else's food
       • The person who refuses to participate
       • The person who is angry and agitated
    C. Wandering behaviors
       • Emergency procedures if a participant wanders
       • Techniques in approaching wanderers
    D. Hallucinations, delusions, and paranoia
    E. Incontinence
       • Causes
       • Toileting procedures
       • Cleaning procedures
    F. Sundowner reactions
  IX. Medical Issues
    A. General medical conditions
    B. Medical emergencies
    C. First aid and CPR training requirements
    D. Medication management
       • Program philosophy
       • Staff responsibility
       • Procedures
   X. Personnel and Center Administration
  XI. Facility Emergency Procedures and Security
 XII. Training Requirements of Staff

New staff member has seen toileting for the following participants:
_____

New staff member has been assisted to fill out daily progress notes.
New staff member has been introduced to family members.

Understanding Normal Aging

Staff should receive at minimum one session on normal aging. Ideally, this session is presented by a medical professional. The topics should include: demographics on aging; functional disability vs. functional limitation; chronic vs. acute conditions; physiological changes associated with aging (skin, brain, bone mass, immune system, homeostatic system, sensory systems, common diseases); and the importance of diet and exercise.

Understanding Alzheimer's Disease and Dementia

This knowledge area should be taught in several sessions, which can include the following elements:

- Specifics about the physiology of dementia and Alzheimer's
- Functional levels—implications for programs
- Differentiation among dementia, depression, delirium
- Use and understanding of assessment tools
- Development and revision of a care plan for dementia
- The basics about activity programs (philosophy, understanding the format, the role of each staff person, how to engage and reengage participants in activities)
- Understanding the family—the stages of grief and the manifestations of grief
- Personal care, especially handling incontinence
- Assisting with activities of daily living, especially eating, walking, transferring
- Basic safety precautions

Handling Communication Problems and Managing Problem Behaviors

These training segments can be the subject of weekly staff sessions designed as a group problem-solving exercise in addition to forming part of the orientation program. The by-product of this experience is team building. The segments should have a staff leader who is trained in brainstorming techniques. The format can be as follows:

1. Staff leader asks the group which participants have problem behaviors that need group attention. Usually staff will agree on who should have priority attention for the session.
2. Staff group assembles in a well-lit room. They are seated around a table or in a circle so that all can face each other.
3. Leader has a white board, black board, or flip chart.
4. Leader explains the structure of the meeting:
   a. Step one will be to identify the problems. Each statement will be written on the board. The group will then reach agreement about the description of the problem.
   b. Step two will be the identification of the antecedents to the behavior. What are the causes or triggers? Leader lists all observations on the board.
   c. Step three will be the analysis of the problem. All suggestions can be listed—no matter how odd or unworkable they may seem. When all suggestions are listed, the group looks at each one. Leader leads the

group in discussion.

d. Step four will be the development of the plan. Leader will write the plan on the board. Group consensus will be solicited. Plan is changed until group consensus is reached.

e. Step five is a plan for evaluation. Leader writes evaluation plan on the board and obtains group consensus.

When this kind of group problem solving is operating on a regular basis, staff burnout ceases to be a major issue because staff feel they are not only "heard" but they are also an important part of the solution. There really is no magical solution to managing problem behaviors; it requires a systematic effort as outlined above.

IN-SERVICE TRAINING

Regularly scheduled in-service training that meets the needs of the individual should be provided to both staff members and volunteers. While an orientation to the program and previous job experience will definitely influence the ability of all staff members to contribute to the function of the center, on-the-job training will probably be one of the most effective ways for staff to learn how to deal with dementia patients in general and with the center's participants in particular. Under the direction and watchful eye of staff who have more seniority and experience, new staff can quickly learn the specific idiosyncrasies of the different program participants and the day-to-day structure of the center. Since a probation period is generally used in most program settings, it can be used in a very positive way as a training period for new staff. This will allow the activity coordinator to work closely with new staff members, providing guidance and assistance while ensuring that participants receive the highest quality of care possible. Regardless of whether training during this introductory period is structured or not, new staff will learn a great deal just by observing and participating in the day-to-day operation of the center.

In-service training may include presentations by staff members or guest speakers, films and videotapes about specific problems of Alzheimer's patients, or lecture/discussions about safety issues. Always useful and informative are updates on stress management ideas and techniques for staff members, families, and caregivers. The better prepared the staff members and volunteers are to do their jobs, the happier and better able they are to express the philosophy of the center to the participants, caregivers, and general public. In addition, appropriate and ongoing training has been shown to reduce staff turnover and increase job satisfaction.

As staff continue to work at the center, it is important to improve and maintain their knowledge, technical expertise, and morale. Appropriate training and support not only improve the quality of the staff, but often contribute to staff retention. All good programs encourage staff development and training.

There are a number of ways in which individuals can learn through in-service programs. In-service sessions may be individualized or conducted in group settings. In-service training should be developed in conjunction with staff and be implemented on an ongoing basis. Sessions intended to build staff *knowledge* can include a number of topics, such as "Alzheimer's Disease and Related Dementias," "Diagnostic Techniques," "Adult Day Care," "Social-Psycho-Biological Dimensions of Aging," and "Caregiver Issues." In other sessions, staff can particularly work on *skills*, such as CPR, first aid, communication with dementia patients, transfer, participant assessment, care plan development, family interactions, physical and art therapeutic activities, counseling, and therapies. While knowledge and skills are very important areas in which to provide staff training opportunities, it is equally important to allow staff to work on *attitudinal and personal characteristics.* Even the best staff can have incorrect perceptions of Alzheimer's patients or may need reinforcement of their interaction with participants and families. All too often, staff can be somewhat paternalistic, patronizing, or pitying. In addition, many individuals have a great deal of anxiety or fear of dementia patients or specific activities. It is important that staff have an opportunity to develop their own self-knowledge and skills in dealing with both participants and their fellow staff. Again, it should be emphasized that staff training, whether it be on-the-job training or in-service training, is highly individual.

TEAM BUILDING/PROBLEM SOLVING

A good training program provides significant benefits to the program itself, its participants, and staff. A key consideration in training is how the executive/program director and other staff serve as role models for new staff and volunteers. It is interesting that the style and approach of an executive/program director can enhance the training environment, as well as the program as a whole. In addition, a program should have weekly sessions or staff meetings, a portion of which is devoted to group problem solving. This third component of a comprehensive training program is the key ingredient in building teamwork and in developing positive staff interactions. Group problem solving also builds the assertive skills staff need to have when they encounter the dozens of unexpected events and behaviors that occur in a typical day. Finally, these sessions enrich the program and give staff an awareness of the broader implications of their work.

Volunteers and students are also in need of training. They should be involved in the same type of orientation programs as paid staff. In fact, volunteers and students may need more on-the-job training than staff if they have no previous experience working with the elderly and/or Alzheimer's patients. It is imperative that volunteers and students be monitored closely in terms of their knowledge levels and ability to work with participants and staff. Just as with paid staff, not all volunteers and students find Alzheimer's day care to be an appropriate place for them.

CONCLUSION

When training is added to the Alzheimer's day care program, staff skills will be constantly refurbished and validated. Training can be conceptualized as having three distinct components. First is an orientation for new staff, including all the information a new staff member needs to know in order to avoid becoming overwhelmed. Second are regular in-service training sessions that can be offered by expert staff as well as outside trainers and professionals. And third are weekly sessions devoted to team building and problem solving. Besides specific training programs, the scheduling of workdays, provision for staff communication time, and staff retreats, can all be used to promote staff development. It is important that all levels of trainees and all training sessions be evaluated to gauge the amount of information that has been learned and retained. This will ensure that the director and other staff do not make incorrect assumptions regarding an individual's knowledge about a specific topic or issue. Training has obvious implications for upgrading and finetuning staff skills. Thorough and ongoing training in the nature of dementia and techniques for working with Alzheimer's patients can also be an important part of improving staff satisfaction and feeling of mission, and preventing burnout.

12

WORKING WITH THE FAMILY

The purpose of this chapter is to help the reader identify the needs of the families served by an Alzheimer's day care program and to learn what day care programs can do to assist these families.

FACTORS THAT MAKE LIFE DIFFICULT FOR FAMILY CAREGIVERS

Disease Duration and Patient Deterioration

The first difficulty comes from two specific characteristics of the process of dementia that are seldom found in other diseases. These are the duration of the disease and the deterioration of the patient. It is hard to take care of someone for what feels like forever, and that may, in fact, be as long as from 5 to 15 (or more) years, when caregiving seems to become a way of life. What makes it worse is the invariable deterioration caused by the disease, where the behavior of the demented person becomes increasingly unadult-like. With a long, debilitating disease like tuberculosis, patients were still left alert, often attractive, personable, and appreciative. When the demented patient loses both mental alertness and personality, the essential components of adult interactions and responsibilities, and when an adult can no longer function independently in the most basic of life's functions and, equally important, cannot show even the slightest appreciation for the effort that others put forth on his or her behalf, those stresses are magnified.

Family's Burden of Care

The second difficulty comes with the placement of the primary burden of care. When a family member has cancer, for instance, early-stage caregiving is often limited to providing transportation, medications, and emotional support; later on, when the patient is most ill, care is often provided by professional health care workers: doctors and nurses or other medical staff or medically supervised assistants. That care is also usually paid for by third-party payers, an insurance company or a government program. When the disease is a dementia, the primary burden of both providing and paying for care is usually on the family member. Not only are family members not trained as caregivers, but also they must assume those responsibilities formerly borne by the patient. An adult child who is used to the parent as a source of wisdom, advice, or emotional or financial support, or a spouse who may have relied on the patient for meal or tax preparation, must now not only provide basic care for the parent or spouse, but must also perform those now neglected tasks himself or herself.

Emotional Baggage

Another difficulty is the emotional baggage the family caregiver carries in relation to the demented person. That emotional baggage comes from the entire previous relationship with the patient and may include love and respect, disagreements and squabbles, expectations and obligations, bitterness and regret, and the whole gamut of feelings. For example, family members have expectations of certain degrees and types of behavioral competence in their relatives, and family members usually feel impatience and frustration at the demented patient's loss of competence. Family members may be convinced—or may try to convince themselves—that their patient could do better if he or she would only try, or would only pay more careful attention. They often want to deny that a disease process is occurring and that their family member can no longer do what he or she could do before, no matter how hard he or she tries. Patients may also feel frustrated both at their loss of competence and their perceptions of their caregiver's impatience. Patient anxiety and stress are likely to contribute to further deterioration of competence.

If the patient was a less-than-perfect parent, a caregiving child may unconsciously (or consciously) attempt to retaliate or, as is often seen, go to extreme lengths to overcompensate, to prove the child a better caregiver of the parent than the parent was to the child. If the parent typically withheld approval from the child, the adult child may overcompensate—try to be a superhuman caregiver—in a final (and usually unsuccessful) attempt to obtain that approval. Whatever the motivation, this puts enormous stress on the caregiving child and will invariably result in failure because the parent is now too demented to be an observer of the adult child's attempts, even if the parent were emotionally inclined to dispense appreciation and approval or acknowledge his or her own past failings. Professional caregivers don't (or shouldn't) have this baggage with their clients.

Adult children rarely anticipate that their parents will become dependent. They expect that their parent will always be parent-like, or at least adult-like, and when the reality is otherwise, the adult child is likely to feel betrayed, angry, and disappointed.

Loss

If the family caregivers are spouses, they have lost the personality of the spouse. Spousal caregivers have lost their companions in life; they have lost their roles as half of a functioning couple. They have lost their partners in such tasks as cooking, gardening, and making repairs and decisions. They may have lost their nutrition consultant, financial manager, housekeeper, or driver. They have lost their freedom to come and go as they wish. They may have lost a sexual partner.

If the caregivers are adult children, they have lost an authoritative parent, perhaps the person who loves them no matter what, or a most important source of pride and approval. They have lost someone who would always listen to woes or offer support. They have lost, perhaps, a "bad" parent to despise and blame for their own failures. They have lost the repositories of their personal childhood histories and of family histories. They may experience themselves as being emotionally orphaned, while having to provide care for the physical body of their parent.

Time Off

Patients' deterioration and caregivers' frustration also, of course, make caring for the patient difficult for the professional caregiver, but the professional usually can leave at the end of the shift. The family member must not only be responsible 24 hours a day, but must be on duty 16 to 24 hours, often after working a full-time job and taking care of other family responsibilities.

Implications

Unlike many (but not all) other diseases, in Alzheimer's disease and other dementias the unit needing care is the family. If the family is to continue bearing the burden and providing most of the care and resources, that family must receive the help and support it needs. Day care is one source of support and help; the degree of that assistance can be enhanced by paying special attention to family needs.

CATEGORIES OF FAMILY NEEDS

Basic emotional needs of caregiving families fall into three categories: respite (time off without worries), information and referrals (where to get help), and understanding of their own emotional reactions to the caregiving situation.

Respite

Basically, respite is what Alzheimer's day care provides—time off from the burden of caregiving, without having to worry that the demented person may get into one sort of trouble or another. Families need other types of respite as well, however. These may include evening or weekend care, or overnight care while they are away on business or vacation trips. Some types of care are likely to be beyond what a day care program can offer.

What Day Care Staff Can Do Identify providers of temporary and overnight respite services in the community, and prepare a listing for the family members. Some staff members may be interested in working evenings or weekends as in-home caregivers. Put them on the list, with telephone numbers and rates, if this is not against agency policy. Churches or senior citizen's centers in the community may have lists of members who are willing to provide respite care. The social service department or discharge planner at local hospitals may also have such a list. Other family members may use or know of appropriate individuals or agencies. Or they may be willing to start a cooperative respite service, taking care of each other's patients periodically. Ask them. Local nursing homes or board-and-care homes may have temporary services for demented patients whose families are out of town briefly. Investigate this, and be forthright to your families regarding how much you know about the people on the list or whether you can recommend them. It may take a full day or two to search out these resources, but it will be a real service to families.

Information and Direction Regarding Patient Care

First of all, families need information about the disorder, which includes as accurate a diagnosis as can be made, not an assumption of "senility" because the person is forgetful. A thoughtful diagnosis is imperative, and must include information from and to the family, so they can understand all of the implications of the disorder, its prognosis, and what they might have to expect. The family has a great deal of information that will contribute to an accurate diagnosis, and should be encouraged to obtain one.

Families need information on how to protect themselves legally and financially in the care of their patient. This means information about Social Security and Supplemental Security Income eligibility, wills and trusts, durable powers of attorney, types of conservatorships, and where to get assistance.

Families need to know where to find emotional support, whether from individual mental health practitioners or the very valuable support groups offered in most communities.

Families need to know what the range of health care professions has to offer them, and how to find these professionals in their communities. They need to know that a registered dietitian can help them with meal planning, feeding, and nutritious and inexpensive meals. A physical therapist can teach them how to help their patient move or transfer from a bed to a wheelchair, for instance, without hurting themselves. A recreational therapist or occupational therapist can give them ideas on how to keep their patient occupied and out of trouble. A speech therapist can help diagnose and plan strategies for dealing with chewing and swallowing problems. A social worker can help them qualify for benefits, or find some of the other professionals for them. A nurse can teach them how to attend to the patient's personal care or nursing needs, or how to administer medications to their patient. In addition, they need to know that residential care—board-and-care, extended care, or skilled nursing care—may be needed by their patient eventually, and how to evaluate a good facility for their needs.

What Day Care Staff Can Do The Alzheimer's day care program should have referrals for the family in all of these areas. Ask family members to share the names of doctors they have been pleased with, along with psychiatrists, psychologists, social workers, and other health care professionals. Ask the closest medical school for the names of professionals specializing in dementia, Alzheimer's disease, or geriatrics; do the same with schools of nursing, social work, or psychology. Ask nurses for names of other professionals; they may have some good referrals. The social service departments of local hospitals, again, may have good lists already prepared. Ask local professional, senior citizens, or dementia organizations for referrals. Provide information concerning a durable power of attorney for health so that families and participants can prepare for future health care decisions.

Associations of residential care facilities often have criteria for evaluating their members, whether they are for-profit or not-for-profit nursing homes, homes for the aged, or board-and-care facilities. Get copies to give to families.

Emotional Reactions

When people experience severe losses, they mourn and grieve. Families need to know that is what they are doing, even if their demented relative is still alive. They need to know that they cannot take care of unfinished emotional business with their demented relative, because the personality with whom they must deal is no longer there.

Families can feel denial, fear, and hope. They deny the illness or the impairment in order to maintain hope for recovery. They fear their patient's pain and suffering or death. They may feel ambivalent, wishing at one moment that the patient would die and at the next wanting every effort to be made to save or cure him or her.

Families can feel vulnerable to a variety of things. They may fear receiving criticism from family members, day care center staff, or the physician. They may worry about being overwhelmed by the responsibilities of caregiving. They may fear developing Alzheimer's disease or dementia themselves. They may worry about care for the patient should they themselves become ill. For some, financial devastation is a real possibility, as is the breakdown of the family unit.

Families can feel anger—at the loss of the love from the patient and at their own loss of love for the patient. They feel anger at the situation they're in. They feel anger because of their frustration—that they've lost control of the situation, that they can't reason with the patient, or that previous methods don't work. They may displace that anger onto the patient, the physician, the day care staff, or onto other relatives. Then they may feel guilty about feeling angry in the first place, or about feeling uncharitable toward their demented relative. The family may feel guilty about decisions that may look self-serving, such as the decision to initiate conservatorship proceedings, to stop the patient from driving, to take over the patient's financial decision making, to enroll the patient in a day care center, or to place him or her in a residential facility.

What Day Care Staff Can Do   Staff members should acknowledge the family member's feelings without judging those feelings. Remember, one's feelings are one's own, and they are perfectly valid, even if one might prefer to feel differently. Staff should not try to talk a family member out of any feeling. Instead, acknowledge the person's right to any feeling he or she has.

Allow reality to intrude—even encourage it. The reality is that it *is* hard to accept the patient's condition; it *is* hard to deal with the problems dementia causes. But it is also a reality that family caregivers must take care of themselves in order to care for their patient adequately. Staff should help caregivers put their patient's needs in perspective by explaining that the patient exists in a system, and that system includes the family, the day care center, the health care system, and any other elements specific to the patient (other family members or friends). The patient is not the center of the universe, but is one element in it.

Families need to be enlightened about the effects that caring for a demented relative has on their own well-being. They need to know that it's normal to feel frustrated and angry some of the time. They need permission to take care of their own emotional and physical well-being and they need reassurance that taking care of themselves will make them better caregivers. Day care staff can point out that an exhausted caregiver snaps and creates anxiety in the patient and other helpers, and this may keep others from offering to assist with the patient. An exhausted caregiver may make mistakes, and this compromises caregiving. Encourage caregivers to take care of themselves. A healthy caregiver takes care of his or her own life and well-being, and makes sure there is enough recreation, fun, and help to make the caregiving hours bearable.

It is important to re-emphasize the importance of individual therapy for caregivers. Individual therapy is provided indirectly by any program staff member who comes into contact with a caregiver. However, it is usually the program director, social worker, or nurse who becomes involved in providing individual therapy to caregivers. Individual therapy can be used to focus on specific behavioral and management issues, personal and family emotional and psychological issues, personal and family needs, and caregiver information needs. Even though appropriate program staff should be able to provide individual therapy, it is worth considering whether a professional from outside the program should be used.

Caregivers have many needs and frustrations, and family caregivers have more than anyone else. The staff of an Alzheimer's day care center program are uniquely positioned to help minimize this burden, by both the care they give the demented person and their attention to the emotional burdens of the caregiver. This is one of the most rewarding aspects of working in the Alzheimer's/dementia day care field.

CAREGIVER SUPPORT GROUPS

One of the primary ways of working with a family is through caregiver or family support groups. While center staff may provide assistance to caregivers individually, group therapies or support groups have been found to be very beneficial to caregivers and their families. As previously mentioned, each caregiver has a unique set of needs, methods of coping, available resources, and type of relationship with patient and program staff. Support groups offer caregivers an opportunity to come together to discuss their individual issues regarding caregiving, to understand their family member's needs and limitations due to the disease, to share their feelings with other caregivers, to communicate with staff, to understand the activities of the center, to reduce their sense of isolation, and to gain reassurance that they are not alone in facing this disease.

Caregiver support groups generally are of two different models: those that are developed by a group of lay persons as a mutual assistance and self-help forum and those that are developed with the guidance of a professional, usually under the auspices of either day care centers or other community organizations, particularly Alzheimer's Association chapters. Day care centers often find caregiver support groups are one of the most requested and effective services they can offer to caregivers after respite. Support groups may be provided solely to caregivers of active program participants or be open to the general community, be on-going open-ended programs or be limited in duration, and be focused on mutual assistance and support and/or information and education. The most important goal for support groups is to meet the needs and interests of the caregivers who participate.

There are several specific issues that must be considered if the board and staff agree to start a caregiver support group, including the type of caregiver support group; the degree of interest on the part of potential members; the availability of community resources; costs to the program in terms of finances, staff time, space, and other resources; the time frame for when the support group will be held; and the need for patient supervision. There are excellent resources available if a program decides to sponsor a support group, including national and local chapters of the Alzheimer's Association, local professionals and community agencies, and numerous books and references (Middleton, 1984).

CONCLUSION

The impact of Alzheimer's disease has a devastating impact upon caregivers and families as well as patients. Families and caregivers of Alzheimer's patients are buffeted by physical, psychological, and financial burdens as well as multiple losses over a continuous and extended period of time. Alzheimer's day care programs can provide special assistance to these individuals, including making referrals to additional types of respite care; offering information and direction regarding patient care, financial and legal services, health care services, and residential care options; and directly (through the establishment of caregiver support groups) or indirectly providing assistance or personal support to help them cope with their emotional reactions to the disease and the burdens of caregiving. Directors and staff of Alzheimer's day care programs have a number of important opportunities to assist caregivers and families, the all too often forgotten victims of this disease, in addition to providing them with respite care.

13

COMMUNITY RESOURCES

While considering the development of an Alzheimer's day care program, planners should be particularly aware of other resources available for professionals in meeting the needs of dementia patients. There is a wide array of supplemental resources available for professionals and families alike. These resources and services cover the entire continuum from home care and community-based care to institutional care, and are under the auspices of a range of organizations. In addition, there are a number of important resources available from national organizations and the federal government.

At present, the accessibility and availability of these resources vary greatly. Only relatively recently have public and private programs been established to meet the needs of professionals who serve dementia patients and their caregivers, much less to meet the needs of professionals who are establishing Alzheimer's/dementia day care programs. In some locations the network of community-based services is extensive, and there is formal training available to meet the needs of professionals. However, while there has been a modest increase in the number of specialized services and resources for professionals serving dementia patients and their caregivers throughout the country, professionals in many states still do not have access to basic services or resources. As with Alzheimer's/dementia day care, there is limited public funding for services that provide supplemental resources to professionals in the field.

The purpose of this chapter is to identify the major generic services and organizations that are available to both professionals working in Alzheimer's day care programs and professionals in related service areas who work with dementia patients and their caregivers (see Table 8). It does not list all the available programs specifically designed to serve as resources for professionals working in dementia, nor does it list those programs that

149

support professionals who work with dementia patients as well as with other populations. The programs mentioned are, however, representative of major public and private services that offer additional support and information for Alzheimer's day care program staff and administrators throughout the country.

There is a wide array of services with which professionals working with patients having Alzheimer's disease or a related dementia generally need to be acquainted. The range of available supportive services varies considerably from community to community and from state to state. In general, the types of services that may be required by patients and caregivers during the course of the disease, and those that may provide supplemental support for professionals, include the following:

physician services
patient assessment
skilled nursing
physical therapy
occupational therapy
speech therapy
personal care
home health aide services
homemaker services
chore services
supervision
paid companion/sitter
congregate meals
home-delivered meals
mental health services
counseling services
telephone reassurance
personal emergency response systems
transportation
recreational services
adult day care
respite care
dental care
legal services
protective services
case management
information and referral
hospice services
education/training

Service providers who deliver any or all of these services to Alzheimer's patients and their caregivers often serve as an important resource for administrators and staff of new or existing Alzheimer's day care programs. In communities where there is a lack of support services, administrators and staff in Alzheimer's day care programs may be able to develop training and formal assistance in a patchwork fashion, turning to local hospitals, nursing homes, colleges, or universities. By working with other organizations with similar technical or training needs, Alzheimer's day care administrators and staff may be able to develop adequate resources to support their program.

INFORMAL SUPPORT

Before approaching organizations, agencies, and individuals in the community who can be of assistance to the center, it is important to look carefully at the informal resources at hand. By *informal resources,* we are referring to family, friends, and neighbors of participants and their caregivers. This also includes organizations or institutions to which a participant belongs or did belong, such as religious organizations, civic organizations, or clubs. These individuals and organizations make up an informal helping network to which participants may have turned in the past, and to which they may turn in the future, for help and support. Members of an individual's informal caregiving network may be able to supplement the efforts of the caregiver and those of the center. In addition, informal caregivers can help ensure that immediate or more subtle problems of participants are not overlooked. Finally, by making an effort to use informal caregivers, center staff may be able to develop more extensive relationships with them and get them involved in center activities and programs as volunteers.

SOURCES OF INFORMATION

To identify community resources, board members, executive/program directors, and staff can turn to a number of existing resources. First, most communities have one or more information and referral systems in place, sometimes coordinated by Area Agencies on Aging, other aging service providers, mental health service providers, hospitals, or social service agencies. Second, staff can use directories of agencies including those of state and local governments, hospitals, health and social service agencies and associations, religious and civic organizations, and local businesses. Even the telephone directory can provide an extensive list of services and contacts to be pursued. And of course, one of the most effective means of identifying resources is through inquiries to steering committee members, board members, the executive/program director, and staff.

TYPES OF COMMUNITY RESOURCES

Community resources should be considered from a number of different perspectives to determine their usefulness to the Alzheimer's day care center and staff. Do they have tangible items that can be of use in program operations, such as equipment or supplies? Can they provide technical assistance, guidance, or access to agencies? Can they provide funds or access to agencies or individuals with funds? Can they provide in-kind support through personnel?

Centers may turn to a wide array of organizations for assistance in providing program activities or for contributions to center resources. Because they are very extensive and differ from community to community, we provide in Table 8 a list of generic organizations or types of organizations. It should be noted that these are by no means mutually exclusive categories since, for example, any organization may provide substantial assistance in a health or social service capacity while at the same time assisting in a center's fund-raising plan. Nor is this an exhaustive list of programs; rather, it represents key areas or types of programs to assist a

TABLE 8   Types of community resources

Category	Examples
Health care	physicians
	nurses
	health departments
	hospitals
	community clinics
	geriatric programs
	professional associations
	visiting nurse associations and registries
	home health agencies and aides
	mental health agencies and professionals
	day care centers
Social care	social workers
	social service departments
	day care centers
	homemaker/chore agencies
	senior centers
	therapists
	social and civic organizations
	church groups
	friendly visitors associations/telephone reassurance
Meals and nutrition	Title III Older Americans Act programs
	home delivered meals programs
	congregate meals programs
	nutritionists/dieticians
	health and social service professionals

TABLE 8 Types of community resources (*Continued*)

Category	Examples
Transportation	van services taxi services public transportation
Family support services	Alzheimer's Association case management social workers/psychologists social service agencies churches civic and social organizations
Legal assistance and consultation	lawyers bar associations Legal Aid Society protective services agencies
Financial assistance and consultation	accountants businesses foundations local, state, and federal agencies benevolent agencies United Way service clubs (Rotary, Elks)
Personnel assistance and consultation	businesses adult education programs community colleges universities Title V employment programs personnel registries United Way
Emergency and safety assistance	police fire departments licensing and certification agencies adult protective services
Program operations	adult day care centers aging service providers Area Agencies on Aging social service and health departments educational institutions adult education institutions
Miscellaneous support	State Department of Rehabilitation (employment counseling, training, and placement) independent living centers specialized dementia nursing homes university hospitals and medical centers

steering committee, board, or executive/program director in identifying the range of possible sources of community assistance.

CONCLUSION

At a minimum, community resources are an important means of expanding the programming of Alzheimer's day care centers. Often their availability and use are vital to the very survival of centers. Community resources run the gamut of informal resources provided by families, friends, and neighbors of participants, to the sophisticated formal resources available through professionals, service agencies, and institutions throughout the community. It is to the advantage of all centers to identify what supportive resources and technical assistance are available in the broader community and to use them to the fullest extent possible in developing and delivering a comprehensive array of services to participants and their families.

14

PROGRAM EVALUATION AND RESEARCH

Program evaluation can provide very helpful information to staff members of Alzheimer's day care programs, in two ways. *Formative evaluation*—that done during the development of an organization or a program—provides information of value in making programmatic decisions and in guiding the direction the program takes. *Summative evaluation*—that done after an organization's programs have been running long enough to have an effect—tells it how well the program is doing and where changes are needed.

Executive/program directors and staff of effective Alzheimer's day care programs utilize program evaluation to improve the day-to-day operations of the program as well as to enhance the program's long-term success. There are a number of ways in which program evaluation can assist staff and administrators:

1. *Planning and outcomes.* Program evaluation can provide descriptive data on the needs and characteristics of the Alzheimer's day care client population and the program service area, identify specific program and participant problems, and pinpoint the strengths and weaknesses of the program.
2. *Quality assurance and accountability.* Program evaluation can provide data to administrators, staff, board members, and funding agencies concerned with the level of program activities and outcomes, ensuring that participants receive the highest level of care possible.
3. *Marketing and public relations.* Program evaluation can provide information that can be used by staff, administrators, and board members to obtain information about the benefits of a program in

a fashion that can be effectively disseminated to caregivers, professionals, supporters, and volunteers.

4. *Staff and program development.* Program evaluation can provide information to staff and administrators that will help them target training needs and identify methods of satisfying those needs.

The major steps in program evaluation are development of specific program goals and objectives, development of an evaluation design, development of data collection instruments, data collection, data analysis, reporting of findings, and utilization of findings for program revisions.

INCORPORATING PROGRAM EVALUATION INTO AN ALZHEIMER'S DAY CARE PROGRAM

Program evaluation should be implemented as early as possible in a program's development to ensure that the program is reviewed using baseline data. The program evaluation should be designed and implemented by an experienced evaluation professional, preferably someone who is not a member of the staff.

There are a number of ways to maximize program resources to conduct an evaluation. First, invite a professional with experience to conduct the evaluation as an in-kind contribution to the program. Second, conduct an evaluation of the program through collaborative efforts with other agencies. Third, involve students or volunteers with appropriate credentials to conduct the evaluation of your program. A local university may help identify a professor interested in research or evaluation who might be willing to assist in order to provide program evaluation experience for students.

CONCLUSION

Although program evaluation and research are often neglected areas for adult day care programs in general and Alzheimer's day care programs in particular, they provide an important means of assessing how well a program is achieving its goals. Program directors are often uncomfortable with or intidimated by program evaluation because they are not familiar with how to conduct an evaluation or are not knowledgeable of evaluation tools. However, the practical outcomes and problem solving that can be achieved far outweigh any difficulties a director may encounter in using program evaluation and research. Using evaluation and research techniques to their fullest requires setting clear achievable goals, identifying practical targets that will benefit from evaluation, collecting accurate data, using staff and other resources efficiently, and carefully incorporating findings in the improvement of program operations.

APPENDIX

SPECIAL RESOURCES FOR ALZHEIMER'S/DEMENTIA DAY CARE

State Alzheimer's Day Care/Respite Programs

The following list identifies state agencies supporting Alzheimer's day care and related respite programs with state general funds. There are many additional Alzheimer's/dementia day care programs supported privately or financed by other funding sources.

Alabama Commission on Aging
136 Catoma Street
Montgomery, AL 36130
205-272-1635

Public Health Nursing Department
P.O. Box H
Juneau, AK 99811-0611
902-465-3151

Aging and Adult Administration
1400 W. Washington, 950A
Phoenix, AZ 85007
602-542-4446

Alzheimer's Program
Slot 622, 4301 W. Markham
Little Rock, AR 72205
501-686-5282

Alzheimer's/Respite Branch
California Department of Aging
1600 K Street
Sacramento, CA 95814
916-323-5170

Colorado Department of Health
Health Facilities Division
4210 E. 11th Ave.
Denver, CO 80220
303-320-8333

Department on Aging
175 Main St.
Hartford, CT 06100
203-566-7728

Department of Health and Social Services
Division of Public Health
Delaware Hospital for the Chronically Ill
Sunnyside Road
Smyrna, DE 19977
302-653-8556

Aging and Adult Services
Department of Health and Rehabilitative Services
1317 Winewood Blvd.
Tallahassee, FL 32399-0700
904-488-2881

Office of Aging
878 Peachtree St., Suite 632
Atlanta, GA
404-894-2041

Executive Office on Aging
335 Merchant St., Room 241
Honolulu, HI 96813
808-548-2593

Idaho Office on Aging
State House
Boise, ID 83720
208-334-2219

Illinois Department of Public Health
421 E. Capitol Ave.
Springfield, IL 62701
217-785-3356 or 800-252-8966

Division of Aging Services
251 N. Illinois St., P.O. Box 7083
Indianapolis, IN 46207-7083
317-232-7020

Iowa Department of Elder Affairs
236 Jewett Building
914 Grand Ave.
Des Moines, IA 50319
515-281-5187

Kansas Department on Aging
Docking State Office Building
915 S.W. Harrison, Room 122-S
Topeka, KS 66612-1500
913-296-4986

Department for Social Services
Division of Aging Services
275 E. Main St.
Frankfort, KY 40621
502-564-7372

Office of Elderly Affairs
P.O. Box 80374
Baton Rouge, LA 70898
504-925-1700

Department of Human Services
Bureau of Maine's Elderly
State House Station #11
Augusta, ME 04333
207-289-2561

Department of Health and Mental Hygiene
Coordinating Council on ADRD, Services to the Aging
201 W. Preston St.
Baltimore, MD 21202
301-225-6770

Executive Office of Elder Affairs
38 Chauncy St.
Boston, MA 02111
617-727-4415

Office of Services to the Aging
P.O. Box 30026
Lansing, MI 48909
517-373-8810

Minnesota Department of Human Services
444 Lafayette Rd.
St. Paul, MN 55155-3819
612-297-1240

Department of Human Development
Mississippi Council on Aging
301 W. Pearl St.
Jackson, MS 39203-3092
601-949-2070

Missouri Division of Aging
2701 W. Main
P.O. Box 1337
Jefferson City, MO 65102
314-751-3082

Department of Family Services
Box 8005
Helena, MT 59604
406-444-5900

Department on Aging
P.O. Box 95044
Lincoln, NE 68509-5044
402-471-2306

Adult Health Section
Nevada Department of Public Health
505 E. King St., Room 101
Carson City, NV 89710
702-885-4210

New Hampshire Department of Health and Human Services
Division of Elderly & Adult Services
6 Hazen Dr.
Concord, NH 03301
603-271-4687

New Jersey Department of Public Health
Gerontology Program, CN 369
Trenton, NJ 08625
609-588-7496

State Agency on Aging
224 E. Palace Ave.
Sante Fe, NM 87501
505-827-7640

New York State Department of Health
Gerontology Program
ESP-Corning Tower Room 523
Albany, NY 12237
518-474-2460

Health and Community Care Section
1985 Umstead Dr.
Raleigh, NC 27603
919-733-3983

Aging Services
Capitol Building
Bismarck, ND 58505
701-224-2577

Ohio Department of Aging
50 W. Broad St., 9th Floor
Columbus, OH 43266-0501
614-466-1220

Oklahoma State Department of Health
Chronic Disease Division
P.O. Box 53551
Oklahoma City, OK 73152
405-271-4072

Senior Services Division
313 Public Service Building
Salem, OR 97310
503-378-3751

Pennsylvania Department of Aging
231 State St.
Harrisburg, PA 17101
717-783-1550

Alzheimer's Disease Crisis Intervention Center
23 Broad St.
Pawtucket, RI 02860
401-725-3870

Commission on Aging
Suite B-500
400 Arbor Lake Dr.
Columbia, SC 29223
803-735-0210

South Dakota Department of Health
Joe Foss Building
523 E. Capitol
Pierre, SD 57501
605-773-3364

Tennessee Department of Mental Health and Mental Retardation
706 Church Street
Nashville, TN 37219
615-741-0980

Texas Department of Health
1100 W. 49th St.
Austin, TX 78756
512-458-7323

Salt Lake County Aging Services
2001 S. State, S1500
Salt Lake City, UT 84190-2300
801-468-2483

Department of Health
60 Main St., P.O. Box 70
Burlington, VT 05402
802-863-7250

Department of Mental Health, Mental Retardation, and Substance Abuse
Office of Geriatric Services
P.O. Box 1797
Richmond, VA 23214
804-786-4837

Aging and Adult Services Administration
HB-11
Olympia, WA 98504
206-753-4925

West Virginia Commission on Aging
Capitol Complex, Holly Grove
Charleston, WV 24305
304-348-3317

Department of Health and Social Services
Bureau on Aging
217 S. Hamilton St.
Madison, WI 53703
608-267-2282

Wyoming Commission on Aging
Room 139 Hathaway Building
Cheyenne, WY 82002
307-777-7986

National Organizations

Alzheimer's Association National Headquarters
70 E. Lake St., Suite 600
Chicago, IL 60601
800-621-0379

The Alzheimer's Association is the national self-help organization for caregivers of Alzheimer's/dementia patients. Its goals are (1) to support research into the causes of and cures for Alzheimer's disease; (2) to aid in organizing family support groups in their own communities so as to give the afflicted families assistance, encouragement, and education; (3) to sponsor educational forums and provide information on Alzheimer's disease for lay and professional people; (4) to advise federal and local government agencies on the needs of afflicted families as well as promote national research; and (5) to offer help in any manner, whenever and wherever needed, to those afflicted by the disease and their loved ones.

The Alzheimer's Association has numerous local chapters across the country whose members offer a wide array of resources for professionals and caregivers.

In addition, the Alzheimer's Association national office has a unit dedicated to working with Alzheimer's day care centers and other respite programs, which also offers a number of day care/respite demonstrations. The association's local chapters often run or collaborate with Alzheimer's day care centers. Chapters provide listings of support group meetings; information on medical and public policy issues; personal telephone contact to help caregivers through stressful times; and information and referral to dementia resources. To contact the nearest chapter office, call 800-621-0379.

The Family Survival Project for Brain-Damaged Adults
425 Bush St., Suite 500
San Francisco, CA 94108
415-434-3388
800-445-8106

The Family Survival Project for Brain-Damaged Adults, which has been designated as the State of California Statewide Resources Consultant for Brain-Damaged Adults, is a nonprofit organization that helps those who care for adult victims of chronic brain disorders. It serves as a clearinghouse for information on brain disorders and as a local resource for caregivers of brain-damaged adults. Its purposes are: (1) to build services where none exist; (2) to assist families directly; and (3) to be a public voice for those suffering emotional and financial distress as a result of caring for an adult who is brain damaged. Local organizations affiliate with the Family Survival Project by joining the Statewide Brain Damage Coalition of California. The Statewide Resources Consultant provides a wide and comprehensive array of literature, research, and listings of supportive services for caregivers and professionals.

California has a unique statewide system of 11 Caregiver Resource Centers (CRCs) modeled after the Family Survival Project offering information about and referrals to all local, state, and federal programs and services available to caregivers of brain-damaged adults. The goals of CRCs are (1) to provide direct services to caregivers; (2) to provide information, supportive services, and training to family and other caregivers and to professionals who work with patients and families; (3) to conduct research into the extent and consequences of brain damage, needed policy reforms, and other related areas; (4) to help secure federal and private financing of services; and (5) to develop and coordinate statewide information, technical assistance, and training about brain damage, the problems it causes, and needed services. Direct services include legal and financial advice, in-home respite care, counseling, and support groups. The CRCs also assist in the identification and documentation of service needs and the development of necessary programs in the service area.

National Institute on Adult Daycare (NIAD)
National Council on the Aging (NCoA)
600 Maryland Ave., S.W.
West Wing 10
Washington, DC 20024
202-479-1200

NIAD is the national voice for adult day care. Membership may be obtained by joining NCoA. NIAD coordinates National Adult Day Care Week each fall and conducts research, assists with legislative advocacy campaigns, and contributes to development of standards for the adult day care field. In addition to publishing a quarterly newsletter for members, NIAD publishes several educational documents including: *Adult Day Care: Annotated Bibliography, Adult Day Care in America, A Survey of Day Care for the Demented Adult in the United States,* and *Standards for Adult Day Care.*

Regional Offices of the Administration on Aging
State Units on Aging (SUAs)
Area Agencies on Aging (AAAs)

State Units on Aging and Area Agencies on Aging can recommend local resources and services that are available to dementia day care directors and staff, and can assist family caregivers in locating appropriate support. In addition, if a patient, family, or caregiver needs help, AAA staff can provide advice about obtaining appropriate services and additional information. Area Agencies on Aging, through their information and referral program, can link older persons with supportive service providers. Further information concerning AAAs may be obtained from Regional Offices of the Administration on Aging or State Units on Aging.

Robert Wood Johnson Foundation Dementia Care and Respite Services
    Program
The Bowman Gray School of Medicine of Wake Forest University
300 S. Hawthorne Rd.
Winston-Salem, NC 27103
919-748-4941

The Dementia Care and Respite Service Program began in August 1988 to demonstrate the benefits of adult day care for persons with dementing illnesses, including Alzheimer's disease. Nineteen sites were selected, and the primary goal is to increase the availability of day programs and other community and in-home respite services for people with dementia. Through enhancing the centers' capacities to meet patient and family needs, the program also hopes to demonstrate that adult day centers can provide these services in an affordable manner. The 19 Dementia Care and Respite Services Program sites will identify the services that caregivers want and will find ways of providing these services cost effectively.

Alzheimer's Disease and Memory Disorder Diagnostic Centers

Statewide networks of regional diagnostic and assessment centers are quite new. Seven states are known to have developed such networks since 1984. These are California, Florida, Illinois, Maryland, New Jersey, Ohio, and Pennsylvania. Other states may be developing similar networks. Listed below are the contacts for several of these centers.

California

Alzheimer's Disease Diagnostic and Treatment Centers (ADDTCs) were established as prototype assessment centers under the auspices of the California Department of Health Services. The goals of the ADDTCs are (1) to provide diagnostic and treatment services and improve the quality of care to dementia patients; (2) to increase research to discover the cause of and cure for Alzheimer's disease; (3) to provide training, consultation, and education to the families of persons with Alzheimer's disease or related dementias; (4) to increase the training of health care professionals with respect to Alzheimer's disease and related dementias; and (5) to collect and analyze more accurate and standardized information relative to Alzheimer's disease and related dementias. ADDTCs serve persons with Alzheimer's disease and other related dementias, their caregivers, and health professionals. Services offered include information and referral, review of medical history, physical examination, neurological and psychological evaluation and testing, home assessment, family conference and treatment planning, follow-up with reevaluation, and autopsy when appropriate. In addition, some ADDTCs provide therapy for caregivers, support groups, ongoing primary care, case management, respite care, and transportation for services. The ADDTCs are located throughout the state.

U.C. Davis–Northern California Alzheimer's Disease Center
Alta Bates-Herrick Hospital
2001 Dwight Way
Berkeley, CA 94704
415-540-4530

University of California, Davis, Alzheimer's Center
2315 Stockton Boulevard
Sacramento, CA 95817
916-734-5496

University of Southern California/St. Barnabas Alzheimer's Disease Diagnosis and Treatment Center
675 S. Carondelet St.
Los Angeles, CA 90057
213-388-4444

Southern California Alzheimer's Disease Diagnostic and Treatment Center
Rancho Los Amigos Medical Center
University of Southern California
12838 Erickson St., Bldg. 301
Downey, CA 90242
213-940-8130

University of California, San Diego, Alzheimer's Disease Diagnostic and Treatment Center, An Extension of Seniors Only Care (SOCARE)
225 Dickinson St., H-204
San Diego, CA 92103
619-543-5306

Program for Alzheimer's Disease Care and Education (PACE)
University of California, San Francisco
1350 7th Ave., CSBS-228
San Francisco, CA 94143
415-476-7605

Stanford Alzheimer's Diagnostic and Resource Center
c/o Palo Alto VAMC
Psychiatry 116A3
3801 Miranda Ave.
Palo Alto, CA 94304
415-494-9108

University of California, San Francisco/Fresno Alzheimer's Disease Diagnostic and Treatment Center
1343 N. Wishon
Fresno, CA 93728
209-233-3363

University of California, Irvine, Alzheimer's Disease Diagnostic and Treatment Center
c/o Department of Psychobiology
University of California, Irvine
Irvine, CA 92718
714-856-6238

Florida

Memory Disorders Clinic
Suncoast Gerontology Center
University of South Florida Medical Center
Box 50
Tampa, FL 33612
813-974-3100
813-974-4355 (Administration)

University of Miami Memory Disorders Clinic
Jackson Medical Tower
University of Miami School of Medicine
1500 N.W. 12th Ave., Suite 1103
Miami, FL 33136
305-547-5883
305-326-1043 (Administration, Center on Adult Development and Aging)

Alzheimer's and Memory Disorders Clinic
Wein Center
Mount Sinai Medical Center
4300 Alton Rd.
Miami Beach, FL 33140
305-674-2543

J. Hillis Miller Medical Center
University of Florida Medical School
Box J-236
Gainesville, FL 32610
904-392-3498

Illinois

Regional Alzheimer's Disease Assistance Center
Southern Illinois University School of Medicine
Springfield, IL
1-800-342-5748 (or 1-800-DIAL SIU)

Regional Alzheimer's Disease Assistance Center
Rush–Presbyterian–St. Luke's Medical Center
Rush Medical College
Chicago, IL 60612
312-942-4463

Maryland

Central Maryland and Maryland/Washington corridor are rich with diagnostic facilities. Most are located within community hospitals. Services are much more restricted in the rest of the state. Persons in western Maryland may contact the Washington County Alzheimer's Disease and Related Disorders Program at Washington County Hospital, 324 E. Antietam St., Hagerstown, MD 21740, 302-582-3080. Persons in eastern Maryland may contact the local Alzheimer's Association chapter or a community hospital in Baltimore or Wilmington, Delaware.

New Jersey

COPSA Institute
Institute for Alzheimer's Disease and Related Disorders
667 Hoes Lane
P.O. Box 1392
Piscataway, NJ 08855-1392
201-463-4430 (within New Jersey, 1-800-424-2494)

Alzheimer's Evaluation Program
University of Medicine and Dentistry
School of Osteopathic Medicine
301 S. Central Plaza, Suite 3100
Stratford, NJ 08084-6843
609-346-6843

In addition to these diagnostic and treatment facilities, New Jersey funds eight additional geriatric assessment centers throughout the state.

New York

New York's Alzheimer's disease diagnostic and treatment centers are called Alzheimer's Disease Assistance Centers (ADACs). They are located throughout the state.

ADAC of Long Island
Department of Psychiatry
Health Science Center, T-10
SUNY at Stony Brook
Stony Brook, NY 11794-8101
516-444-2570, ext. 1618

ADAC of Central New York
SUNY Health Science Center at Syracuse
750 E. Adams St.
Syracuse, NY 13210
315-464-6097

ADAC of the Finger Lakes
Monroe Community Hospital
University of Rochester
School of Medicine and Dentistry
435 E. Henrietta Rd.
Rochester, NY 14603
716-442-7319

ADAC of North Eastern New York
SUNY at Plattsburg
Plattsburg, NY 12901
518-564-3377

ADAC of Western New York
Deaconess Center
1001 Humboldt Parkway
Buffalo, NY 14208
716-886-4400

ADAC of Brooklyn
SUNY Health Science Center at Brooklyn
450 Clarkson Ave., Box 50
Brooklyn, NY 11226
718-270-2452

ADAC of the Hudson Valley
Burke Rehabilitation Center
785 Mamaroneck Ave.
White Plains, NY 10605
914-948-0050, ext. 2375 or 2419

ADAC of the Capital Region
The Eddy
2256 Burdette Ave.
Troy, NY 12180
518-272-1777

Pennsylvania

Pennsylvania has 20 comprehensive geriatric assessment programs located throughout the state. These centers provide full diagnoses of memory disorder problems, and offer treatment to patients and support for caregivers. In addition, a directory of Alzheimer's disease support services has been published. To obtain a copy of this directory, contact the Project Office for the Alzheimer's Disease Initiative for the Commonwealth of Pennsylvania, 231 State St., Harrisburg, PA 17101 or call 717-783-1550.

SAMPLE PROGRAM FORMS

Intake

INTAKE/SCREEN

In Re Dis Read
1. Form# (Circle one) 1 2 3 4

California Department of Aging
FORM 100
Revised 12/89

COUNTY NO. ___ PROGRAM OR PROJECT NO. ___ SITE NO. ___ 2. PARTICIPANT NO. _____ — _____

3. DATE _____ TIME:_____ a.m. / p.m. MODE Letter Drop In Telephone RESPONSE Emergency Normal
MM/DD/YY

Site No.   SSA

APPLICANT NAME: Last _____ First _____ Mi _____ SYSTEM NO. (SN)

RESIDENT ADDRESS: Street _____ City _____ State ___ 4. ZIP _____ *Tel. No. (   )

MAILING ADDRESS:

5. DOB MM/DD/YY	AGE	6. SEX 1 2 M F	7. MARITAL STATUS 1 2 3 4 5 Mr Wd Sp Sg Dv	8. RACE/ORIGIN 1 2 3 4 5 6 7 W B A/PI AI/NA Oth F Hisp	

TRANS. LANG. Y N | 9. LIVES ALONE Y 1 N 2 3 4 | 10. PHYS IMP 1 2 Y N | 11. RESIDENCE 1 2 3 4 5 6 7 8 9 Hse Apt MH Htl B&R RCF SNF Hmls Oth | PROPERTY Rent Own Oth

SOCIAL SECURITY NO. | MEDICARE/RRB NO. | HEALTH INSURANCE NAME AND NO.

MEDI-CAL NO. Y N | VETERAN NO. Y N

| 12. SSI/SSP 1 2 Y N | 13. LOW INCOME 1 2 Y N | |

REGULAR PHYSICIAN: Name _____ Address _____ Tel. No. (   )

EMERGENCY CONTACT: Name _____ Relationship _____ Address _____ Tel. No. (   )

14. REFERRAL SOURCE: Type: 1 2 3 4 5 6 7 8 9 10 11 12 13 14 15 16   Name _____

Address: Street _____ City _____ State ___ ZIP ___ Tel. No. (   )

15. REASON FOR REFERRAL: (Circle one) 1 2 3 4 5 6 7 8 9 10

*PRESENTING PROBLEM/SERVICES REQUESTED/COMMENTS/FOLLOWUP

16. DIAGNOSIS: (Circle one) 1 2 3 4 5 6 7 8 9 10 11 12 13 14

17. DISENROLLMENT - Out of home placement: (Circle one) 1 2 3 4 5 6 7

18. DATE OF DISENROLLMENT _____
MM/DD/YY

COMPLETED BY: Program/Name _____

Staff Code No. _____ 19. Date and Signature _____ ▶ _____ Tel . No. (   )
MM/DD/YY

FUNCTIONAL ASSESSMENT

IN RE DIS READ

1. Form # (circle one): 1 2 3 4

| COUNTY NO. | PROGRAM OR PROJECT NO. | 2. Participant #: ___ - ___ - ___ |
| | | Site #   Social Security # |

| Participant Name | Last | First | Mi |

| 3. Assessment Date | Assessment Seq. No. (1=First) | Enrollment Date | |

1.1 with ease
1.2 some difficulty
1.3 very difficult

4. ADL*/IADL FUNCTIONING	INDEPENDENT	VERBAL ASSISTANCE	SOME HUMAN HELP	A LOT OF HUMAN HELP	DEPENDENT	PARAMEDICAL	DEVICE	HAS FORMAL HELP	HAS INFORMAL HELP	HAS NO HELP	NEEDS (MORE) HELP	COMMENTS
	1.	2	3	4	5	6						
A. HOUSEWORK	1.	2	3	4	5							
B. LAUNDRY	1.			4	5							
C. SHOPPING & ERRANDS	1.		3		5							
D. MEAL PREP & CLEAN UP	1.	2	3	4	5	6						
E. MOBILITY INSIDE*	1.	2	3	4	5							
F. BATHING*	1.	2	3	4	5							
G. GROOMING/	1.	2	3	4	5							
H. DRESSING*	1.	2	3	4	5							
I. BOWEL, BLADDER, & MENST*	1.	2	3	4	5	6						
J. TRANSFER*	1.	2	3	4	5							
K. EATING*	1.	2	3	4	5	6						
L. RESPIRATION	1.				5	6						
M. MEDICATIONS	1.	2	3		5	6						
N. STAIRCLIMBING*	1.	2	3	4	5							
O. MOBILITY OUTSIDE*	1.	2	3	4	5							
P. TRANSPORTATION	1.	2	3	4	5							
Q. TELEPHONE	1.	2	3		5							
R. MONEY MANAGEMENT	1.	2	3		5	6						
S. CONTINENCE: BOWEL*		1	2	3	4							
T. CONTINENCE: BLADDER*		1	2	3	4							

6. Level of severity of care needs: (circle one)

Mild	Moderate	Severe
1	2	3

5. MENTAL FUNCTIONING	No Problem	Mild	Moderate	Severe		No Problem	Mild	Moderate	Severe	
A. MEMORY	1	2	3	5	E. Anxiety	1	2	3	5	
B. ORIENTATION	1	2	3	5	F. Combativeness	1	2	3	5	
C. JUDGEMENT	1	2	3	5	G. Wandering	1	2	3	5	
D. COMMUNITCATION	1	2	3	5	H. Personality Changes	1	2	3	5	

COMPLETED BY: Tel. No.
                                                            (   )

Staff Code No.   Date and Signature (If applicable)

ALZHEIMER'S FAMILY CENTER, INC.
PATIENT PROFILE/SOCIAL HISTORY

NAME _____

AGE _____

BIRTH DATE _____

MEDICAL INFORMATION

Mobility: ambulatory _____ walker _____ cane _____ wheelchair _____

Vision: normal _____ normal with glasses _____ poor _____ blind _____

Hearing: normal _____ impaired _____ deaf _____ hearing aid _____

Hand dominance _____ Special diet _____

BACKGROUND

Living arrangements _____ Local family support _____

Level of education _____ Languages spoken _____

Former occupation _____ Other skills _____

Other jobs held _____

Place of birth _____ Siblings _____

Marital status M ____ W ____ D ____ Sp ____ Sg ____ Length of time _____

No. of marriages _____ No. of children _____ religion _____

Significant historical events:

_____

_____

INTERESTS

Please specify:

Art _____ Crafts _____ Cooking _____ Carpentry _____

Games _____ Music _____ Instrument played _____

Animals _____ Sports _____ Travel _____ Reading _____

Volunteer service or social clubs _____

Hobbies _____ Other _____ Gardening _____

Socially active? _____ Prefers group or individual activity? _____

COMMENTS

_____

_____

_____

_____

_____

_____

_____

ALZHEIMER'S FAMILY CENTER, INC.
CAREGIVER STRESS INTERVIEW

STRESS SCORE _____   DATE OF INTERVIEW _____

INSTRUCTIONS: The following is a list of statements that reflect how people sometimes feel when taking care of another person. After each statement, indicate how often you feel that way. There are no right or wrong answers.

1. Do you feel that your relative asks for more help than he/she needs?

    0. Never   1. Rarely   2. Sometimes
    3. Quite Frequently   4. Nearly Always   _____

2. Do you feel that, because of the time you spend with your relative, you don't have enough time for yourself?

    0. Never   1. Rarely   2. Sometimes
    3. Quite Frequently   4. Nearly Always   _____

3. Do you feel stressed between caring for your relative and trying to do other responsibilities for your family or work?

    0. Never   1. Rarely   2. Sometimes
    3. Quite Frequently   4. Nearly Always   _____

4. Do you feel embarrassed over your relative's behaviors?

    0. Never   1. Rarely   2. Sometimes
    3. Quite Frequently   4. Nearly Always   _____

5. Do you feel angry when you are around your relative?

    0. Never   1. Rarely   2. Sometimes
    3. Quite Frequently   4. Nearly Always   _____

6. Do you feel that your relative currently affects your relationship with other family members or friends in a negative way?

    0. Never   1. Rarely   2. Sometimes
    3. Quite Frequently   4. Nearly Always   _____

7. Are you afraid what the future holds for your relative?

    0. Never   1. Rarely   2. Sometimes
    3. Quite Frequently   4. Nearly Always   _____

8. Do you feel your relative is dependent upon you?

    0. Never   1. Rarely   2. Sometimes
    3. Quite Frequently   4. Nearly Always   _____

9. Do you feel strained when you are around your relative?

    0. Never   1. Rarely   2. Sometimes
    3. Quite Frequently   4. Nearly Always   _____

10. Do you feel your health has suffered because of your involvement with your relative?

    0. Never   1. Rarely   2. Sometimes
    3. Quite Frequently   4. Nearly Always   _____

11. Do you feel you don't have as much privacy as you would like, because of your relative?

    0. Never   1. Rarely   2. Sometimes
    3. Quite Frequently   4. Nearly Always   _____

12. Do you feel your social life has suffered because you are caring for your relative?

    0. Never   1. Rarely   2. Sometimes
    3. Quite Frequently   4. Nearly Always   _____

13. Do you feel uncomfortable about having friends over because of your relative?

    0. Never   1. Rarely   2. Sometimes
    3. Quite Frequently   4. Nearly Always   _____

14. Do you feel your relative seems to expect you to take care of him/her, as if you were the only one he/she could depend on?

    0. Never   1. Rarely   2. Sometimes
    3. Quite Frequently   4. Nearly Always   _____

15. Do you feel you don't have enough money to care for your relative in addition to the rest of your expenses?

    0. Never   1. Rarely   2. Sometimes
    3. Quite Frequently   4. Nearly Always   _____

16. Do you feel you will be unable to take care of your relative much longer?

    0. Never   1. Rarely   2. Sometimes
    3. Quite Frequently   4. Nearly Always   _____

17. Do you feel you have lost control of your life since your relative's illness?

    0. Never   1. Rarely   2. Sometimes
    3. Quite Frequently   4. Nearly Always   _____

18. Do you wish you could just leave the care of your relative to someone else?

        0. Never   1. Rarely   2. Sometimes
        3. Quite Frequently   4. Nearly Always   _____

19. Do you feel uncertain about what to do about your relative?

        0. Never   1. Rarely   2. Sometimes
        3. Quite Frequently   4. Nearly Always   _____

20. Do you feel you should be doing more for your relative?

        0. Never   1. Rarely   2. Sometimes
        3. Quite Frequently   4. Nearly Always   _____

21. Do you feel you could do a better job in caring for your relative?

        0. Never   1. Rarely   2. Sometimes
        3. Quite Frequently   4. Nearly Always   _____

22. Overall, how burdened do you feel in caring for your relative?

        0. Never   1. Rarely   2. Sometimes
        3. Quite Frequently   4. Nearly Always   _____

Based on Zarit Burden Instrument adapted for Alzheimer's Day Care Resource Center. Original version copyright 1983 by Steven H. Zarit and Judy M. Zarit.

ALZHEIMER'S FAMILY CENTER, INC.
PHYSICIAN'S REPORT

NOTE TO PHYSICIAN:

    The person whose name appears below is an applicant for a licensed day care program. This facility provides the personal care and supervision normally provided by a relative to a member of the family. A current health report is required.

Name and _____ Date of exam: _____

address: _____ Date of birth: _____

_____ Sex: _____

Length of time under your care: _____

Primary Diagnosis: _____

Secondary Diagnosis: _____

Tuberculosis Clearance: _____

                    Date of last negative chest x-ray (within 1 yr)

                    Date of last negative skin test (within 1 yr)

HEALTH HISTORY:

    Past illness, medical treatments, hospitalizations: _____

    History of present illness: _____

    Current medications: _____

    Allergies: _____

PHYSICAL ASSESSMENT:

    General appearance: _____

    Integument: _____

    Head, eyes, ears: _____

    Nose: _____

    Mouth, throat: _____

    Respiratory: _____

    Cardiovascular: _____

    Gastrointestinal: _____

    Genitourinary: _____

    Musculoskeletal: _____

    Neurological: _____

_____ Name _____

Signature   Address _____

Date _____ Phone No. _____

STATE OF CALIFORNIA
HEALTH AND WELFARE AGENCY

PREPLACEMENT APPRAISAL INFORMATION

Admission - Residential Care Homes

NOTE: *This information may be obtained from the applicant, or his/her authorized representative. (Relatives, social agency, hospital or physician may assist the applicant in completing this form.) This form is not a substitute for the Physician's Report (LIC 602).*

APPLICANTS NAME	AGE

HEALTH (Describe overall health condition including any dietary limitations)

PHYSICAL DISABILITIES (Describe any physical limitations including vision, hearing or speech)

MENTAL CONDITION (Specify extent of any symptoms of confusion; forgetfulness, participation in social activities (i.e., active or withdrawn)

HEALTH HISTORY (List currently prescribed medications and major illnesses, surgery, accidents (specify whether hospitalized and length of hospitalization: in last 5 years.)

SOCIAL FACTORS (Describe likes and dislikes, interests and activities)

BED STATUS

- [ ] OUT OF BED ALL DAY
- [ ] IN BED PART OF TIME
- [ ] IN BED ALL OR MOST OF TIME

COMMENT

TUBERCULOSIS INFORMATION

ANY HISTORY OF TUBERCULOSIS IN APPLICANT S FAMILY	DATE OF TB TEST	[ ] POSITIVE
[ ] YES [ ] NO		[ ] NEGATIVE
ANY RECENT EXPOSURE TO ANYONE WITH TUBERCULOSIS?	ACTION TAKEN (IF POSITIVE)	
[ ] YES [ ] NO		

GIVE DETAILS

LIC 603 (11-82)

(Over)

FUNCTIONAL CAPABILITIES (Check all items below)

YES NO

☐ ☐ Active, requires no personal help of any kind - able to go up and down stairs easily

☐ ☐ Active, but has difficulty climbing or descending stairs

☐ ☐ Uses cane or crutch

☐ ☐ Feeble or slow

☐ ☐ Uses walker? If Yes, can get in and out unassisted?   ☐ Yes ☐ No

☐ ☐ Uses wheelchair? If Yes, can get in and out unassisted?   ☐ Yes ☐ No

☐ ☐ Requires grab bars in bathroom

☐ ☐ Other: (Describe) _____

_____

_____

_____

SERVICES NEEDED (Check items and explain)

YES NO

☐ ☐ Help in getting in and out of bed and dressing _____

☐ ☐ Help with bathing, hair care, personal hygiene_____
☐ ☐ Does client desire and is client capable of doing own personal laundry and other household tasks (specify) _____

☐ ☐ Help with moving about the facility _____

☐ ☐ Help with eating (need for adaptive devices or assistance from another person) _____

☐ ☐ Special diet/observation of food intake _____

☐ ☐ Toileting including assistance equipment, or assistance of another person _____
☐ ☐ Continence, bowel or bladder control. Are assistive devices such as a catheter required? _____
☐ ☐ Help with medication _____

☐ ☐ Needs special observation/night supervision (due to confusion, forgetfulness, wandering) _____
☐ ☐ Help in managing own cash resources _____
☐ ☐ Help in participation in activity programs _____

☐ ☐ Special medical attention _____

☐ ☐ Assistance in incidental health and medical care _____

☐ ☐ Other "Services Needed" not identified above _____

Is there any additional information, which would assist the facility in determining applicant's suitability for admission?   ☐ Yes ☐ No
If Yes, please attach/comments on separate sheet.

To the best of my knowledge; I (the above person) do not need skilled nursing care.

SIGNATURE	DATE COMPLETED
APPLICANT (CLIENT) OR AUTHORIZED REPRESENTATIVE	

SIGNATURE	DATE COMPLETED
LICENSEE OR DESIGNATED REPRESENTATIVE	DATE COMPLETED

180

ALZHEIMER'S FAMILY CENTER, INC.
EMERGENCY MEDICAL INFORMATION

Name _____ Phone _____

Address _____ Start Date _____

_____ Living Arrangements _____

Diagnosis (primary) _____

Diagnosis (secondary) _____

M __ F __ DOB _____ M __ W __ D __ S __ Social Security # _____

Medicare # _____ Secondary Ins. Co. and # _____

Emergency contacts:

_____

_____

_____

Name   Relationship   Phone #

Primary physician _____ Specialty _____

Address _____ Phone _____

Secondary physician _____ Specialty _____

Address _____ Phone _____

Hospital records at _____ Phone _____

Drug allergies _____

Food allergies _____ Diet _____

Dentures _____ Glasses _____ Contacts _____

Current medications:

Name _____ Dosage _____ Times _____

Name _____ Dosage _____ Times _____

Name _____ Dosage _____ Times _____

Name _____ Dosage _____ Times _____

Name _____ Dosage _____ Times _____

Other significant information: _____

_____

_____

ALZHEIMER'S FAMILY CENTER, INC.
ADMISSION AGREEMENT

---   ----------------------
Patient Name   Date of Admission

I. Program
    The basic services provided at the Alzheimer's Family Center are directed toward
    maintenance of independence and self-care. Services shall be provided to the patient
    without discrimination as to race, religion, or national origin.

    The following services will be provided as required by California Administrative
    Code, Title 22:

    A. Basic Services
        1. Observation and supervision.
        2. Supervision of meals and snacks by professional staff.
    B. Basic Health Services
        1. Daily observance of the patient's general health.
        2. Assistance with personal care needs.
        3. Assistance with obtaining medical care as needed.
        4. Assistance with taking prescribed medications as ordered by a physician.
        5. Bedside care for temporary illness until the caregiver can be contacted to
            take the patient home.
    C. Emergency Care
        The Center will obtain emergency services via Paramedic services in the event
        of an emergency medical problem.

II. Center Policies
    A. The Center shall have the right to consult with the patient's attending physician
        regarding medications, and to assist in the supervision of such medication, if in
        the opinion of the Center's administration it is necessary. The Center is not
        licensed for and will not provide nursing care.
    B. The Center shall have the right to ask a patient to leave for failure to adhere to
        those items agreed to in Policy F of this agreement. A 30-day written notice will
        be given unless the cause for leaving is a doctor's recommendation. Prior to any
        eviction the Center must notify the patient's designated representative or
        placement agency.
    C. No patient will be summarily evicted unless behavior is threatening property or
        the safety of other persons in the facility.
    D. If rates are increased, 30 days' written notice will be given.
    E. The Center will not be responsible for any money, valuables, or personal effects
        brought into the Center.
    F. _____ will:
        Name of patient or patient's representative
        1. Cooperate with the general policies of the Center that make it possible for
            patients to be together.
        2. Not bring medication, special foods, or beverages into the Center without the
            knowledge of the Center Manager.
        3. Respect the property of the Center and other patients.

182

G. My signature as "Patient or Patient's Representative" below indicates that I have read, or have had read and explained to me, the provisions of this agreement.

III. Fees
I understand that the fee for each day of attendance is $ _____

_____
Patient or Patient's Representative   Date

_____
Center's Representative (signature and title)

PERSONAL RIGHTS — COMMUNITY CARE FACILITIES
AND CHILD DAY CARE FACILITIES

Explanation

California Code of Regulations, Title 22,, requires that persons admitted to a facility (or their representative) must be advised of their personal rights. In addition, facilities shall post these rights in areas accessible to clients, children and visitors.

This form has been designed to meet the requirements of this regulation, and a copy has been supplied to each facility. A facility may photocopy as many copies as it may need. If your facility is required to post these rights, you may wish to display the copy which has been provided. The front of this form is to be reviewed with the client and/or parent/guardian at the time of admission. This back portion will verify that the rights have been reviewed and the client and/or parent/guardian advised of complaint procedures. A completed copy is to be given to the person(s) who has/have signed the acknowledgment. A completed copy should also be retained in the client's/child's personal file maintained by the facility.

As mentioned above, THE CLIENT AND/OR PARENT(S)/GUARDIAN HAS THE RIGHT TO BE INFORMED OF THE APPROPRIATE LICENSING AGENCY TO CONTACT REGARDING COMPLAINTS WHICH IS:

Name _____

Address _____

City, Zip Code _____

Area Code/Telephone Number _____

ACKNOWLEDGMENT: I have been personally advised and have received a copy of these rights at the time of my admission to

_____

_____   _____
(Signature of Client)   (Date)

and/or

I, as the designated representative and/or parent/guardian of _____
                                                                                                        (Name of Client/Child)

have been personally advised and have received a copy of these rights at the time of his/her admission to

_____
(Name of Facility)

_____   _____   _____
(Signature of Designee)   Title: (Parent, Guardian, etc.)   (Date)

LIC 613 (12/89) (Confidential)

184

PERSONAL RIGHTS
Community Care Facilities and Child Day Care Facilities

Personal Rights. See Section 86072 for waiver conditions applicable to rehabilitation facilities. See Section 101223 for waiver conditions applicable to Child Day Care Facilities.

(a) All Facilities. Each person receiving services from a community care facility and/or a child day care facility shall have rights which include, but are not limited to, the following:

(1) To be accorded dignity in his/her personal relationship with staff and other persons.

(2) To be accorded safe, healthful and comfortable accommodations, furnishings and equipment to meet his/her needs.

(3) To be free from corporal or unusual punishment, infliction of pain, humiliation, intimidation, ridicule, coercion, threat, mental abuse, or other actions of a punitive nature, including but not limited to: interference with the daily living functions, including eating, sleeping, or toileting, or withholding of shelter, clothing, medication or aids to physical functioning.

(4) To be informed, and to have the authorized representative informed by the licensee of the provisions of law regarding complaints including, but not limited to, the address and telephone number of the licensing agency's complaint receiving unit, and of information regarding confidentiality.

(5) To be free to attend religious services or activities of his/her choice and to have visits from the spiritual advisor of his/her choice. Attendance at religious services, either in or outside the facility, shall be on a completely voluntary basis. (In child day care facilities, decisions concerning attendance at religious services or visits from spiritual advisors shall be made by the parents or guardians of the child.)

(6) To leave or depart the facility at any time, except for house rules for the protection of clients or for minors and others from whom legal authority has been established. (Pertains to Community Care Facilities only.)

(7) Not to be locked in any room, building, or facility premises by day or nights.

(8) Not to be placed in restraining devices without advance approval by the licensing agency.

(b) Residential Facilities. See Section 86072 for waiver conditions applicable to rehabilitation facilities. In addition to (a) above, each person provided services by a residential facility should have and may exercise the following rights:

(1) To visit the facility with his/her relatives or authorized representative prior to admission.

(2) To have his/her relatives or authorized representative regularly informed by the facility of activities related to care and supervision including but not limited to modifications to needs and services plan.

(3) To have communications to the facility from his/her relatives or authorized representative answered promptly and completely.

(4) To be informed of the facility's policy concerning family visits and other communication with clients. This policy shall encourage regular family involvement and provide ample opportunities for family participation in activities at the facility.

(5) To have visitors, including advocacy representatives, visit privately during waking hours provided such visitations do not infringe upon the rights of other clients, unless prohibited by court order or the authorized representative.

(6) To wear his or her own clothes, to possess and control his/her own cash resources, to possess and use his/her own personal items, including his/her own toilet articles.

(7) To have access to individual storage space for his/her private use.

(8) To have access to telephones, to make and receive confidential calls, provided such calls do not infringe on the rights of other clients and do not restrict availability of telephone in emergencies.

(9) To mail and receive unopened correspondence unless prohibited by court order or by the authorized representative and for children to have ready access to letter writing materials and stamps.

(10) To receive assistance in exercising the right to vote.

(11) To receive or reject medical care or health-related services, except for minors and others from whom legal authority has been established.

(12) To move from the facility in accordance with the terms of the admission agreement.

Reference: California Code of Regulations - General Licensing Regulations, Sections 80072, and 101223; Section 83072, Small Family Homes; Section 84072 Group Homes; 85072 Adult Residential Homes; Section 87072 Foster Family Homes; Section 87144 Residential Care Facilities for the Elderly; and Section 102423 Family Day Care Homes.

ALZHEIMER'S FAMILY CENTER, INC.
ACKNOWLEDGMENTS

Statements to be Acknowledged	Initials	Date

Received and understand AFC Medication Policies:

    Only medications in a licensed pharmacy container will
be accepted. _____ _____

    Medication left 30 days post-discharge will be disposed
of according to regulations. _____ _____

Publicity Release:

    I hereby give _____ or do not give _____ my permission
for _____ to be photographed for
publicity for the Alzheimer's Family Center. _____ _____

Personal Rights:

    I have received a copy of my personal rights.

Agreement to participate in State of California and AFC Research:

    The Alzheimer's Family Center is required to supply the
California Department of Aging under its Alzheimer's
Day Care Resource Center (ADCRC) grant with
information obtained from personal interviews and data
collection of its patients and their families. Records will
be kept completely confidential and I understand that
my identity and that of the patient will not be disclosed
without my written consent unless required by law.
If I agree to participate with the patient in this data and
information collection, the following tests will be given:

       1. Functional Assessment

       2. DOARS (Mini-Mental Status)

       3. Burden Inventory

    A social work–related and medical history of the family
and patient (ADCRC Intake/Screen) will be obtained.
Participation is voluntary. I may refuse to participate or
withdraw at any time without jeopardy to the care of
the patient. _____ _____

_____   _____   _____

Signature   Witness   Date

_____

Relationship

Assessment

ALZHEIMER'S FAMILY CENTER, INC.
PHYSICAL INFORMATION

HEALTH HISTORY

1. Local medical doctor

2. Consulting physician(s)

3. Past illness, medical treatments, hospitalizations

4. History of present illness

5. Current medications

PHYSICAL ASSESSMENT

1. General appearance

2. Integument (Describe any breakdown)

3. Head, eyes, ears

4. Nose

5. Mouth, throat

6. Respiratory

7. Cardiovascular

8. Gastrointestinal

9. Genitourinary

10. Musculoskeletal

11. Neurological

SELF-CARE CAPACITY (circle one):

1. Is able to care for all personal needs	yes no
2. Can administer own medication	yes no
3. Bathes self	yes no
4. Dresses self	yes no

5. Feeds self   yes   no
6. Cares for toilet needs   yes   no

REQUIRES ASSISTANCE FOR:

1. Ambulation   yes   no
2. Bladder control   yes   no
3. Bowel control   yes   no

TUBERCULOSIS EXAMINATION
     active or quiescent   inactive or none

OTHER CONTAGIOUS OR INFECTIOUS DISEASES
     none   if any, specify:

_____

Signature

Phone number _____

All Rights Reserved. Copyright 1988 by Alzheimer's Family Center, Inc. Reprinted by permission.

ALZHEIMER'S FAMILY CENTER, INC.
LEVEL OF SEVERITY RATING SCALE

_____
Date

_____
Patient Name

_____
Severity Rating

LIGHT STAGE

Activities of Daily Living

_____ Eating: Feeds self without help or supervision; may require some assitance with cutting food

_____ Transfer: Transfers in and out of chairs, car, etc., without assistance or with help of equipment only

_____ Mobility/walking outside: Walks without assistance from a person but may use equipment (e.g., cane)

_____ Mobility/walking inside: Walks without assistance from a person but may use equipment

_____ Dressing: Dresses and undresses without assistance; may need help in selecting clothing

_____ Grooming: Aware of grooming needs and manages grooming without assistance; may need reminders

_____ Bathing: Bathes without assistance but may need reminders

_____ Toileting: Uses toilet room without help but may need reminders

_____ Continence care: Full control of bowel and bladder but may have occasional urinary accident

Instrumental Activities of Daily Living

_____ Shopping: Able to tag along and can make small decisions about purchases

_____ Meal preparation: Able to prepare meals with minimal supervision

_____ Housework: Can handle housework but may need supervision

_____ Laundry: Can do laundry but may need supervision

_____ Transportation: Can handle public transportation or taxis without assistance

_____ Telephone: Can make and receive telephone calls

_____ Medications: Handles own medications with minor help

_____ Money management: Can make small purchases but needs close supervision for money management matters

Behaviors

_____ Anxiety: Low level; demonstrates appropriate motor activity but may have some nervous movements or anxious questions

_____ Alertness: Exhibits high level of awareness and appropriate orientation to person and place

_____ Concentration: Able to concentrate on tasks until completion even if frustrated

_____ Interaction: Initiates conversations with others or does not initiate conversations but responds appropriately

_____ Language: Has no problems expressing or receiving verbal communications; can follow a three-step direction; makes appropriate substitutions for mistakes in words

_____ Participation: Participates in groups readily and with enthusiasm

MODERATE STAGE

Activities of Daily Living

_____ Eating/feeding: Feeds self but may have difficulty with utensils and requires supervision

_____ Transfer: Needs help from a person to transfer from bed, chair, etc.

_____ Mobility/walking outside: Needs assistance of a person

_____ Mobility/walking inside: Needs assistance of a person

_____ Dressing: Clothing must be selected by another person and assistance is required to complete the dressing task

_____ Grooming: Has some interest in remaining well-groomed, but needs supervision and assistance

_____ Bathing: Can wash some parts of self but requires assistance including reminding and supervision

_____ Toileting: Needs help of a person or can handle toileting but needs supervision and assistance with wiping and cleaning self

_____ Continence care: Soils or wets either day or night or both more than once a week

Instrumental Activities of Daily Living

_____ Shopping: Cannot participate in shopping; may have lost interest but is able to tag along for short periods of time. Cannot handle long shopping excursions

_____ Meal preparation: Cannot prepare meals without one-on-one supervision for every step

_____ Housework: Can handle simple tasks but forgets how to complete the tasks without supervision and reminding

_____ Laundry: Can handle simple aspects (e.g., folding clothes) but only with supervision and may periodically forget how to continue with the task

_____ Transportation: Cannot handle transportation on public conveyances without personal help

_____ Telephone: Cannot answer telephone, make calls, or receive messages

_____ Medications: Supervision must be handled by others, but does not resist taking medications

_____ Money management: Cannot handle small change or any management matters

Behaviors

_____ Anxiety: Moderate level with some pacing, wandering, or anxious questioning, but is still able to sit down and be distracted from agitations; may be combative if provoked

_____ Alertness: Not orientated to person, place, or time during the day but some awareness of activities

_____ Concentration: Intermittent attention span—very easily distracted by external or internal stimuli

_____ Interaction: Cannot initiate verbal communication and makes some inappropriate responses to conversations

_____ Language: Is not aware of mistakes; cannot substitute appropriately; invents words or events; repetition and confusion in story

_____ Participation: Cannot initiate activity; may be reluctant to participate in activities but can be engaged in activities with coaxing or other enticing strategies

SEVERE STAGE

Activities of Daily Living

_____ Eating/feeding: Has to be fed or can feed self but only with intensive one-on-one supervision in which food is placed in the hand, with constant reminders to continue to put food into mouth

_____ Transfer: Cannot transfer in and out of bed or chair without total assistance from a person

_____ Mobility/walking inside: Needs physical support of a person or must be moved by a wheelchair

_____ Mobility/walking outside: Needs physical support of a person or must be moved by a wheelchair

_____ Dressing: Cannot handle dressing needs at all; may resist efforts to be dressed

_____ Grooming: Completely unaware of grooming needs and cannot handle any grooming tasks

_____ Bathing: Cannot assist with bathing needs and must be totally bathed by others

_____ Toileting: Needs complete help with toileting, including reminders, clothing, seat placement, and cleaning

_____ Continence care: No toileting control; has accidents or uses diapers

Instrumental Activities of Daily Living

_____ Shopping: Unable to shop

_____ Meal preparation: Unable to participate in meal preparation—can perform only very rudimentary meal preparation functions with intensive supervision (e.g., stirring)

_____ Housework: Unable to perform housework tasks; can handle rudimentary functions with intensive supervision but performance will only approximate the true nature of the task (e.g., folding clothes will consist of placing clothes around the room or folding them in assorted angles)

_____ Laundry: Does not do any laundry

_____ Transportation: Travels only with intensive supervision

_____ Telephone: No ability or awareness about use of phone

_____ Medications: Handled entirely by others and refuses or resists when medicine is offered

_____ Money management: No awareness about money matters

Behaviors

_____ Anxiety: Rarely sits; wanders and paces throughout day and often night as well; constant or repetitive anxious questions; strong potential for violence or combativeness

_____ Alertness: No orientation to time, place, or person

_____ Concentration: Pays no attention to task; needs constant supervision to attend to any activity

_____ Interaction: Always inappropriate with no ability to send or receive verbal messages

_____ Language: Severe verbal limitations: usually incoherent

_____ Participation: No participation in activities without intensive supervision; wanders aimlessly or with agitation; may sleep or look chronically bored

ALZHEIMER'S FAMILY CENTER, INC.
DEMENTED OLDER ADULT RATING SCALE (DOARS)

Name _____

Date _____

Please write in actual patient responses in pencil.

Score Range	Score	Statements
2-0	_____	1. "Please sit down." _____
5-0	_____	2. "What is the year?" _____ "Season?" _____ "Month?" _____ "Date?" _____ "Day of the week?" _____ "Part of the day?" _____ "Time of day?" _____
5-0	_____	3. "What is the name of this place?" _____ "What street is it?" _____ "What floor are we on?" _____ "How long have we been here?" _____ "What is the name of this city?" _____ "County?" _____ "State?" _____
3-0	_____	4. "Please repeat after me: shirt, brown, honesty."
3-0	_____	5. "I would like you to remember these three words." "What are they?" _____ Immediate recall _____ Repeat the words until the patient learns all three. "What are they?" _____ Number of trials _____
5-0	_____	6. "Spell the word *world*." _____ "Now spell the word *world* backwards." _____
3-0	_____	7. Do you remember the 3 words I gave you a few minutes ago?" _____ _____ _____
3-0	_____	8. Show the client a pencil, watch, button. Ask: "What are these?" _____ _____ _____
2-0	_____	9. "Please repeat the following phrase:" "I would like to go home." _____ "No ifs, ands, or buts." _____
3-0	_____	10. "Take this piece of paper with your left hand, fold it in half, and give it back to me." _____
2-0	_____	11. "Read this sentence aloud and do what it says." (Close your eyes.)
2-0	_____	12. "Write your name and a sentence: 'This is a very nice day.' " (Or ask the patient to write a sentence spontaneously.)
2-0	_____	13. "Copy this design." (intersecting pentagons)
2-0	_____	14. "Touch your knee."
2-0	_____	15. The rater has seen the client show an active interest in participating in daily activities.
2-0	_____	16. The rater has seen the client begin conversations with staff and other clients daily.
2-0	_____	17. The rater has seen the client listen when spoken to and respond daily.
2-0	_____	18. Rate the client's vision.
2-0	_____	19. Rate the client's hearing.

Score Range	Score	Statements
4-0	_____	20. The rater has seen the client: Request help from others. _____ Seek emotional support from others. _____ Help others. _____ Show an awareness of past or present abilities and/or accomplishments. _____

TOTAL _____

Adapted from the Adult Day Care Environment for the Demented Older Adult, Illinois Department on Aging, 1987. Reprinted by permission.

CLOSE YOUR EYES

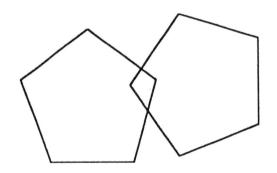

DOARS SCORING WORKSHEET

Verbal	Sensory-Motor	Cognitive	Coping	Psychosocial
(1) ＿＿	(1) ＿＿			
		(2) ＿＿		
		(3) ＿＿		
(4) ＿＿		(4) ＿＿		
(5) ＿＿		(5) ＿＿		
(6) ＿＿		(6) ＿＿		
(7) ＿＿		(7) ＿＿		
(8) ＿＿				
(9) ＿＿				
(10) ＿＿	(10) ＿＿			
(11) ＿＿				
	(12) ＿＿	(12) ＿＿		
	(13) ＿＿			
(14) ＿＿	(14) ＿＿			
				(15) ＿＿
				(16) ＿＿
				(17) ＿＿
	(18) ＿＿			
	(19) ＿＿		(20) ＿＿	
Total ＿＿	Total ＿＿	Total ＿＿	Total ＿＿	Total ＿＿

Verbal % Correct (Total/28) × 100 = ＿＿%
Sensory-Motor % Correct (Total/15) × 100 = ＿＿%
Cognitive % Correct (Total/26) × 100 = ＿＿%
Coping % Correct (Total/4) × 100 = ＿＿%
Psychosocial % Correct (Total/6) × 100 = ＿＿%

ALZHEIMER'S FAMILY CENTER, INC.
DEMENTED OLDER ADULT RATING SCALE (DOARS)
AND MINI-MENTAL STATES EXAMINATION

Patient ID # _____

Date _____

Please write in actual patient responses in pencil.

DOARS SCORE		ADCRC MINI-MENTAL
(2) _____	1. "Please sit down." _____	
(5) _____	2. "What is the year?" _____ "Season?" _____ "Month?" _____ "Date?" _____ "Day of the week?" _____ "Part of the day?" _____ "Time of day?" _____	(5)_____
(5) _____	3. "What is the name of this place?" _____ "What street is it?" _____ "What floor are we on?" _____ "How long have we been here?" _____ "What is the name of this city?" _____ "County?" _____ "State?" _____	(5)_____
(3) _____	4. "Please repeat after me: shirt, brown, honesty."	
(3) _____	5. "I would like you to remember these three words." "What are they?" _____ Immediate recall _____ Repeat the words until the patient learns all three. "What are they?" _____ Number of trials _____	(3)_____
(5) _____	6. "Spell the word *world*." _____ "Now spell the word *world* backwards." _____	(5)_____
(3) _____	7. "Do you remember the 3 words I gave you a few minutes ago?" _____ _____ _____	(3)_____
(3) _____	8. Show the client a pencil, watch, button. Ask: "What are these?" _____ _____ _____	(2)_____
(2) _____	9. "Please repeat the following phrase:" "I would like to go home." _____ "No ifs, ands, or buts." _____	(1)_____
(3) _____	10. "Take this piece of paper with your left hand, fold it in half, an give it back to me." _____	(3)_____
(2) _____	11. "Read this sentence aloud and do what it says." (Close your eyes.)	(1)_____
(2) _____	12. "Write your name and a sentence: 'This is a very nice day.'" (Or ask the patient to write a sentence spontaneously.)	(1)_____
(2-0) __	13. "Copy this design." (intersecting paragons)	(1)_____
(2-0) __	14. "Touch your knee."	
(2-0) __	15. The rater has seen the client show an active interest in participating in daily activities.	
(2-0) __	16. The rater has seen the client begin conversations with staff and other clients daily.	
(2-0) __	17. The rater has seen the client listen when spoken to and respond daily.	
(2-0) __	18. Rate the client's vision.	
(2-0) __	19. Rate the client's hearing.	

(2–0) ___ 20. The rater has seen the client:
_____ Request help from others.
_____ Seek emotional support from others.
_____ Help others.
_____ Show an awareness of past or present abilities and/or
accomplishments.

(53) ___ TOTAL DOARS   TOTAL MINI-MENTAL (30) _____

This is a modification and fusion of DOARS and the California State ADCRC Mini-Mental Assessment Instrument. Adapted from the Adult Day Care Environment for the Demented Older Adult, Illinois Department on Aging, 1987, and Folstein, M. R., Folstein, S., & McHugh, P. R. (1975). Mini-Mental state: A practical method for grading the cognitive state of patients for the clinician. *Journal of Psychiatric Research, 12,* 189–198.

CLOSE YOUR EYES

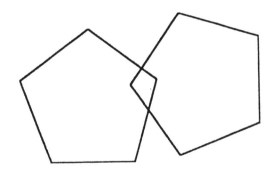

GUIDE FOR SCORING DOARS AND MINI-MENTAL

Item	DOARS		Mini-Mental
1	2 points if responds readily 1 point if responds after prompting 0 if no response to request	(2)	0
2	1 point for year 1 point for season 1 point for month 1 point for date or day of week 1 point for part of day or time of day	(5)	5 points—same
3	1 point for name of place or street 1 point for floor or how long we've been here 1 point for city 1 point for county 1 point for state	(5)	5 points—same
4	1 point for each word repeated	(3)	0
5	1 point for each word immediately recalled	(3)	3 points—same
6	2 points if spelled correctly frontwards 3 points if 5 letters correct and in order backwards 2 points if 4 letters correct 1 point if 2–3 letters correct	(5)	5 points—same
7	1 point for each word remembered	(3)	3 points—same
8	1 point for each correct identification	(3)	2 points for 2 correct identifications
9	1 point for each correct repetition	(2)	1 point for both
10	1 point for each direction correctly followed	(3)	3 points—same
11	1 point if sentence read 1 point if direction followed	(2)	1 point for total response
12	1 point if name correctly written	(2)	
	1 point if sentence correct		1 point for sentence
13	2 points if figures are pentagons and are intersecting	(2)	1 point for totally correct
	1 point if any shaped figures intersect		
14	2 points if correct immediate response 1 points if response after prompting 0 points if prompting does not produce results	(2)	0
15	2 points if 100% of time 1 point if 50% of time 0 points entirely passive	(2)	0

Item	DOARS		Mini-Mental
16	2 points if 100% of the time 1 point if 50% of the time	(2)	0
17	2 points if 100% of the time 1 point if 50% of the time	(2)	0
18	2 points if excellent 1 point if good 0 points if poor	(2)	0
19	2 points if excellent 1 point if good 0 points if poor	(2)	0
20	1 point for first two items 1 point for last two items	(2)	0
Total		53	30

Locate a comfortable and quiet area.

Use a dark pen for the patient to write and draw.

If stress is high during the examination it may be broken down into parts and done over a period of several days if necessary.

In the case of language, hearing, or visual deficits, other forms of testing may need to be devised.

Adapted from the Adult Day Care Environment for the Demented Older Adult, Illinois Department on Aging, 1987, and Folstein, M. R., Folstein, S., & McHugh, P. R. (1975). Mini-Mental state: A practical method for grading the cognitive state of patients for the clinician. *Journal of Psychiatric Research, 12,* 189–198.

ALZHEIMER'S FAMILY CENTER, INC.
BEHAVIOR ASSESSMENT SCALES

ANXIETY: Level of anxiety or nervousness expressed in motor activities and/or anxious questions and comments

    Very high   Appropriate motor activity....................................4
    High   Nervous movements and anxious questioning are occasional; no agitated wandering......................................3
    Moderate   Some pacing, wandering, or anxious questioning..................2
    Low   Rarely sits, paces most of the day, constant or repetitive anxious questions/comments......................................1

ALERTNESS: Level of awareness of things, people, activities

    Very high   Notices almost everything 4
    High   Mostly aware 3
    Moderate   Intermittent awareness.......................................2
    Low   Generally unaware throughout the day...........................1

CONCENTRATION: Ability to concentrate on task suited to functioning level

    Very high   Focuses on task until complete even if frustrated.................4
    High   Shortened attention span; focuses on task with assistance.............3
    Moderate   Intermittent attention, easily distracted by nonobvious stimuli such as own thoughts 2
    Poor   Oblivious to task, pays no attention 1

EATING: Ability to function appropriately and independently during meals

    Very high   Eats lunch by him/herself.....................................4
    High   Eats lunch but needs supervision...............................3
    Moderate   Needs constant supervision or will take food from others, wander while eating, or needs to be coaxed to eat 2
    Low   Wanders from table, must be fed or handed food, unable to tolerate group eating 1

GROOMING: Awareness of dress and personal care

    Very high   Concerned about grooming; attempts to maintain good grooming habits 4
    High   Somewhat aware of growing needs, but may have trouble handling some of the activities of grooming................................3
    Moderate   Almost no awareness of grooming; will be disheveled and unclean unless assisted by caregiver 2
    Low   No awareness of grooming; totally dependent on caregiver for grooming needs; does not assist in any way with grooming 1

INTERACTION: Degree of verbal interactions with others

    Very high   Initiates conversations with others 4
    High   Responds appropriately when others initiate talk 3
    Moderate   Some inappropriate responses to conversations initiated by others......................................2

Low   Constantly inappropriate or no response to conversations
initiated by others 1

LANGUAGE: Ability to communicate meaning to others

Very high   Has no problems or has some search for synonyms or word
substitution; awareness of mistakes. 4
High   Loses thread of thought, noticeable vocabulary loss, some
awareness of mistakes but unable to correct 2
Moderate   Poor syntax and sequence, invents words, repetition and
confusion in story. 3
Low   Parrots words, mostly incoherent, mostly uncomprehending,
severe verbal limitations 1

MOBILITY: Degree of physical independence and coordination

Very high   Walks and sits independently including stairs .4
High   Walks and sits independently but needs some help with stairs 3
Moderate   Walks and sits with occasional assistance from physical
aides or persons 2
Low   Can't walk or sit without full support and help 1

PARTICIPATION: Degree of enjoyment, interest, enthusiasm while
participating in appropriate activity

Very high   Participates readily with interest and enthusiasm. 4
High   Participates on own in a perfunctory manner 3
Moderate   Participates reluctantly or only after urging .2
Low   No participation, looks bored or unhappy; may wander aimlessly
or sleep 1

TOILETING: Ability to carry out bathroom functions independently

Very high   Toilets self independently, needs no reminders 4
High   Needs minimal help with toileting, including reminders, seat
placement 3
Moderate   Needs complete help with toileting, including reminders,
clothing, seat placement 2
Low   No toileting control, has accident, or only uses diapers. 1

Adapted from the Adult Day Care Environment for the Demented Older Adult, Illinois
Department on Aging, 1987. Reprinted by permission.

ALZHEIMER'S FAMILY CENTER, INC.
PROGRESS NOTES

PATIENT #: _____

NAME: _____

Date and Initial	Type of Contact	Comments

Daily Roster/Client and Staff Schedules

ALZHEIMER'S FAMILY CENTER, INC.
DAILY ROSTER

Date _____   Location _____

Patients	Caregiver**	In	Out	Personal Belongings	Code
A, Doris					L
C, Della					M
C, Joe					L
C, Alice					M
C, Ed					T
*deL, Bill					L
D, Victor					S
*G, Elise					T
H, David					L
H, Daisy					L
*K, Florence					M
K, Bert					T
K, Jack					M
*K, Sylvia					T
M, Helen					T
N, Alta					M

Note: In case of an emergency evacuation, this register MUST accompany patients by assigned staff member for a patient count at designated regrouping area. Code: L = light, M = moderate, S = severe, T = temporary. * = Van services. ** = Today's designated emergency contact.

ALZHEIMER'S FAMILY CENTER, INC.
STAFF SCHEDULE

STAFFING FOR _____

                (day)   (date)

STAFF _____ _____ _____

          _____ _____ _____   COMMENTS

Time	Task		Comments
9:00–9:30	Greet, socialize	_____	
	Put lunch away, serve coffee	_____	
9:30–10:00	Program: Newspaper	_____	
	Program Support	_____	
	Greet, Put lunch away	_____	9:45 Set up Patio _____
	Wanderers and Door	1. _____	
		2. _____	
10:00–11:00	Program _____	_____	
	Program Support	_____	
	Wanderers and Door	1. _____	
		2. _____	
Approx. 11:00	WALK: Make assignments	_____	
11:00–12:00	Program _____	_____	
	Program Support	_____	
	Wanderers and Door	1. _____	11:15/30 Fix Lunches____
		2. _____	
12:00–12:30	LUNCH: Break 12:20	_____	SPECIAL LUNCH NEEDS:
	Break 1:00	_____	
	Break 1:30	_____	
12:30–1:00	Program: Massages/Music	_____	
	Move people to Music Room	_____	
	Wanderers and Door	1. _____	
		2. _____	
1:00–2:00	Program _____	_____	
	Program Support	_____	
	Wanderers and Door	1. _____	
		2. _____	
2:00–3:00	Program _____	_____	
	Program Support	_____	
	Wanderers and Door	_____	
Approx. 2:30	WALK: Make assignments	_____	
3:00–3:30	SNACK: Prepare	_____	
	Serve	_____	
	Wanderers and Door	1. _____	
		2. _____	
3:30–5:00	Program _____	_____	
	Program Support	_____	
	Wanderers, Doors, and	1. _____	
	check signouts	2. _____	

ALZHEIMER'S FAMILY CENTER, INC.
TOILETING SCHEDULE

Name	Time	Results	Staff
Daisy	after lunch assist		
Marion (colostomy)	11-1-3 assist		
Chris	prn (check pad)		
Rufino	remind prn		
Elsie	remind prn		
Della	remind prn		
Louise	remind assist with clothing		
Ed	11 + 3 remind		
Howard	remind + 1 person assist		
Bertha	after lunch (assist)		
Ann	remind		
Ed	11-1-3 remind/assist		
Frank	after lunch (remind) (assist)		

Code to be used: 0 = No Void, V = Voided, R = Refused.

prn = take as required.

Care Plan

PATIENT CARE PLAN

Patient's Name _____Helen_____   Date _____July 17, 1987_____

Staff: _____, Soc. Wk; _____, Activities; _____, Nursing

Problem	Goals	Plan and Approaches	Staff
I. *Physical* Needs supervision in bathroom Inability to clean self	Keep her clean and free of odor and dry	Place her on bathroom list for supervision—immediately and ongoing	R.N.
Possible limited mobility	Determine mobility status	Observe and record daily in progress notes—by August 1, 1987	R.N. Actv.
II. *Psychosocial* Limited social contacts	Increase socialization by ensuring at least one morning and one afternoon one-on-one	Special greeting upon arrival; introduce them to each other. Assign a volunteer, staff, or patient to a minimum 5-minute conversation for A.M. and P.M.	Actv.
Limited ability to initiate activities or to be involved in activities	Will participate in planned center activities	Encourage with positive reinforcement when she participates and follows through in activities Record participation on daily program sheet	Act. Actv.
III. *Family* No contact with family	To develop a regular contact with family	Set up an interview with family by August 1, 1987 Invite family to group therapy sessions with psychiatrist	Soc. Wk. Soc. Wk.

Monthly Review
Outcome: _____

_____

_____

Daily and Monthly Plan Plan

A GENERIC LOOK AT THE DAILY PLAN

Arrival	Introductions, socialization, self-esteem building
Schedule planning	Staff discuss with the group the plan for the day's activities—which are written on the blackboard
Reality orientation	Reading of newspaper—with emphasis on patient participation
Exercise	To provide sensory stimulation and to maintain strength and range of motion
Group time	Activity selected according to group's ability to respond for that day. Includes crafts, cooking, and games
Lunch	Socialization plus patient participation in preparation and clean-up—as part of activities of daily living
Rest and relaxation	With music and massage
Afternoon exercise group activity	Similar to morning exercise Determined by patient functional levels
Individual projects	Games, special interests, etc.
Physically active Group activity	Bowling, shuffleboard, volleyball, throw and toss, ball games, etc.
Small group activity	Same as above
Departure	Positive feedback to families

The program places a strong emphasis on sensory stimulation. Taken as a whole, every sensory level is stimulated through one or more programs: visual, auditory, tactile, vestibular, and kinesthetic. There is also a balance between cognitive or fine motor activities that are more sedentary and large motor activities that are more physically demanding.

At the end of each day, staff record the progress of each patient using a Behavior Assessment Scale, which looks at the following areas:

Anxiety	Alertness
Concentration	Eating
Grooming	Interaction
Language	Mobility
Participation	Toileting

In this way, patient progress toward goals can receive daily attention.

JUNE 1990

MONDAY	TUESDAY	WEDNESDAY	THURSDAY	FRIDAY
	June Birthdays Peggy C. 6/8 Peg P. 6/11 Barb H. 6/26	**Daily Routine** 9:00 Arrive, Socialize, Coffee 9:30 Current Events 10:00 Group Activity 11:00 Walk 12:00 Lunch 1:00 Group Activity 2:00 Walk 3:00 Snack 4:00 Group Activity 5:00 Center Closes		**1** 10:00 Get Strong with M.J. 1:00 Music Therapy with Alice 3:30 Happy Wedding Bells to Ann! 4:00 Sound of Moods Game
NATIONAL FAMILY DAY 4 10:00 Physical Fitness 1:00 Art with Mary 2:50 Discussion and Collage: Families 4:00 Lawrence Welk	**5** 10:30 Sing-A-Long with Jane and special guest Jeane Coleman 11:30 Hymn Singing 1:00 Tone your Muscles 4:00 Jane's Piano	**Covered Bridge Day 6** 10:00 Shape Up with M.J. 1:00 Alice's Music 3:30 Discussion: Covered Bridges 4:00 Reminiscing with Slides FAMILY MTG: Dr. Goodrich	**7** 10:00 Musical Fun with Alice 1:00 Physical Fitness with M.J. 3:15 Crafts with M.J.: Place Settings	**8** 10:00 Exercise with M.J. 1:00 Alice's Guitar and Flute Fest 3:30 Balloon Game 4:00 Bob's Musical Memories
HUG DAY – GIVE SOME¹ ONE A HUG!! 10:00 Physical Fitness 2:30 Humane Society 3:50 Hugging Exercise 4:00 Lawrence Welk	**12** 10:30 Accordionist David Hubbel 11:30 Hymn Singing 3:30 Discussion: I Remember Dad 4:00 Sing with Jane ***** C E L E B R A T E F A T H E R S !! *****	**13** 10:00 Physical Fitness with MaryJane 1:00 Music with Alice 3:30 Father's Day Poetry/Collage 4:00 FAMILY MEETING: Dr. George and Joy Glenner	**FLAG DAY! 14** 10:30 Musical Trivia with Jane 11:30 Sing-A-Long 1:00 Exercises 3:30 Crafts	**FRIENDSHIP DAY 15** 10:30 Exercise with Julia 11:30 Discussion: Friends 1:00 Sing-A-Long with Bob 2:30 Bean Bag Toss 3:30 Musical Memories
18 10:30 Singing and Dancing with Musical Memories 2:50 Ring Toss Game 3:50 Stretching 4:00 Lawrence Welk	**19** 10:30 Music and Movement with Ann 11:30 Sing-A-Long with Jane 1:00 Physical Fitness 3:30 Discussion: Stop and smell the Roses 4:00 Sing with Bob	**20** 10:00 Get Fit with M.J. 1:00 Alice's Music 3:30 What's Different? 4:00 Discussion: Flowers FAMILY MEETING: Dr. Goodrich	**21** 10:00 Music Therapy with Alice 1:00 Physical Fitness with Mary Jane 3:30 Crafts with M.J.: Rose Sachets National Rose Month	**22** 10:00 Get Strong with Mary Jane 1:00 Alice's Guitar and Flute Fest 3:30 Bean Bag Toss 4:00 Bob's Music
25 10:00 Physical Fitness 1:00 Art with Mary 2:30 Poetry with Ann 3:30 Balloon Game 4:00 lawrence Welk	**26** 10:30 Musical Trivia 11:30 Sing with Jane 3:30 Word Game 4:00 Sing-A-Long with Bob and dance with Jane	**27** 10:00 Shape Up with M.J. 1:00 Music with Alice 3:15 Guitar Sing-A-Long with Ollie Shaffer 4:00 FAMILY MEETING: Judy Joiner	**28** 10:00 Musical Fun with Alice 1:00 Physical Fitness Mary Jane 3:30 Crafts with M.J.	**29** 10:00 Stretch and Tone with MaryJane 1:00 Music Therapy with Alice 4:00 Bob's Musical Memories

ALZHEIMER'S FAMILY CENTER, INC.℠
3686 Fourth Avenue, San Diego, CA 92103
Phone (619) 295-2419

Monthly Program Report

1.Site No: ....
2.Reporting Period: .... / ....   FY: .... - ....
month   year

Participation:

A. Monthly participants count:
1. Participants count on last day of the previous month . . . . _____
2. Participants admitted . . . . _____
3. Participants readmitted . . . . _____
4. Participants discharged . . . . _____
5. Total number of participants enrolled in the program . . . . _____
B. Unduplicated count: Year to date
6. Unduplicated count on last day of prior month . . . . _____
7. Total unduplicated count (Add #2 to #6 for unduplicated total). . . . . _____
C. Waiting list:
8. Participants on the waiting list from previous month. . . . . _____
9. Participants removed from the waiting list . . . . _____
10. Participants added to waiting list. . . . . _____

Attendance:

11. Total hours of operation . . . . _____
12. Total days of operation . . . . _____
13. Days of day care operation . . . . _____
14. Number of participant days . . . . _____

Operations:

15. Number of paid staff hours. . . . . _____
16. Number full-time staff . . . . _____
17. Number part-time staff . . . . _____
18. Number of volunteer staff hours. . . . . _____
19. Number of volunteers . . . . _____

Support:

20. Hours of in-service training. . . . . _____
21. Number of trainees . . . . _____
22. Hours of training for families . . . . _____
23. Number of trainees . . . . _____
24. Hours of support group . . . . _____
25. Number attending support groups . . . . _____
26. Hours of counseling . . . . _____
27. Number counseled . . . . _____
28. Hours of community education. . . . . _____
29. Number attending community education. . . . . _____
30. Hours of professional training. . . . . _____
31. Number attending. . . . . _____
32. Hours of intern orientation . . . . _____
33. Number attending . . . . _____
34. Hours of consultation. . . . . _____
35. Number of consultations. . . . . _____

Program:

36. Number of home visits . . . . _____

PREPARED BY:...................................   **REVIEWED BY**: ....
DATE:........../........./.........   **(SITE DIRECTOR'S SIGNATURE)**

SAMPLE JOB DESCRIPTIONS

Executive/Program Director

1. *Qualifications:* Applicants for the position of Executive/Program Director must have a master's degree in a human services field *or* equivalent experience; be able to supervise paid personnel and volunteers; be knowledgeable about basic office procedures, administration, and personnel activities; have fiscal and budgeting experience; have experience with grants and fund raising; be proficient at community relations and coordination; have experience with outreach and marketing techniques; and have demonstrated aptitude for working with caregivers, seniors, handicapped, and/or demented patients. Experience in adult day care, or in working specifically with Alzheimer's patients, is preferred. Must be able to assist with participant transfer and have valid driver's license.

2. *Job Description:* The Executive/Program Director will be responsible for the daily operation of the Alzheimer's Day Care Center. The Executive/Program Director reports to the Center Board of Directors.

3. *Duties:* The Executive/Program Director's duties include the following:

A. *Administration and Personnel*
   Supervises program staff.
   Advertises, interviews, and hires for positions below Executive/
      Program Director.
   Does written evaluations of staff annually, and at the end of the probationary period for new employees.
   Coordinates fringe benefits.
   Provides staff with personnel manuals.
   Provides staff a list of board members.
   Provides orientation and training for newly hired staff.
   Has responsibility for recruiting, training, and supervising volunteers.
   Terminates staff.
B. *Record Keeping*
   Maintains all data and reports required by board, foundation, state and
      federal government agencies, and other funding sources.
   Maintains attendance records.
   Maintains supportive records (schedules, teacher hours, volunteers, interns, students, etc.)
   Maintains registration cards, assessment sheets.

This description combines duties of an Executive Director (administration) with those of a Program Director (program). Adapted by permission from the Berkeley Alzheimer's Family Respite Center.

Approves and signs time cards.

Keeps telephone log.

Maintains client behavior/problem log.

Completes outreach reports.

Maintains data required by funding sources.

C. *Program*

Supervises client intake.

Assists with program activities as necessary, including transferring participants.

Supervises personal assessment or re-evaluation of clients as necessary.

Maintains client files and emergency records.

Terminates inappropriate clients from program as necessary.

Administers and supervises administration of required measurement instruments.

Supervises program schedule.

Supervises nutrition program.

Supervises transportation services.

D. *Budgeting and Fiscal Activities*

Accounts for money collected.

Keeps individualized records of client fees and determines fee schedule.

Reconciles totals and deposits at the end of each month.

Shall be knowledgeable of content and format and able to produce accurate and timely end-of-month reports.

Makes regular deposits.

Shall be knowledgeable of methods, format, and content of contracts and budgets of program, and act in conformance with their contents.

Coordinates purchase and reimbursement of supplies and equipment.

E. *Community Relations and Coordination, Outreach, and Marketing*

Acts as liaison with all dementia, long-term care, and agency providers.

Acts as liaison with Adult School Coordinator, Meals Program, and Transportation Program.

Coordinates marketing and outreach efforts for program referrals.

Develops Center brochure.

Develops and maintains Center mailing list.

F. *Fund raising and Grants*

Identifies and writes appropriate proposals.

Implements and coordinates fund-raising activities.

G. *Site*

Serves as liaison to the host institution.

Maintains security of buildings.

Has responsibility for physical appearance of program site.

Supervises site maintenance.

H. *Other duties as assigned.*

Activity Coordinator

1. *Qualifications:* This person must have a working knowledge of Alzheimer's disease and related dementias, be experienced in organizing activities and supervising other staff, obtain a CPR card and keep it current, and have a demonstrable aptitude for working with elderly, handicapped, or demented patients.

2. *Job Description:* The Activity Coordinator will supervise daily activities, develop and maintain a structured activity program, set up and plan for special events, assist in care and personal hygiene of patients, coordinate instructors and volunteers, and serve as an assistant to the Director. He/she will take over the daily operations of the Center when necessary.

3. *Duties:* The duties of the Activity Coordinator are:

A. Works with Director to complete daily paperwork.
   Ordering lunches and snacks
   Collecting and recording fees
   Daily scheduling
   Client behavior log
   Telephone log
B. Supervises overall program to ensure that all patients remain inside designated areas.
C. Helps set up and serve lunches and snacks.
D. Supervises mealtime activity, assists with eating/clean-up.
E. Provides programming for teachers when absent, and at other times when teachers are not scheduled.
F. May open and close premises.
G. Monitors activity of patients—wandering, disposition, etc.
H. Plans, organizes, and does follow-up of special events and parties.
I. Assists in bathing, showering, toileting, and basic personal care and hygiene of patients.
J. Other duties as assigned.

Program Aide/Specialist

1. *Qualifications:* A Program Aide/Specialist should have a high school diploma and a demonstrable aptitude in working with victims of Alzheimer's disease and related disorders. He/she must obtain a CPR card and keep it current and attend training and in-service sessions. The Program Aide/Specialist must be responsible and work well with others. Expe-

Job descriptions for Activity Coordinator, Program Aide/Specialist, and Volunteer reprinted by permission of the Berkeley Alzheimer's Family Respite Center.

rience in working with the elderly, handicapped, or demented patients is preferred.

2. *Job Description:* The Program Aide/Specialist will provide personal care for patients in the program and assist the staff and teachers with daily activities and meals.

3. *Duties:* The duties of a Program Aide/Specialist are:

A. Sets up the room for the daily program.
B. Maintains neatness and order in rooms.
C. Assists patients to and from their cars.
D. Assists patients with personal care
E. Organizes and distributes lunches and snacks.
F. Assists patients with eating and clean-up.
G. Helps teachers and staff with daily activities.
H. Assists Activity Coordinator with special events/parties.
I. Takes patients for walks outside.
J. Keeps Director and Activity Coordinator informed of needed supplies.
K. Socializes with patients.
L. Monitors behavior of patients (disposition, wandering).
M. Helps maintain behavior log and client files.
N. Supervises overall activities to ensure that patients remain inside designated areas.
O. May open and close premises.
P. Other duties as assigned.

Volunteer

POSITION TITLE: Alzheimer's Day Care Center Volunteer

PROGRAM DESCRIPTION: The Alzheimer's Day Care Center provides day care for individuals with Alzheimer's disease or related dementias. The purpose of the program is to enhance the demented participant's quality of life and to ease the family's burden of caring for the individual with dementia. Volunteers play a key role and will be used in all aspects of the program. Volunteers bring extra energy, ideas, and motivation to the program. They can offer warmth and support to program participants. The Center is currently open five days a week, Monday through Friday, from 7:30 A.M. to 6:00 P.M.

VOLUNTEER TASKS: Volunteers will work under the supervision of the Activity Coordinator.

- Volunteers will be offered opportunities to conduct small group activities, lead exercises, help in meal preparation, and discuss the news and day's events.

- Volunteers will offer reassurance and companionship to the participants. Volunteers can work one-on-one with an individual or with groups.
- Those volunteers who do not wish to work directly with the participants can help by answering telephones, typing letters, preparing mailings, and designing fliers and notices.
- Volunteers will be used to make creative bulletin boards, calendars, and a monthly newsletter for families.
- Volunteers will organize birthday parties, holiday celebrations, and other social events.
- Volunteers with special skills can share them with the participants. These special skills may include musical, gardening, cosmetology, and/or massage skills.

TRAINING PROVIDED: Volunteers will work with the Activity Coordinator to select an appropriate schedule based on volunteers' interest and program needs. Training will be provided by the Center staff. A volunteer manual will be given to all volunteers. Volunteers will participate in an orientation and training session. Volunteers are encouraged to attend all staff meetings and follow-up training sessions. The Activity Coordinator will be available to talk with volunteers on an individual basis as needed.

REQUIREMENTS: Volunteers are required to:

- promptly notify the program if they cannot attend their scheduled session.
- attend orientation and training sessions.
- have a current TB skin test.

QUALIFICATIONS: Volunteers should show a concern for and interest in older people along with an ability to work cooperatively with the program staff and other volunteers.

FOR MORE INFORMATION, please call (telephone number) and talk to the Activity Coordinator.

SAMPLE TABLES OF CONTENTS FOR POLICY AND PROCEDURE MANUALS

Sample Program Policies and Procedures Manual Table of Contents

SECTION I: Philosophy, Goals, and Objectives

A. Philosophy and mission statement of the dementia day care center
B. Goals and objective of the dementia day care center

SECTION II: Program Organization

A. Organizational Policies
   1. By-laws and membership list of the Board of Directors
   2. Committees and functions of the Board of Directors
   3. Advisory committee functions and membership list
   4. Organizational chart
   5. Other related committees, subcommittees, affiliated organizations, etc.
B. Operations and Management Policies and Procedures
   1. Hours and days of operation
   2. Official closing days/unscheduled closings
   3. Attendance
   4. Volunteers and other professionals
   5. Program format
C. Budget Policies and Procedures
   1. Description of budget planning process
   2. Description of budget oversight responsibilities
   3. Description of bookkeeping, accounting, auditing procedures
   4. Fee structure/sliding fee scale
   5. Participant payment mechanism
D. Personnel Policy and Procedures
   1. Personnel policies and guidelines
   2. Job descriptions

SECTION III: Program/Services Policies and Procedures

A. List of Services
B. Admission
C. Care Plan
D. Discharge

Reprinted by permission of the Berkeley Alzheimer's Family Respite Center.

E. Waiting List Policies
F. Medication Management
G. Medical Emergencies
H. Transportation
I. Nutrition/Meals
J. Participant Records
K. Insurance and Liability Policies
L. Family and Caregiver Responsibilities
M. Interorganizational Relations with Other Community Agencies

SECTION IV: Administrative Records

A. Personnel and Payroll Records
B. Administrative Documents (attendance, travel, training, etc.)
C. Insurance and Professional Documents
D. Manual and Automated Record Keeping Policies and Procedures
E. Equipment, Key, and Other Inventories

SECTION V: Physical Plant Policies and Procedures

A. Building/Structural Licenses and Regulations
B. Program Safety Policies and Procedures/Security
C. Building Maintenance and Housekeeping

SECTION VI: Disaster Preparedness Plan

A. Fire Safety Plan
   1. Fire marshal approval
   2. Fire drills
   3. Inspections
B. Disaster Plans
   1. Procedures for staff
   2. Procedures for participants

SECTION VII: Quality Assurance Policies and Procedures

A. Confidentiality
B. Internal and External Quality Assurance Requirements
C. Participant Record Review
D. Program Evaluation and Research

SECTION VIII: Appendices

A. Program Forms
B. Complete Participant Chart

Sample Personnel Policies and Procedures Manual
Table of Contents

Reprinted by permission of the Berkeley Alzheimer's Family Respite Center.

   2. Workers' Compensation
   3. State Disability Insurance
   4. Disability Income Protection
   5. Health/Dental/Vision/Life Insurance
   6. Retirement Annuity
E. Leaves of Absence
   1. Sick Leave/Leave of Absence
      a) Sick Leave
      b) Personal and Emergency Leave
      c) Termination
      d) Military Leave
      e) Jury Duty Leave
   2. Medical
      a) General
      b) Definition
      c) Procedure
      d) Medical Leave and Vacation Time
   3. Maternity
      a) General
      b) Definition
      c) Procedure
      d) Medical Leave and Vacation Time
   4. Work-Related Injury or Illness
      a) General
      b) Definition
      c) Procedure
      d) Work-Related Leave
   5. Personal Leave of Absence
      a) General
      b) Definition
      c) Procedures
      d) Personal Leave

SECTION VI: Performance Evaluation

A. Principle
B. Procedure

BIBLIOGRAPHY

Adapting the adult day care environment for the demented older adult. (1986). Springfield, IL: North Shore Senior Center, Parkside Human Services Corporation. (For copies, write to the Illinois Department on Aging, 421 E. Capitol Ave., Springfield, IL 62701.)

Adult day care in the United States: A comparative study (final report). (1975). Transcendency Corporation for the National Center for Health Services Research.

Bachner, J. P., & Cornelius, E. *Activities coordinator's guide: A handbook for activities coordinators in long-term care facilities.* Washington, DC: U.S. Government Printing Office. (This book is for sale by the Superintendent of Documents, U.S. Government Printing Office, Washington, DC 20402.)

Berman, S., Delaney, N., Gallagher, D., Atkins, P., & Graeber, M. P. (1987). Respite Care: A partnership between a Veterans Administration nursing home and families to care for frail elders at home. *The Gerontologist, 27*(5), 518–584.

Besdine, R. W. (1983). The educational utility of comprehensive functional assessment in the elderly. *Journal of the American Geriatrics Society, 31*(11), 651–656. (Address correspondence and reprint requests to Richard W. Besdine, M.D., Hebrew Rehabilitation Center for the Aged, Harvard Medical School, 1200 Centre St., Boston, MA 02131.)

A brief overview of requirements to become an adult day health care (ADHC) provider (revised). (1984). Sacramento, CA: California Department of Aging. (For copies, write to the California Department of Aging, 1600 K St., Sacramento, CA 95814.)

Burdz, M. P., Eaton, W. O., & Bond, J. B. (1988). Effect of respite care on dementia and nondementia patients and their caregivers. *Psychology and Aging, 3*(1), 38–42.

Calkins, M. P. (1988). *Design for dementia: Planning environments for the elderly and the confused.* Owings Mills, MD: National Health Publishing.

Capitman, J. A. (1982). *Evaluation of adult day health care programs in Califor-*

nia pursuant to Assembly Bill 1611 Chapter 1066, Statutes of 1977. Sacramento, CA: California Department of Health Services.

Capitman, J. A. (1984). *Supplemental report on the adult day health care programs in California: A comparative cost analysis.* Sacramento, CA: California Department of Health Services.

Carroll, K. (Ed.). (1978). *Compensating for sensory loss.* Minneapolis: Ebenezer Center for Aging and Human Development. (This book may be obtained by writing the Ebenezer Center for Aging and Human Development, Minneapolis, MN 55407.)

Caserata, M. S., Lund, D. A., Wright, S. D., & Redburn, D. E. (1987). Caregivers to dementia patients: The utilization of community services. *The Gerontologist, 27*(2), 209–214.

Cohen, D., & Eisdorfer, C. (1988). Depression in family members caring for a relative with Alzheimer's disease. *Journal of the American Geriatrics Society,* October 1988, 885–889.

Corby, N. H., Downing, R., & Lindeman, D. A. (1988). *Alzheimer's day-care resource center guide: Starting a dementia day-care program in California.* Sacramento, CA: California Department of Aging. (This book may be obtained through the Alzheimer's Branch, California Department of Aging, 1600 K St., Sacramento, CA 95814 or by calling 916-323-5170.)

Crepeau, E. (1980). *Activities programming—Serving the elderly. The technique: Part 5.* Durham, NH: New England Gerontology Center. (This book may be obtained by writing the New England Gerontology Center, 15 Garrison Ave., Durham, NH 03824.)

Davis, L. J., & Kirkland, M. (Eds.). (1986). *The role of occupational therapy with the elderly.* Rockville, MD: The American Occupational Therapy Association, Inc. (This document may be obtained by writing the American Occupational Therapy Association, Inc., 1383 Piccard Dr., Rockville, MD 20850.)

Directory of state small business programs, 1980 edition. (1980). Washington, DC: Small Business Administration. (This document may be obtained by writing to the Small Business Administration, Office of the Chief Counsel for Advocacy, Washington, DC 20416.)

Doty, P. (1986). Family care of the elderly. *Milbank Memorial Fund Quarterly, 64*(1), 34–75.

Ernst, M., & Shore, H. (1978). *Sensitizing people to the processes of aging: The inservice educator's guide.* Denton, TX: Center for Studies in Aging Resources. (This book may be obtained by writing the Center for Studies in Aging Resources, P.O. Box 13438, NT Station, Denton, TX 76203.)

Evans, D. A., Funkenstein, H. H., Albert, M. S., Scherr, P. A., Cook, N. R., Chown, M. J., Hebert, L. E., Hennekens, C. H., & Taylor, J. O. (1989). Prevalence of Alzheimer's disease in a community population of older persons. *JAMA, 262*(18), 2551–2556.

Fact sheet: Alzheimer's disease. San Francisco, CA: Family Survival Project. (This is available from the Family Survival Project, 425 Bush St., Suite 500, San Francisco, CA 94108.)

Falcone, A. (1983). Comprehensive functional assessment as an administrative tool. *Journal of the American Geriatrics Society, 31*(11), 642–650. (Address correspondence and requests for reprints to Angela R. Falcone, BSN, MPH,

Executive Director, Long-Term Care Assessment Training Center, Department of Public Health, Cornell University Medical College, 421 E. 70th St., New York, NY 10021.)

Feil, N. (1988). *Validation: The Feil Method.* Cleveland, Ohio: Edward Feil.

Fletcher, K. B. (1987). *The 9 keys to successful volunteer programs.* Washington, DC: The Taft Group.

Folstein, M. R., Folstein, S., & McHugh, P. R. (1975). Mini-Mental State: A practical method for grading the cognitive state of patients for the clinician. *Journal of Psychiatric Research, 12*:189–198.

French, C. J. (1986). The development of special services for victims and families burdened by Alzheimer's disease. *Pride Institute Journal of Long Term Home Health Care,* Summer 1986, 19–27.

George, L. K., & Fillenbaum, G. G. (1985). OARS methodology: A decade of experience in geriatric assessment. *Journal of the American Geriatrics Society, 33*(9), 607–615. (Address correspondence and requests for reprints to Linda K. George, Ph.D., Box 3003, Duke University Medical Center, Durham, NC 27710.)

Glenner, J., Moses, D. V., & Sanborn, B. (1986). *Alzheimer's respite aide—Training manual.* San Diego, CA: Alzheimer's Family Center, Inc. (This book is for sale from the Alzheimer's Family Center, Inc., 3686 Fourth Ave., San Diego, CA 92103.)

Goldston, S. M. (1989). *Adult day care—A basic guide.* Owings Mills, MD: National Health Publishing.

Gonyea, J. G., Seltzer, G. B., Gerstein, C., & Young, M. (1988). The acceptance of hospital-based respite care by families and elders. *Health and Social Work, 13*(3), 201–208.

Gwyther, L. (1986). Introduction: What is respite care? *Pride Institute Journal of Long Term Health Care,* (5), 5–6.

Hamill, C. M., & Oliver, R. C. (1980). *Therapeutic activities for the handicapped elderly.* Rockville, MD: Aspen Systems Corporation.

Herman, J. L., Morris, L. L., & Fitz-Gibbon, C. T. (1987). *Evaluator's handbook.* Beverly Hills, CA: Sage Publications.

Holmes, D., Abbott, K., & Holmes, M. (1978). *Planning guide to day care services for older persons.* New York: Community Research Applications, Inc. (This document is available from Community Research Applications, Inc., 1560 Broadway, Suite 1214, New York, NY 10036.)

Jacobs, B. (1974). *Involving men: A challenge for senior citizens.* Washington, DC: The National Council on the Aging, Inc.

Jacobs, B. (1976). *Working with the impaired elderly.* Washington, DC: The National Council on the Aging, Inc.

Judd, M. W. (1979). *Why bother? He's old and confused.* Winnipeg: Mary W. Judd. (This book may be purchased from Mary W. Judd, Winnipeg Municipal Hospital, Morley Ave. E., Winnipeg, Manitoba, Canada R3L 2P4.)

Kane, R. L., Ouslander, J. G., & Abrass, I. B. (1984). *Essentials of clinical geriatrics.* New York: McGraw-Hill, Inc.

Katz, S. (1983). Assessing self-maintenance: Activities of daily living, mobility, and instrumental activities of daily living. *Journal of the American Geriatric Society, 331*(2), 721–727.

Kotler, P., & Bloom, P. N. (1984). *Marketing professional services.* Englewood Cliffs, NJ: Prentice Hall, Inc.

Lawton, M. P., Brody, E. M., & Saperstein, A. R. (1989). A controlled study of respite service for cargivers of Alzheimer's patients. *The Gerontologist,* February 1989, 8–16.

Lewis-Long, Madelyn. (1989). *Realistic Alzheimer's activities.* Buffalo, NY: Potential Development, Inc. (This report may be obtained by writing to Potential Development, Inc., 775 Main St., Buffalo, NY 14203.)

Light, E., & Lebowitz, B. D. (1989). *Alzheimer's disease treatment and family stress: Directions for research.* Rockville, MD: U.S. Department of Health and Human Services.

Lindeman, D. A., Benjamin, A. E., Fox, P. J., Bogaert-Tullis, M., & Berkowitz, G. (1986). *California Alzheimer's day care resource centers: Preliminary report.* San Francisco: Institute for Health & Aging. (This report may be obtained by writing the Institute for Health & Aging, University of California, San Francisco, CA 94143.)

Lyman, K. (1989). Day care for persons with dementia: The impact of the physical environment on staff stress and quality of care. *Gerontologist, 29*(4), 557–560.

Mace, N., & Rabins, P. V. (1984). *A survey of day care for the demented adult in the United States.* Washington, DC: National Council on the Aging.

McKhann, G., Drachman, D., Folstein, M., Katzman, R., Price, D., & Stadlan, E. (1984). Clinical diagnosis of Alzheimer's disease. *Neurology, 34,* 939–944.

Mehnert, T., & Krauss, H. H. (1989). Cost benefits of a medically supervised day treatment program for patients with Alzheimer's disease and other forms of dementia. *The American Journal of Alzheimer's Care and Related Disorders and Research,* July/August 1989, 34–36.

Merrill, T. (1975). *Activities for the aged and infirm: A handbook for the untrained worker.* Springfield, IL: Charles C Thomas.

Middleton, L. (1984). *Alzheimer's family support groups: A manual for group facilitators (Vol. III).* Washington, DC: U.S. DHHS, Administration on Aging.

Miller, D. B., & Goldman, L. (1989). Perceptions of caregivers about special respite services for the elderly. *The Gerontologist, 29*(3), 408–410.

Montgomery, R. J., & Borgatta, E. F. (1989). The effects of alternative support strategies on family caregiving. *The Gerontologist,* August 1989, 457–464.

Multidimensional functional assessment: The OARS methodology. (1978). Durham, NC: The Duke University Center for the Study of Aging and Human Development. (Address correspondence to the Center for the Study of Aging and Human Development, Duke University Medical Center, Durham, NC 27710.)

Neustadt, L. A. (1985). Adult day care: A model for changing times. *Physical and Occupational Therapy in Geriatrics, 4*(1), 53–66.

O'Brien, C. L. (1982). *Adult day care: A practical guide.* Monterey, CA: Wadsworth Health Sciences Division.

On Lok Senior Health Services manual. (1978). San Francisco: On Lok Senior Health Services. (This manual may be obtained from On Lok Senior Health Services, 1490 Mason St., San Franciso, CA 94133.)

Padula, H. (1983). *Developing adult day care: An approach to maintaining inde-*

pendence for impaired older persons. Washington, DC: The National Council on the Aging, Inc.

Panella, J. (1987). *Day care programs for Alzheimer's disease and related disorders.* New York, NY: Demos Publications.

Panella, J., & McDowell, F. H. (1983). *Day care for dementia.* White Plains, NY: The Burke Rehabilitation Center Auxiliary. (This book may be obtained from the Burke Rehabilitation Center, Dementia Research Service, White Plains, NY 10605.)

Pfeiffer, E. (1976). *Day care for older adults: A conference report.* Durham, NC: Center for the Study of Aging and Human Development. (This book may be obtained by writing the Center for the Study of Aging and Human Development, Duke University, Durham, NC 17706.)

Rader, J., & Doan, J. (1985). How to decrease wandering, a form of agenda behavior. *Geriatric Nursing, 6*(4), 196–199.

Rousseau, P. (1987). Comprehensive evaluation of the geriatric patient. *Postgraduate Medicine, 131*(1), 239–246.

Sanborn, B. (1988). Dementia day care: A prototype for autonomy in long term care. *The American Journal of Alzheimer's Care and Related Disorders and Research,* July/August 1988, 23–33.

Sands, D., & Suzuki, T. (1983). Adult day care for Alzheimer's patients and their families. *The Gerontologist, 23*(1), 21–23.

Sands, D., & Suzuki, T. (1984). The Harbor Area Adult Day Care Center: A model program. *Pride Journal of Long-Term Health Care, 3*(4), 44–50.

Sarason, S. B. (1972). *The creation of settings and the future societies.* San Francisco, CA: Jossey-Bass, Inc.

Scharlach, A., & Frenzel, C. (1986). An evaluation of institution-based respite care. *The Gerontologist, 26*(1), 77–82.

Schwartz, R. (1979). Multi-purpose day centers: A needed alternative. *Journal of Gerontological Nursing, 5*(1), 48–52.

Sheridan, C. (1987). *Failure-free activities for the Alzheimer's patient: A guidebook for caregivers.* Oakland, CA: Cottage Books.

Specifications for making buildings and facilities accessible to and usable by physically handicapped people. (1980). New York, NY: American National Standards Institute. (For copies write the American National Standards Institute, 1430 Broadway, New York, NY 10018.)

Standards for adult day care. (1984). Washington, DC: National Council on the Aging, Inc. (For information write to the National Institute on Adult Day Care, National Council on the Aging, 600 Maryland Ave., S.W., West Wing 100, Washington, DC 20024.)

Szekais, B. (1985). Using the milieu: Treatment-environment consistency. *The Gerontologist, 25*(1), 15–16.

Von Behren, R. (1978). *On Lok Senior Health Services: Adult day health care: From pilot project to permanent program* (final report). Sacramento, CA: California Department of Health Services.

Von Behren, R. (1986). *Adult day health services* (final report—APS and Sacramento centers). Sacramento, CA: California Department of Health Services.

Von Behren, R., & Duveneck, M. (1978). *Adult day health care: Nursing home alternatives* (final report—Garden-Sullivan and Mt. Zion centers). Sacramento, CA: California Department of Health Services.

Webb, L. C. (1989). *Planning and managing adult day care: Pathways to success.* Owings Mills, MD: National Health Publishing.

Zachary, R. A. (1984). Day care within an institution. *Physical and Occupational Therapy in Geriatrics, 3*(4), 61–67.

Zarit, S., & Zarit, J. (1983). *The memory and behavior problems checklist and the burden interview.* Unpublished manuscript, University of Southern California, Department of Psychology.

Zawadski, R., & Von Behren, R. (1990). *Adult day service—A descriptive report 1990.* National Adult Day Care Census Project. Topical report prepared for the Health Care Financing Administration under Contract #500-89-0024. San Francisco, CA: Institute for Health & Aging, University of California, San Francisco.

Zgola, J. M. (1987). *Doing things: A guide to programming activities for persons with Alzheimer's disease and related disorders.* Baltimore: The Johns Hopkins University Press.

INDEX